The Mill

Fifty years of pulp and protest

with a foreword by Elizabeth May

Joan Baxter

Pottersfield Press, Lawrencetown Beach, Nova Scotia, Canada

Library and Archives Canada Cataloguing in Publication

Baxter, Joan, author
      The mill : fifty years of pulp and protest / Joan Baxter.
ISBN 978-1-988286-17-4 (softcover)
1. Northern Pulp (Pictou, N.S.). 2. Pulp mills--Nova Scotia--Pictou.
3. Pulp mills--Nova Scotia--Pictou--History.
4. Wood-pulp industry--Environmental aspects--Nova Scotia-- Pictou.
5. Wood-pulp industry--Social aspects--Nova Scotia--Pictou.
6. Pictou (N.S.)--Social conditions. I. Title.
HD9769.W53N67 2017   338.4'7676120971613   C2017-902768-9

Cover image: Dr. Gerry Farrell

Cover design: Gail LeBlanc

Pottersfield Press gratefully acknowledges the financial support of the Government of Canada through the Canada Book Fund for our publishing activities. We also acknowledge the support of the Canada Council for the Arts and the Province of Nova Scotia which has assisted us to develop and promote our creative industries for the benefit of all Nova Scotians.

Pottersfield Press
83 Leslie Road
East Lawrencetown, Nova Scotia, Canada, B2Z 1P8
Website: www.PottersfieldPress.com
To order, phone 1-800-NIMBUS9 (1-800-646-2879) www.nimbus.ns.ca

Printed in Canada   FOREST STEWARDSHIP FSC COUNCIL

Pottersfield Press is committed to preserving the environment and the appropriate harvesting of trees and has printed this book on Forest Stewardship Council® certified paper.

Dedicated to all those who have struggled so long and so hard to protect our air, water, health, and biodiverse forests in Nova Scotia, and elsewhere on this precious, much-abused planet.

Table of contents

"They don't do that no more"

by Dave Gunning and Jim Dorie
from Dave Gunning's CD *Lift*

They walked everywhere they went and sailed on the wind
Wasn't even that long ago some still remember when
You could drink the rivers and eat from every shore
Well the tides come and go they don't do that no more

There were dance halls all around
There was one on Green Hill
Where the good old boys and folks from town
And all the women dressed to kill
Many met their sweethearts wrote letters back and forth
Now that's all been changed they don't do that no more

They don't do that no more they don't do that no more
They don't write letters back and forth
They don't do that no more

Every family had a garden somewhere in the yard
Comforting to know you'd always eat if times got hard
And homemade bread was common so was being poor
Now there's credit cards and big-box stores
They don't do that no more

They don't do that no more they don't do that no more
They spend more than they can afford
They don't do that no more

They used to camp there with their kids
They'd play in the water
The Landing had a fishing fleet she was good as any other
They'd swim out to Pine Island boil fresh dug clams on shore
Then the big mill started going they don't do that no more

They don't do that no more they don't do that no more
There's poison on the harbour floor
They don't do that no more
They don't do that no more
They don't do that no more

Foreword

First, let me declare my bias. Even before I read the volume you hold in your hands, I hated that damn mill.

When my family first visited Nova Scotia, back in the summer of 1972, we stayed at a beautiful spot along the warm waters of the Northumberland Strait in Pictou County. The cottages were lovely, right along the water. I remember my parents marvelling that they were not fully booked. We awoke in the middle of the night to a stench so foul we could not get back to sleep. In the morning my father asked the owner if a sewer line had broken in the night. The poor fellow shook his head sadly. "No," he said. "That's the pulp mill. I used to have a good business here, but we're on our last legs now. When the wind shifts no one wants to stay ... and I really can't blame them."

Within a few years of my parents' decision to live on Cape Breton Island, from 1975 to 1979, I fought the forest industry in order to protect our community from overhead aerial spraying of toxic insecticides. It was a huge victory when a group of local residents forced the Nova Scotia Cabinet to overturn its initial approval of the spray program.

The purpose of the planned spraying was to eradicate a naturally occurring forest insect – the spruce budworm. I started learning from foresters about how forest management practices had changed our forest composition and increased the damage caused by the budworm. Over decades, deliberate decisions had preferred fir and spruce for pulp over hardwood (deciduous) species for saw logs and building materials. While foresters in the 1950s had called for "budworm proofing" the forest with mixed species of different ages, the government had gone in the other direction. It was in aid of getting Scott Paper to open the mill in Pictou County that the provincial government of the day repealed the Small Tree Act – a piece of legislation that had protected the immature hardwood until it was ready to be cut as valuable saw logs. The repeal of that act was all about converting Nova Scotia's forests to lower value softwood for clear cutting and pulp, instead of selective logging and saw mills.

One of my teachers in understanding the value of saw logs was Murray Prest, then president of the Nova Scotia Woodlot Owners and Operators Association. I will never forget the word he used to describe what happened to Nova Scotia forests after the arrival of Scott Paper. "It was a blitzkrieg," he said. "A wholesale assault on our forests."

Then I began to hate the mill.

In 1982, Scott – along with what was then Stora Forest Products in Port Hawkesbury on Cape Breton Island and Bowater Mersey in Brooklyn, near Liverpool on Nova Scotia's South Shore – asked for and received permits to spray Agent Orange. This time the target was small hardwood growth that "interfered" with the growth of the planted conifers for future pulp and paper. The use of one of the most infamous herbicides known was euphemistically described as "conifer release."

We went to court. That is another and longer story. Initially we sued all three pulp companies to get an injunction to stop the spraying of Agent Orange. After preliminary rounds of applications, all that was left was Stora. The case took two years before the Nova Scotia judge ruled Agent Orange was "safe." But after the first round, Scott Paper, no longer a defendant in the court case, pursued us plaintiffs for costs of their two days at a preliminary hearing. To raise the $15,000 Scott demanded, my parents sold our land on Cape Breton. After that, I hated the mill a bit more.

But it wasn't until I started working on the Boat Harbour

issue, as Executive Director of the Sierra Club of Canada – long before becoming involved in the Green Party – that I began to grasp the full horror of the mill. I had been working on toxic contamination of the area surrounding the coke ovens and steel mill in Sydney for years (the "Tar Ponds") when I began to hear about the cancer rates in Pictou. The violation of First Nations rights and the scandalous lies told to the Mi'kmaq First Nation of Pictou Landing were breathtaking. I couldn't understand why I had not heard of Boat Harbour before.

The incredible deal set out for Scott Paper included that it would bear no responsibility for the mill's pollution. The Nova Scotia Department of Environment would essentially own and manage the discharge of water pollution into Mi'kmaq fishing grounds. No wonder the laws were so egregiously abused – the polluter was the regulator. The fox wasn't running the chicken house metaphorically. It ran it literally.

I moved to New Glasgow and started working to clean up the mill. I began to hear from more local residents that the causeway crossing Pictou Harbour, again built for the convenience of the mill, had caused the loss of salmon and created extensive algae upstream. But as drivers crossed over the causeway, the scene still looked beautiful. This ecological destruction was nothing compared to what lay hidden – out of sight and out of mind – in Boat Harbour.

Working with Jonathan Beadle and the Pictou Landing First Nation, I went back through the woods and for the first time actually saw Boat Harbour. I literally could not believe it. The stench was unreal. The noxious gases billowed off the surface of the water as the aerators churned the fetid toxic cocktail. As we watched, workers in open boats went about adjusting the equipment. To my horror, they wore no protective masks to keep the gases out of their lungs. It was a Dickensian nightmare, but this was 2007.

It was then I decided to ask Dr. John O'Connor to visit the area and hold a town hall meeting for local residents concerned about their health. Friends in Pictou were dying of cancer at rates that reminded me of the Sydney Tar Ponds. But no level of government would respond.

Local opposition began to increase. The lure of the jobs in the mill declined as the jobs declined. Local residents began to demand what had been unthinkable in the 1970s and '80s: close the mill. Nevertheless, the mill seemed to hold the secrets to political power. Environmental practices remained negligent, bordering on criminal. But regardless of what political stripe was in power – Liberal, Progressive Conservative, or New Democrat – the mill's owners, also a changing cast of characters, continued to receive government handouts.

I really hate that damn mill.

Joan Baxter has done all of Canada a service in meticulously documenting the scandal. My personal brushes with that loathsome pollution source, economic basket case, and recipient of seemingly endless governmental largesse are as nothing compared with what Joan Baxter has uncovered. Our stories mesh along the way. For instance, some of the key figures played roles in my stories and also in this book. I had not realized the Deputy Minister for the Environment Department who approved the Agent Orange spraying in 1982 was the same man who defended the Boat Harbour pollution scheme in 1966, E.L.L. Rowe.

The heroes are the same as well. The local champions for sustainability – Bob Bancroft, Mary Gorman, Matt Gunning, Bob Christie, Dave Gunning, Jonathan Beadle, and many more – continue to fight for justice.

I hope this book will make a difference. More people need to understand the political deals that brought this mill into being and protect it still. Can nothing change the political culture of Nova Scotia to protect its citizens?

– Elizabeth May

Introduction

The day the mill came calling

The myth of progress has sometimes served us well – those of us seated at the best tables, anyway – and may continue to do so. But I shall argue ... that it has also become dangerous.

— Ronald Wright[1]

It was one of those stunningly clear, blue-sky mornings that nature sometimes bestows on Nova Scotia, especially when a north wind ushers in a mass of cool, clean air from Labrador. Such was the day that dawned over the province's northern shore on the second of June in 2016. The sun was still shinnying its way over the treetops and the thermometer told me it was chilly out there. Overnight, temperatures had dipped to near zero and a glaze of frost glistened on the dandelions and on the fledgling makings of the meadows that would, in the full bloom of summer, become a swell of wildflowers. It was glorious. Or so it looked, from inside the house.

Then I opened the door, stepped outside, and took a breath. The air was acrid, a noxious blend of sulphur overlaid with something acidic and metallic. It came as a bit of a shock, but it wasn't unfamiliar; the telltale odour from the pulp mill at Abercrombie Point in Pictou County did, from time to time, wend its way over hill and dale to our neck of the woods some forty kilometres away. But the mill's plume normally rode towards us on an easterly wind that came with clouds and heralded rain. This was the first time that the stench had settled over us on such a clear, wondrous day. And I didn't recall it ever being so powerful that it made it painful to breathe.

I started to jog – very slowly, because that's my speed – down the dirt road. After a few hundred metres my eyes were stinging, watering so heavily I could hardly see. My head began to pound, then to ache. Then my nose started to bleed.

I turned around, went home, and looked up the phone number for the Pictou pulp mill. Eventually I was passed on to an affable man, the mill's environmental leader. I told him about the stench, the headache, and the nosebleed, and asked him if something had gone wrong with the mill that it was poisoning the air so far away from Pictou. He said something about the direction the wind was blowing. Oh, I said, did he mean that on days when we weren't getting the pernicious plume, others were? He didn't seem to have an answer, so I asked if there were plans to do anything to reduce the odour from the mill and could he point me to a place where I could find a record of the chemicals that were being emitted.

He said he wasn't aware of any plans that would alter the mill's smell, but offered to send me the most recent results of the stack emissions tests if I gave him my email, which I did. I made another call to Nova Scotia Environment, and left a message with my concerns on their answering machine.

The pulp mill had been a fixture in northern Nova Scotia for as long as I could remember. As children, we commented on how it reeked when we passed Pictou on our way to Cape Breton or summer camp in Big Cove. As an adult, I'd never had much interest in spending time in or around the town because, well, it usually stank. In the summer of 2000, I'd taken a friend from South Africa to Pictou for a lobster meal. She took one look at the mill across the harbour, a few whiffs of the air, and declared that this was not a place she intended to eat lobster, or anything else for that matter. As soon as we drove away from the town and the smell, I tucked the mill quickly out of mind.

Unlike people who lived in and around Pictou, for whom it was either an inescapable, unpleasant fact of life or a lifeline to a job (or both), I had the luxury of not paying the mill any heed. I'd spent a lot of time far from Nova Scotia, almost half my adult life in various countries in Africa with my husband and kids. I'd done a fair amount of research and reporting on foreign investment in extractive industries such as logging and mining in Mali, Ghana, Cameroon, and Sierra Leone, and documented how exploitative and destructive some of them were.

I'd written about the ways some foreign investors, sometimes aided and abetted by governments and local elites, were causing environmental and social mayhem by grabbing forests and huge tracts of land from local communities, and transforming them into giant industrial plantations, producing palm oil or sugarcane for export. Sometimes the companies were part of incredibly and deliberately complex corporate webs of shell and holding companies and subsidiaries scattered all over the world in tax shelters, so they paid very little – if any – tax anywhere. And sometimes they pillaged and plundered and made off with all the profits, leaving the human, social, and environmental costs behind.

I'd had occasion to speak to a few Canadians involved in these mining, logging, and land deals who told me they liked doing business in Africa because they didn't have to abide by all the regulations that they feared would hamstring them in Canada. Some said Canada had too much red tape. If red tape meant regulations that protected people and the environment, I mused, then surely it was a good thing and we should be glad to have it.

I'd been lazy, lulled into a complacent and comfortable zone of unasked questions, assumed that unlike governments in non-democracies or very young ones on other continents, ours in Canada – federal and provincial – were doing a good job of reining in corporations at home, that we had lots of strong regulations to protect people and the things we need to live – clean water and air, healthy landscapes with biodiverse forests that capture carbon and slow global warming. This is certainly what I *wanted* to believe.

Of course I knew our country had committed horrific crimes against the aboriginal peoples of Canada, and against other minority groups over the years, and there were still a lot of amends to be made, reconciliation to be done, and new leafs to be turned over. And more than a few Canadian companies – in mining, infrastructure, and energy sectors – had tarnished our reputation internationally.[2] But Canada was a mature democracy, a member of the G7 and G20. It sent out observers to monitor elections and promote government accountability in young or fragile democracies; I'd met Canadian election observers in Ghana, in Mali, and Sierra Leone. It dispatched international development experts to developing countries to undertake projects to promote good governance, public health, and environmentally sustainable development.

Surely Canada was doing at home what its emissaries preached abroad. Surely I didn't need to pay as much attention to these issues in Canada as I'd been doing in Africa for so many years. Surely if a pulp mill were truly causing harm, it would not be allowed to operate.

Or so I had always thought – if I thought about it at all. Mostly I hadn't. Whenever the smell of the mill reached us over in Colchester County, I noticed it, sometimes commented on it, but I didn't think about it. Same with the logging trucks, sometimes half a dozen in just a few minutes, which roared past on the back roads during my morning jogs, loaded with trees that were pencil-thin. There had long been criticism of forest policies in the province, so I knew there were problems. It made me sad watching those trucks roar by. But never for very long.

In 2014, a friend had signed me up to a Facebook page

called "Clean Up The Pictou County Pulp Mill," which appeared on my news feed from time to time.[3] From afar in Kenya, where I'd been working for international forestry and agroforestry research organizations, I'd been vaguely aware that back home in Nova Scotia the pulp mill had been causing quite a stink – literally and politically. There had been lots of discussion about a concert in Pictou to protest the pollution from the mill, and reports about the new equipment the mill had installed to reduce its emissions. But I had always followed the online discussion and the media reports the same way I would listen to election results from a place I knew nothing about and would have trouble locating on a map. In one ear, out the other.

Then came the morning in June. I'll never know whether the headache and nosebleed that day were caused by the mill's emissions. But I do know they came as a wake-up call that belatedly triggered my overdue curiosity.

Following the phone calls to the mill and provincial environment department, I went online. Northern Pulp's website portrayed the company in glowing terms, highlighting an economic impact study it had commissioned to prove its immense economic worth to the area.[4] It was committed "to achieving excellence in environmental management for its pulping operations" and to many other laudable things as well. I recognized the hand of a communications specialist at work in the fine art of spinning; I'd been doing some of that massaging of messages myself as part of my work in Kenya.

Then I perused the website developed by a group called Clean The Mill.[5] It was chock-a-block with research reports, government documents, studies full of facts and figures about emissions, media articles, and interviews with mill managers and politicians, timelines and factsheets. The Clean The Mill website contained enough material for a dissertation or two. But it seemed not to have been updated for a year or so, and it promised a lot of source material in PDFs that had yet to be posted. I sent an email to the contact given on the page, saying it would be great to learn more about the group and progress on cleaning the mill, so would they please get back to me?

A few minutes later my phone rang. It was Dave Gunning, a native of Pictou and an internationally acclaimed folk singer and songwriter. I'd met him a decade earlier when I was writing a book about Willard Kitchener MacDonald, a local legend known as the Hermit of Gully Lake. Gunning had composed a poignant ode to MacDonald called "Let Him Be," which he kindly allowed me to use in the book.

On the phone that morning, he said my email had been forwarded to him because he did a lot of work for the Clean The Mill group. He'd gotten involved a couple of years earlier through his brother Matt and sister-in-law Bobbi Morrison, who had co-founded the group with the siblings Paul and Kathy Gregory. Gunning started rattling off facts and figures about the mill's effluent and emissions and the work of the Clean The Mill group. "And I'm not even an environmentalist!" he said at one point.

It seemed an odd thing for him to say; he sounded like someone deeply immersed in environmental issues. Gunning said the Facebook page had garnered more than 4,500 followers in less than three years, including people on all sides of the issue, from those who didn't believe the mill could be cleaned up and just wanted it closed, to those who wanted it to remain open but only if it reduced its environmental footprint, to others who supported the mill no matter what, and some who disparaged the work of the group.[6]

But he was unequivocal about the goal of the Clean The Mill group itself; it was to get the mill cleaned up, not closed. Too many people depended on it for their livelihoods, he said. Among them, many were his friends and neighbours, the parents of his kids' friends and members of their hockey teams. Gunning was passionate; he listed off the names of a dozen people he thought I should contact, people in all walks of life with a range of views on the mill. By the time he had finished, I'd filled several pages with notes. But, he said, this was just a beginning. There was so much more. He would email me some documents. It took hours to download them. Weeks to study them.

At the risk of overdramatizing what happened as I delved and listened in the next few months, it felt as if the proverbial scales were dropping from my eyes. I'd had no idea that the mill had been the focus of so much investigative reporting, and featured in so many media reports, essays, opinion pieces, letters to the editor, studies, and reports. No idea of the extent of the controversies that swirled around it, the public protest it had spawned. The more I learned, the bigger the story grew, the more it looked like a vortex of human stories spanning half a century, with the mill the epicentre.

The mill may be in Nova Scotia, but its story has no borders. With its absentee corporate landlords, it seemed a microcosm of the globalized economy that exploits and extracts to maximize, channel upwards, and then export profits. It is about governments caught between their constituents and corporate power. It symbolizes much of what has happened on the planet in the past century, and the mindset that sees economics as something separate from the environment, that puts profits before people and the natural world that sustains us, that views citizens as mindless consumers. It is about environmental racism underlying decisions about how and where to dispose of toxic waste. But it is also a story about public determination and civic courage, about ordinary citizens devoting years of their lives, often at great emotional and personal expense, to take up the struggle, to try to understand some of the wrongs and right them. And it's about many good, law-abiding people who hold their noses and keep their mouths closed because they have a mortgage to pay and a family to feed, and the mill provides them the income to do so.

At the heart of it all is the pulp mill. Where better to begin the tale than in Pictou, with a walk on the boardwalk and a long look at the thing?

1

The smell of money

In Campbell River both day and night,
The pulp smell's much worse than the sight,
You may get cancer, but that's all right,
'Cause that's the smell of money.

— Smokey Dymny[7]

t's not pretty, the pulp mill on Abercrombie Point, and no vigorous stretching of the imagination can make it so. It looms large just across the harbour from the picturesque town of Pictou, which bills itself as the birthplace of New Scotland. From the vantage point of the Pictou waterfront, with its seafood eateries, charming historic buildings, scenic boardwalk, and the replica of the ship *Hector* that brought 189 Highland Scottish immigrants to these shores in 1773, the mill hogs the horizon and renders it almost Dickensian.

It belches smoke and fumes from a conglomeration of stacks. It can consume up to 92.3 million litres of clean fresh water every day and pipe almost as many back out again as toxic effluent. The *Lonely Planet Travel Guide* dissuades would-be visitors who might be tempted to make a stop in Pictou on their way from the Prince Edward Island ferry to

Cape Breton or Halifax, by advising them that although its main street is "lined with interesting shops and beautiful old stone buildings," its sea views are unfortunately "blighted" by the "giant smoking mill in the distance."[8]

So no, not a pretty thing.

"Big stinky cloud factory" is what my brother dubbed it when his daughters were small and asked, each time they drove past Pictou, what that smelly building was. "Poop mill," is what Dave Gunning says they called it when he was young. "Mordor, it looks like Mordor," according to a friend of mine who recently went to Pictou with her partner for a day's outing, then cut short the visit because of the smell of the mill. A bit over-the-top, perhaps, to suggest that a simple pulp mill belongs in the fictional Land of Shadow ruled by the Dark Lord Sauron in J.R.R. Tolkien's *Lord of the Rings*. But the mill has always generated strong and often opposing views.

Shortly before it went into production in September 1967, Scott offered the media a "familiarization tour" of the plant and reassured them about its emissions. A staff writer for *The Chronicle Herald*, Clarence Johnson, had this to say about the new mill: "Some small amount of odour, which originated from the sulphur-containing compounds, might be detected." However, he added, such odours in the kraft bleaching process would be "substantially reduced by modern process design and increasingly effective control."[9]

On the day the mill opened in 1967, a special supplement of Nova Scotia's leading daily newspaper offered this description: "The attractive brick complex and several supporting buildings were designed to be compatible with the beauty and charm for which Pictou County is widely known," and concluded that "in all respects" the mill is "worthy of pride, not only by company officials but by Pictou County and the province of Nova Scotia as a whole."[10]

Fifty years on, the original company is long gone and it might be tricky to find many in Nova Scotia who would use the word "pride" to describe their feelings about the pulp mill. A large welcome sign at the entrance says "Local product. Global reach," but in 2016 it still proclaimed, "This is our time. We have the right product. We have the right owner and the right people." Nevertheless, the early euphoria about the mill has long since dissipated.

The $50-million mill was built during a golden era for pulp that gained momentum during the last half of the twentieth century. I'm inclined to think that the global pulp rush may have inspired Dr. Seuss in 1971 to pen his book *The Lorax* about greed, a consumer "need," and the environmental devastation those caused. In it, a character called Once-ler discovers a natural wonderland inhabited by marvellous creatures, with a "rippolous" pond full of splashing Humming-Fish and an abundance of sweet-smelling "Truffala Trees." The soft-as-silk tufts of the trees knit up nicely into consumer items called "Thneeds." The Once-ler goes into mass production, felling ever more trees to make ever more Thneeds, "shipping them forth," and growing the business ever bigger. The Thneed factory pollutes the air and water, drives living things from the landscape, and eventually, inevitably, the very last tree falls to the Super-Axe-Hacker.

Throughout it all, the Lorax, speaking for the trees, begs the Once-ler to stop the destruction. His pleas are in vain, and finally he gives up, leaving behind just a small pile of rocks with the word "unless" written on them. The Once-ler frets over what this means until one day, in telling the whole sorry story to a visitor, he has an epiphany. Unless he finds someone to whom he can give the last Truffala seeds, and unless that person cares an awful lot and will plant those seeds and grow back the forest and bring back life, nothing will get better. So he gives his visitor the seed, sowing hope. The End.

Okay, yes, I know. It's a children's story. Simplistic. Sheer fantasy. But there are some parallels. I contemplate a few of them as I sit at a picnic table on the boardwalk on the Pictou waterfront, gazing across at the mill. This morning its plumes are brownish, yellowish, and grey, creating a haze that is lazing its way north towards Pictou Landing and the Northumberland Strait, a dark smudge stretched across the sky. Whether the mill's emissions are within approved limits or not – and members of the Clean The Mill group say that's a big "if" given the way the testing is done and how often it has exceeded limits and not been sanctioned by the government – it still pumps pollutants into the air and water. It transforms trees into pulp that is used in all manner of consumer products, some useful and necessary, others not so much. And the pulp industry as a whole has not been kind to the Acadian forests, the woodlands ecosystem unique to Canada's Maritime provinces, a small portion of the northeastern United States, and southern Quebec.

From the waterfront today in Pictou I've watched as truck after truck pulled up to the wharf, each piled sky-high with white packages of pulp from the mill. The pulp was then loaded onto the large ship docked there. Headed for export, just like the profits. If any of that pulp ever makes it back to Nova Scotia's sea-bound coast, it's probably going to be as a component in products such as toilet paper, disposable diapers, wet wipes, and paper towels. And unless something is done to restore Acadian forests and reduce the harm that the mill does to the environment and is believed to do to human health, then – just as Seuss writes – "… nothing is going to get better. It's not."

But this likely reads like fanciful nonsense and completely beside the point for those who depend on the mill and the pulp industry for their livelihoods. Pulp is an economic mainstay here in Pictou. Throughout the province and indeed across the country, the pulp industry has shaped forestry policies and practices for many years, been a major employer and source of economic growth. So the mill doesn't have to be pretty. It may not be the newest or the cleanest or the most efficient, it may even be an eyesore and dirty and old, but it's a pulp mill, for heaven's sake. Its job is to make pulp, which we need for paper products, and it provides some well-paying jobs. And that god-awful stench? It's just the "smell of money," a mantra that has been used for fifty years to defend the mill. "The greatest stink of all," according to a former labour leader in Pictou, is "the stink of unemployment."[11]

The numbers have varied over the years, but in 2016 the company said the mill directly employed over 300 people. It provides pensions for many who went before them, and indirect jobs for hundreds more who work in the forestry or service industries. While many other mills across Canada have closed in recent years, victims to downturns in the global pulp market and to increasing competition from new producers and raw materials, the mill at Abercrombie Point is still there and still pulping away.

In Nova Scotia, politicians win elections with promises of jobs, jobs, health care, and more jobs. Woe unto any government that dares to come down hard on, even tiptoe over, the knuckles of any large company that employs hundreds and wields immense control over an entire industry. The economic dependence on the mill in and around Pictou means that anyone who does raise a fuss, criticize it for whatever reason, risks causing dissension in the community. To call for an end to the status quo can be a very difficult thing to do.

And yet, that is exactly what people have been doing for many years. Even before the mill went into operation, worries about its potential to damage air, water, forests, and fisheries began to percolate just below the normally placid surface of small-town and rural life along the Northumberland Shore of Nova Scotia. Since then, people have watched as government after government doled out loans and grants and Crown land leases to the mill's owners, going to great lengths to protect jobs while taxpayers were charged with the expensive health and environmental liabilities.[12] And almost like clockwork, every few years, the ripples of public discontent and frustration have welled up, created powerful swells, and crested in waves of peaceful protest.

Over the lifetime of the mill, thousands of people have struggled to pressure one government after another to make the mill clean up its act, to stop the pollution, protect human health and the environment, and to play its role as regulator rather than financier and friend of the pulp industry. People from all backgrounds and walks of life – Pictou Landing First Nation, farmers, fishers, owners of woodlots and local businesses, academics, lawyers, artists, doctors, ecologists and biologists, even some politicians (generally while they were in opposition) – have joined forces to lead these protests and movements.

There have been court cases, blockades, letter-writing campaigns, petitions, public meetings and consultations, even a concert and a photo exhibit. Citizen groups have expended untallied amounts of energy and used up endless hours of their own time to do research, write reports and press releases, hold meetings, pen letters to politicians and articles for the media, put together scrapbooks and amass dauntingly large collections of files that document their struggles. The electronic files that Dave Gunning sent to me, put together by the Clean The Mill group, take up nearly two gigabytes on my computer. The scrapbooks and physical files I've been given fill several bankers boxes.

In its lifetime, the mill has had five different corporate owners, four of them American and one Asian. It has seen ten Canadian prime ministers and twelve provincial premiers come and go. It has received many hundreds of millions of dollars worth of concessions, loans, and grants from governments, many of them intended to help it clean up its environmental act. And at least a dozen different groups and three successive generations of concerned citizens have taken up the same cause. For the sake of social harmony, many people have learned to studiously avoid discussing the smelly elephant on Abercrombie Point except in the privacy of their homes, lest they create ugly rifts in their neighbourhood and community.

But rifts are inevitable, and they can be exacerbated when

the mill goes on the offensive, as it did in 2016 with a PR blitz of television, radio, and newspaper advertisements. In the company's newsletter in late 2015, Northern Pulp's communications director Kathy Cloutier wrote, "For a while, someone else has been telling Northern Pulp's story," and then, "Not any longer. Not on my watch."[13] She and Northern Pulp's board and executive declined to be interviewed for this book.[14]

The reality is that the story of the mill goes back a long way, long before the current mill owners came on the scene and reignited the same old struggle that citizens had been waging for decades, and history started to repeat itself – yet again. The mill may belong to Northern Pulp now, but its story belongs to the people of Nova Scotia, and to tell it, we need to go back a half-century to where it all began, as a political dream of creating riches in Nova Scotia.

2

A Christmas present (1955-1965)

Santa Claus will be bringing a unique gift to Pictou County this year – a pulp and paper mill...
                                                            – Ron MacDonald[15]

I t was late 1964, a momentous year for Canada. In Ottawa, Parliament had passed a new bill that would give Canada its own flag that would feature the red maple leaf, as a nod to the native tree that crimsons so many Canadian landscapes each autumn. A report recommending the formation of a universal Medicare program had been tabled in the House of Commons. Canadian literature was blossoming with new books from Irving Layton, Leonard Cohen, Margaret Atwood, Margaret Laurence, and Marshall McLuhan. And Prime Minister Lester Pearson was a year into his first term in office with a Liberal minority government.

Out on the east coast, Nova Scotia's Premier Robert L. Stanfield was enjoying his eighth year in office and his fourth consecutive Progressive Conservative majority. Stanfield, the son of the founder of a very successful textile company known for its woollens, underwear, and T-shirts, had in his youth called himself a socialist, much to the dismay of his politically conservative family who called him a "parlour pink" or a "damned Grit."[16] Although he remained a decidedly liberal-minded man of great humility and modest living throughout his life (walking home to lunch every day in Halifax and travelling in the back of the plane with economy-class passengers even in later years when he became head of the federal Progressive Conservative Party), once he became premier his economic outlook and policies seem to lean solidly in more conservative directions. By the early 1960s, he was setting his sights on luring big money to the province. In 1964, rumours were rumbling about a big industrial project in the offing, possibly a new mill.

On December 23 that year, Stanfield called a press conference that put an end to the speculation. Standing alongside Paul C. Baldwin, Executive Vice President of the large American company Scott Paper of Philadelphia, Stanfield told reporters Scott would be building a large pulp mill in the province.[17] It would use a sulphate chemical process known as "kraft," from the German word for strength, to dissolve and bleach wood fibre and transform it into 500 tons of pulp a day, doubling the value and volume of Nova Scotia's pulp production.[18] It would be built in the heart of Pictou County and employ 350 people when it went into production in 1967.

This must have sounded like very good news to many in the province. The economy of the town of Pictou, like the whole of the county, had been struggling since the end of the Second World War. There had been a sharp downturn in local industries that had once flourished in the region – coal mining, shipbuilding, and steelmaking. Premier Stanfield and his government had been aggressively pursuing foreign investment and new industries that would stimulate the economy and create jobs.

In neighbouring New Brunswick, K.C. Irving had already set the precedent when, in 1951, he expanded the pulp mill in Saint John, renaming it Irving Pulp and Paper Ltd., negotiating generous tax concessions from the municipal and provincial governments, while getting immunity from nuisance lawsuits, rights to dump waste in the river, and the right to expropriate additional land for future expansion. As journalist and author Jacques Poitras noted, "New Brunswick could not afford to be choosy when it came to industrialists."[19]

Perhaps Nova Scotia felt the same. In 1957, Stanfield had created the Crown corporation Industrial Estates Limited to woo big investors and help build and finance plants for companies that were willing to locate to Nova Scotia. He hand-picked a prominent Nova Scotian entrepreneur, Frank Sobey, to head the corporation. Sobey was the founder of the grocery chain that would eventually become a nationwide empire, a conglomerate appropriately named Empire Company.

Sobey, who hailed from Pictou County, had been instrumental in getting Scott to set up the new mill on Abercrombie Point and also in securing it a break on its property taxes.[20] Scott already owned a small mechanical mill in Sheet Harbour on the Atlantic coast of the province, which had been in operation since the 1920s. That mill had been bought in 1963 by the Fraser Companies of New Brunswick, and a year later, Fraser sold the Sheet Harbour mill to Scott Paper.[21]

The big American company had had its sights set on Nova Scotia for years. A decade earlier, during the time the province was governed by the Liberals under Premier Henry Hicks, Scott had already purchased 400 acres at Abercrombie Point for a future mill site.[22] According to Dr. John Seaman Bates, who would come to play a pivotal role in the history of the mill, he was the one who originally found the site for the mill in Pictou County. In a memoir he published much later in life, Bates wrote that in 1953, Hick's predecessor, Premier Angus L. MacDonald, had asked him to recommend sites for pulp and paper in northeastern Nova Scotia. Bates studied five sites in the province. His first choice had been Point Tupper near Port Hawkesbury in Cape Breton, the location that would later be chosen by the Swedish company Stora Kopparberg for its pulp mill. But in March 1955, while engaged as a consultant for Scott Paper of Philadelphia, Bates took a Scott engineer to another of the potential sites, Abercrombie Point, wading through hip-deep snow to get there. The location would provide the company with access to vast quantities of fresh water and the trees it would need, and according to Bates, the Scott representative was ecstatic, saying, "John, this is the best pulp mill site I have ever seen."[23]

In early 1956, it looked as if Scott was ready to build the mill. Bates, Scott consultants, and several provincial cabinet ministers travelled to company headquarters in Pennsylvania and spent a morning discussing the proposal with "high hopes of signing an agreement." At the last minute, however, the president of Scott decided to defer the project for another decade.[24]

So it happened that by the time Scott was ready to go ahead with its mill in Nova Scotia in the mid-1960s, Stanfield and Sobey would be the ones handling – and credited for – the investment. Walter Miller, the first manager of the mill and the president of Scott's Nova Scotian subsidiary, Scott Maritimes, later praised Frank Sobey for all the "courtesies and helpfulness" and "advice, consultation and assistance" that he and Industrial Estates lavished on his company.[25]

In hindsight, it seems unlikely that Sobey realized just how smelly a neighbour the mill would be; Abercrombie Point was in his own backyard. In 1963, he had built Crombie House – a mansion replete with gold-plated bathroom fixtures, an outdoor swimming pool, and enough room to hang his fine collection of Canadian paintings – just over a kilometre from the site where the new Scott mill would be built.[26] If he had known that the mill emissions would make the paint peel off walls, something he reportedly acknowledged and regretted later in life, perhaps he might have dealt a little differently with the powerful American investor.

When Stanfield introduced Scott to Nova Scotians, he described it as one of the "greatest forest products companies in the world."[27] He wasn't exaggerating; the company had been growing for almost a century. Scott Paper was founded in 1879 by the Scott brothers, Clarence and E. Irwin. As the story went, they had launched the business with "a pushcart and a loan," and with a little audacity on the side that they needed to overcome prudish attitudes to the product for which they would become famous – toilet paper.[28] Scott was the first company to market toilet paper in a roll, before it branched out into paper towels, tissues, sanitary pads, and disposable diapers in the twentieth century. At one point it had even tried out a line of paper apparel, creating a disposable party dress.[29]

In the 1950s, it merged with Hollingsworth & Whitney Limited of Boston, Massachusetts, which had been acquiring large land holdings in New Brunswick and Nova Scotia since the 1920s to feed its mill in Winslow, Maine. After the merger, these assets were transferred to the Scott name and by the 1960s it had become, as Stanfield said, one of the world's largest producers of pulp and paper.

In addition to mills in the United States and two it partially owned in Australia and Britain, the company had also been investing heavily north of the border in Canada. It owned mills in British Columbia and Quebec, and seemed to be on an acquisition spree in Nova Scotia. It already owned the mill in Sheet Harbour, which included 110,000 acres of timberland, and it had purchased 450,000 acres in the province years earlier.[30] Scott also held a minority interest – a 20 percent investment – in the Swedish Stora Kopparberg pulp mill that had opened in 1961 near Port Hawkesbury, across the Canso Strait from mainland Nova Scotia.[31]

But the new mill on Abercrombie Point, said Premier Stanfield, would be far bigger than any of the other four mills operating in the province – in Liverpool, Hantsport, Sheet Harbour, and Port Hawkesbury. It would need 400,000 cords of wood a year for its round-the-clock pulp production. A standard lumber truck at the time could hold only about eight cords of wood – a cord being a stack four feet by four feet by eight feet. So about 50,000 truckloads would be delivered each year to the mill at Abercrombie Point, which would consume nearly as much wood as the other four mills combined.

Stanfield also took advantage of the occasion to warn small woodlot owners that they would have to adopt more modern methods to increase their own production of pulp-wood if they were to keep up with the new mill's voracious appetite. By this he meant harvesting should be done with chainsaws and large machines rather than axes, handsaws, and horses. To quell concerns about the effect this might have on the forests, the premier assured reporters the new pulp mill would not overtax the province's woodlands.

Whether he really believed this or not, we'll never know. It certainly contradicted the views of many with a longer per-spective than the government of the day. Those who knew the Acadian forest knew it took more than a century to grow trees in the forests of Nova Scotia, and that with pulp they would be trying to alter that reality. At public hearings in Cumberland County about plans to clear cut in the area in advance of the new pulp mill in Pictou, a forester from Parrsboro wryly com-mented, "You can't grow a 150 year-old tree in 50 years."[32]

The notion that the province could handle the new pulp mill also went against the view of forestry experts in the prov-ince, including Wilfrid Creighton, then a senior manager in the Department of Lands and Forests who was opposed to the unbridled growth in pulp processing.[33] It also countered the findings of R.M. Bulmer and Lloyd Hawboldt, two forestry ex-perts whom Stanfield's government had asked a year earlier to assess remaining forest resources in the province. Their mandate was to prepare a report showing whether mainland Nova Scotia had the wood reserves for the new large mill. They concluded that it didn't, even with Crown lands includ-ed,[34] which constituted 3.8 million acres or about 29 percent of the province.

Unhappy with the naysaying duo and apparently deter-mined to go ahead with the giant new mill no matter what they said, Premier Stanfield ordered Minister of Lands and Forests E.D. Haliburton to "get those people of yours 'thick as sweat' down to the [Hotel] Nova Scotian and lock em up until they come up with an answer."[35]

Deputy Premier and Minister of Finance George Isaac (G.I.) Smith then summoned Bulmer and Hawboldt to a meet-ing at the Hotel Nova Scotian in Halifax. Notably absent from the meeting was Wilfrid Creighton, another dissenter on pulp, who later said he wasn't invited.[36] Nevertheless, there were se-nior staff from the Department of Lands and Forests and they defended the Bulmer and Hawboldt report, arguing against a new pulp mill. Deputy Premier Smith was having none of it.

G.I. Smith had been a trial lawyer and after he began his career in politics, he came to be known as Premier Stanfield's "hatchet man" because he could be counted on to handle "the unpleasant jobs with a minimum of fuss, leaving his chief free for loftier matters."[37] At the meeting in Halifax, Smith cross-examined the report's authors like a "Grand Inquisitor," as Hawboldt recalled years later for Sandberg and Clancy, when they interviewed him for *Against the Grain*, their landmark book on foresters and politics in the province.[38] The deputy premier, Hawboldt said, could be "belligerent and nasty."[39] The meeting dragged on for a week, and in the end, politics and the lure of economic development based on pulp – and pulp industry jobs – prevailed. Science and scientific advice about sustainable management of forest resources in the province be damned. It was a pattern that would persist.

That initial opposition from forestry experts worried about the state and future of Nova Scotia's forests effective-ly quashed, the deal was sealed for the mill at Abercrombie Point. Smith prepared his own report for Premier Stanfield, who then approved a lease for a vast swath of Crown land for Scott, following the precedent set when the province gave Stora a fifty-year lease on a million acres of Crown land (11 percent of Nova Scotia's land mass), thus paving the way for Stanfield's triumphant announcement and the mill itself.

Hyberbole became the language of the day. Newspapers reported that the announcement was "hailed jubilantly from all parts of the county," that it brought to the province "the chance to work, grow and earn," and offered the "opportunity for the community to expand with the presence of an industry known to be steady and solid."[40] As for the premier, he called the new mill "a very pleasant Christmas present for Nova Scotia."[41]

3

A very expensive welcome mat (1965-1967)

The industrial climate of Nova Scotia is very good and our company received only the best of assistance and co-operation from local and provincial agencies.

– Walter Miller, General Manager
Scott Maritimes Limited[42]

At first, it did look like the mill was the Christmas gift that Stanfield had promised. It certainly was for Donald Burt MacKenzie, who today lives with his wife Rose, well off the beaten path in the charming hamlet of Lorne, Pictou County, on a farm with beef cattle, sheep, and a couple of horses. Back in 1965, though, MacKenzie was a newly minted engineer and for him the mill was a "real boom." The contract for the construction of the Scott mill went to a giant American engineering firm, Charles T. Main, one of the world's largest at the time, and MacKenzie went to work for them at Abercrombie Point. He was earning $900 a month, which was nothing to be sneezed at for a young graduate in the 1960s.

It's a very warm day in August 2016 when the MacKenzies invite me into the cool comfort of their living room for a trip down MacKenzie's lane of amazing memories. Their house is part rambling farmhouse, part art gallery with its walls adorned with paintings by Rose, a retired teacher and former municipal councillor. It's also part museum of globe-trotting adventure, full of photographs and mementos and trophies that MacKenzie has collected over the decades when he travelled the world, often piloting his own planes, working for billionaires, and meeting dignitaries while working as an engineer on six continents.

MacKenzie settles into a plush leather armchair, looking every bit the seasoned gentleman traveller in his jeans, white dress shirt, and black suspenders, his greying hair swept back in dashing waves. He regales me with stories of the incredible ventures and antics of one of his employers, the American tycoon and shipping magnate Daniel K. Ludwig, a real "character," MacKenzie says, who "had more money than Howard Hughes and Aristotle Onassis together," something a later Internet search confirms.

None of this was easily imaginable when MacKenzie was growing up in Pictou Landing in the 1940s. The family lived in a small one-and-a-half storey house that was shared by twelve children and two grandparents, his mother, and also his father when World War II ended and he returned home after six years of service. Although they had no indoor plumbing, central heating, or running water, MacKenzie says they lived and ate "very, very well."

"We had a farm, we used to make our own butter, carried water from the spring," he tells me. "We made all our own hay with a scythe and the wheelbarrow to put it in, and we killed chickens every week – that was the kids' job, to kill the chickens and pluck them – and we made all our own butter." His grandfather would fish in the Northumberland Strait and bring home fresh flounder. And he has particularly vivid memories of his grandmother's cakes. "My grandmother would make chocolate cake with frosting on it," he says. "You'd never believe what you can make with an old woodstove."

He went off to study, first to St. Francis Xavier University in Antigonish and then to the Technical University of Nova Scotia in Halifax for his engineering degree, after which he landed the job with Charles T. Main. The Scott pulp mill turned out to be a launching pad for his career that spanned the globe. Once the mill was complete in 1967, Main invited MacKenzie to the United States to work, and he headed there with his wife and three small kids. Just eighteen days later, he tells me, he got a notice that he was being drafted into the American military to go to Vietnam, but in the end he was classified as 5A, too old for active service duty. "I was only twenty-seven," he says with a great guffaw. After that, he and several of the core members of the Main team that worked on the Scott mill wound up working together on pulp mills all over the world – from the Brazilian Amazon, to South Africa, to the former Czechoslovakia.

He says that when they were building the mill in Pictou, it was modern and state-of-the-art; they were looking at a twenty-year lifespan. This meant they figured it would last until 1985 or so. But, as he says, "We're not in 1985 anymore." MacKenzie tells me it would be possible to reduce the odours the mill produces, the amount of water it uses, and the effluent it produces – he has worked on mills elsewhere in the world that have done that. So can it be cleaned up, I ask him. "Of course you can clean it; it's just a matter of money," he says. And while it was "a good job" when they built it in 1967, it was intended to run for about twenty years, so up until 1987 or 1990. And, he adds, we're now in 2016, so "… yeah, it has passed its life."

Still, he has nothing but gratitude for the experience that he got working on the new mill at Abercrombie Point. And he says it has provided work and good income for many people, and many of his own relatives, including his son who works there today, president of the union.

Beth Henderson is another who remembers the early and heady days when the mill felt like a true gift. Henderson is a retired banker born and raised in Pictou, and she takes great interest in the rich history of the county, founding the Pictou County Historical Photograph Society that collects and curates its photos.

It's high summer along the northern shore when she welcomes me into her lovely country home; the tidy and homey interior she and her husband have crafted is as immaculate as the gardens outside. We're in the community of Three Brooks, just a few kilometres from Pictou and out of sight of the mill. A cup of tea and a delicious homemade muffin appear in front of me, and Henderson summons her memories of the halcyon times in the county when the mill was in its youthful heyday.

"It was a joy ride," she says. For her husband, who worked on the mill's construction, it meant a steady paycheque and good money even before it opened. After it did, things really boomed. As loans officer at the local bank, she enjoyed watching people coming in with big paycheques and she enjoyed being able to give out lots of loans that they had no trouble paying back. As she says, "People had money."

And if the mill smelled bad, which it did, then so be it; as they all said, that was the price to be paid – it was the smell of money. "We had so little of it back then," says Henderson. "So we didn't look to see if there were many detrimental effects of the mill. There were great pensions, great benefits. It was like a gift from God if you could work at the mill."

These days, she describes herself as "neutral" on the subject of the mill; she has family members who work there and so is glad they've been able to stay in Pictou to raise their families rather than heading to Halifax or out west to find a job, as so many others have. And she's grateful for her own long career in a bank in Pictou, which benefitted from the presence of the mill. But she admits that a lot has changed and a lot has been learned; there is much about the mill that belies its early promises – the toxic effluent, the money that both federal and provincial governments have pumped into it, the clear cutting it has promoted in the province's forests, and also the way it has divided the people of Pictou County. She worries that Nova Scotia, a "have-not province," has been too anxious to give money away to foreign owners to encourage business.

In 1965, when he presented the mill as a "very pleasant" Christmas gift to the province, Stanfield neglected to mention what the province was giving Scott for Christmas. As part of the deal, enshrined in the Scott Maritimes Limited Agreement Act of 1965, was the offer from the province to Scott of 230,000 acres of Crown land in Halifax County,[43] on which grew some of the finest standing timber left in the province.[44] Later, this increased to 250,000 acres.[45] This was in addition to about a million acres that the company already owned in Nova Scotia and some 30,000 acres it owned in New Brunswick.[46] The Act also stated the lease would be for fifty years and construction of the mill would start by the end of March 1967.

Scott would also enjoy a tax holiday for twenty years on all forest land owned by or leased to the company, including on the site of the new mill. And then there were the giveaway rates that Scott would be paying for wood it harvested on Crown land. The standard stumpage rate had been set in the late 1950s when the provincial government was negotiating a deal with the Swedish company, Stora, although in hindsight it's not obvious on whose side the provincial negotiators were really negotiating. Not only did they offer Stora long-term leases on 1.5 million acres of Crown land – almost 40 percent of all public land in Nova Scotia – but they did so at rates that had been set for the Bowater-Mersey plant back in the 1920s, almost four decades earlier.

John Bigelow, a very experienced forester who had been engaged by the Nova Scotia Department of Trade and Industry as an expert to oversee the development of the pulp and paper industry, suggested the province charge Stora $4.40 per cord of wood from the Crown lease. At a cabinet meeting, Premier

Stanfield and two of his ministers questioned that amount, and recommended the stumpage be set at just $1 per cord, so as not to upset Stora by charging it more than Bowater-Mersey was paying. Stora's Karl Clauson had been prepared to pay more so he was reportedly – and not surprisingly – "delighted" by this offer.[47] And so, one can only imagine, were the Scott executives ten years later when the government of Nova Scotia also gave them the great deal on the stumpage it would charge on Crown land of just $2 per cord, less than half what Bigelow had recommended back in the 1950s.

The generosity of the people of Nova Scotia didn't stop there. When John Bates was helping Scott find a suitable site for the mill with access to lots and lots of fresh water, he had devised the plan for a causeway across Pictou Harbour, the estuary formed by the confluence of the East, Middle, and West rivers. When the deal was signed, the province agreed to construct and pay for that causeway. And just upstream from that, it would build a new dam across Middle River.[48] It would also install and run the pumping station to provide the pulp mill with fresh water; enshrined in the Agreement was a guarantee to Scott that it would have access to 25 million Imperial gallons (about 114 million litres, enough to fill more than 45 Olympic-sized swimming pools) of fresh water every day for the pulping process, all for an annual cost of just $100,000 or for $18.53 per million Imperial gallons, whichever was greater.[49]

In its official offer to Scott, the Nova Scotia government said it was "pleased" to make this fresh water available by building the dam across the Middle River.[50] It was directing the Department of Highways to "so construct a causeway across Pictou Harbour" to create an "impervious dam" to ensure an adequate water level, and directing the Nova Scotia Water Authority to provide all "facilities necessary for the delivery of water from the reservoir created by the Middle River dam and the reservoir created by the Pictou Harbour Causeway dam, or either of them, to the mill."[51]

In addition, the province said it would "cost, own, operate and maintain" the system that would handle all the mill's effluent, which involved a toxic mix of wastewater, wood fibre, and chemicals. For this service, Scott would pay the government just $12.03 per million Imperial gallons, or $100,000 a year, whichever was highest.[52] And like the cherry on top of the huge and sweet cake that the province was baking for Scott, the government said it would also "indemnify and save harmless" the company from all claims relating to the effluent.[53]

Expensive infrastructure at no cost to the company, vast tracts of forest for the cutting, massive amounts of inexpensive water, and many millions of litres of toxic waste in return – for which Nova Scotians would be left picking up the very hefty tab. As if this weren't enough, for good measure, the federal government also kicked in $5 million and an additional five-year holiday on income tax for Scott.[54]

Watching the whole deal unfold was Robert (Bob) Christie, a lifelong resident of Pictou Landing. Today, Christie lives in the farmhouse his family built back in 1837. His life has been intimately connected to the mill, which, when the trees around his property are bare in winter, he can see clearly from his front step. In 1965 and 1966, he worked for Tidewater, which had the contract to do the clearing and ground preparation for the new mill.[55] Later Christie went to work for the Canso Chemicals plant right beside it, which would produce chemicals needed for the pulping process.

Christie worked nine years for Canso Chemicals, and although he says he had a number of reasons for leaving, the prime one was the accident – the day he was gassed. He was standing outside the plant when the head operator blew the safety valve of a chlorine tank, allowing the gas to leak. Christie was not wearing any safety equipment; they didn't even think about things like that back then, he says. He wound up in hospital and lost the use of half a lung.

Later, in the 1980s, he became a strident critic of the

mill, particularly the toxic effluent it was pumping, via pipe-line, into Boat Harbour, just a hundred metres or so behind his house. Later still, his stance softened towards the mill after he became the Executive Director of the Pictou Harbour Environment Protection Program, which was funded by the federal government to look at pollution hot spots in Canada, of which the Pictou area was considered one. Today he sits on the Community Liaison Committee of Northern Pulp, the current owner of the mill, as an invited member of the company-chosen group. He still describes himself as an environmentalist, but he alternates between defending the mill and laughing loudly as he recounts his own long history of fighting hard against it.

And he still has nothing good to say about the sweet deal that the government of the day handed to Scott. He says the province had no business damming a river to give the "water monster" all the fresh water it needed. He's even more critical of the province's unprecedented offer to take complete responsibility for the mill's toxic effluent.[56] This, for him, is the crux of what he sees as the biggest problem with the mill.

It's a beautiful summer day in 2016 when I visit him in his farmhouse, and we sit at the table in a roomy and modern kitchen that somehow still retains the cozy feel of a large country kitchen from another century. Christie is dapper in a well-pressed, short-sleeved plaid shirt and khaki trousers, and very chipper as he summons memories that are decades old.

He recalls a conversation he had with the president and general manager of Scott Maritimes, Walter Miller, shortly after Miller's retirement party. As he remembers the occasion, he had been playing shuffleboard with some friends in the Bluenose Tavern in the nearby town of Stellarton when he spied Miller in a corner. He decided to ask the outgoing mill manager what his plans were, if he was going to stay on in Pictou after his retirement. Miller, who hailed from the United States, replied he wasn't going to live any longer in Nova Scotia. And he informed Christie that during his time as mill manager, his pay package had included a monthly bonus of $5,000, "isolation pay" for living in Pictou.

Christie then remarked to Miller that he'd never in all his years heard of a government offering such huge incentives to get an industry to set up in Pictou County, particularly a pulp industry, and what did he think of that? Miller confirmed that Scott had secured a very good deal indeed. Thanks to the concessions the government offered, the company had saved at least $5 million a year. If Scott had set up a similar mill in the United States, Miller said, they would have had to treat their own effluent and that would have cost between $3 and $5 million, and they would have had to buy their own water for another couple of million dollars.

According to Christie, when all of this was being hammered out in meetings at Scott's headquarters in Philadelphia, "They couldn't believe how stupid the government was up here."[57] He laughs, but wryly, when he repeats what Miller said to him all those years ago about the huge incentives the government of Nova Scotia offered to Scott in exchange for its decision to locate in Pictou: "Bob, they're still laughing in Philadelphia."

4

Water woes in "the other room" (1965-1970)

A'se'k and its recreational, physical, mental, spiritual, and emotional purposes have been compromised since a pulp and paper mill was built nearby and began dumping its effluent into this cherished body of water. For nearly 50 years, we – our Elders, our leaders, all of us – have been trying to redress this environmental and social injustice.[58]

She doesn't want her name to appear in any books, and she is cagey about her age, but the Mi'kmaq Elder welcomes me into the living room of her bungalow and seems happy to recall what life was like for the Pictou Landing First Nation when she was growing up. She looks fit and well. And despite her claim that her memory is failing, she has no trouble summoning clear pictures of Boat Harbour years before the mill came to Abercrombie Point and before it became a receptacle for its waste. For her, it was the "best place in the world."

The Pictou Landing Reserve where she lives is an exceptionally beautiful spot on the shore of the Northumberland Strait, a part of the world where there is no shortage of beautiful beaches and vistas. It offers a panorama of sandstone shoreline and enticing blue water. Across the Strait, Prince Edward Island is just barely visible on the horizon, a sliver of land separating azure sea from sapphire sky. Pictou Landing is the mainland anchor for a long, white sandy strip known as Lighthouse Beach that reaches out into the Strait like a protective arm at the mouth of Pictou Harbour. On the other side of the Reserve is Boat Harbour, which the Elder remembers when it was still a tidal estuary connected to the Northumberland Strait by a narrow channel.

The whole area had always been an important hunting and fishing ground for the Mi'kmaq. The estuary was so valuable to them, so much a part of their lives and livelihoods, that they viewed it as part of their home, calling it "A'se'k," or "the other room."[59] The Elder tells me it was packed with fish, all kinds of them, with lots of streams, large and small, feeding into it.

"You just go in there and you don't need nets or anything, you just pull your fish out," she says. "That's how we used to do it. As a little girl, I would say I'm going to have fish today and I'd take my basket and go there and get my supply and go home. The whole community did that, eh."

"For us, that was Sobeys," she says, chuckling, as she refers to the supermarket chain. "You go shopping there and come home with lots of fruit and fish." People had root cellars, where they stored the food they harvested in and around Boat Harbour, hunting and trapping in the woods that surrounded the estuary. The fields in the area were full of medicinal plants and berries. There were also many vegetable gardens in the community and people shared their harvests with each other. She attributes her health even today to the traditional, natural diet of her childhood, much of which came from the estuary and its surroundings.

A'Se'k was a safe haven for fishing boats, and it was a popular recreational area for both First Nation and other residents of the area who hunted and fished there. It was also a safe haven for the Mi'kmaq themselves, the place they took their children to try to hide them from government agents who came to Pictou Landing to take them away to residential schools.[60]

In the 1900s, many people from the nearby towns of Stellarton and New Glasgow as well as from more distant towns such as Truro, purchased cottages along the Pictou Landing shoreline and many more flocked to Lighthouse Beach on warm summer days. For decades, it was a favourite spot for picnics and for a time looked like it was set to develop into a popular resort with a hotel, lobster bar, shops and canteens, yacht club, twice-daily train service, and also a ferry that took passengers and vehicles to and fro between Pictou Landing, the town of Pictou, and Abercrombie Point.[61]

The whole area – the Boat Harbour tidal inlet, the rivers, the forest, and miles and miles of sandy beaches along the Northumberland shoreline – was considered one of such natural beauty that there had been talk in the 1920s of creating a national park to preserve it for posterity.[62] Instead, in 1967, it became a dumping ground for poisonous waste from the pulp mill.

"Well, almost a week after they got that mill going, the change started to come right away," the Elder tells me. The previously clear, pure water turned dark and began to smell. Children who swam in it came home with what looked like burns on their skin. The estuary became a no-go area, and not just for human beings.

Where the estuary met the Northumberland Strait, just beside an existing highway bridge in Pictou Landing, a dam had been built to control the release of the effluent from Boat Harbour and keep the water levels high in the harbour, where the effluent was supposed to sit for twenty-one days before it flowed into the Strait. The Elder recalls walking to the dam and recoiling as she looked down at the brown water behind the dam.

"And the fish, honest to goodness that's the saddest sight

I've seen," she says. "The fish were trying to get out of the water, all their little heads were, well it was packed, packed, packed with fish trying to get, I don't know, trying to get oxygen or whatever. Whatever it was, it wasn't available for them in the water, so they had to stick their little heads up. And there's no way they can stay like that, that's what killed them, eh. And in just a few short days the shores were just covered with dead fish." The effluent, laden with wood fibre, had robbed the water of oxygen, suffocating the fish.

The Elder says no one in the area had any idea how the effluent was going to affect Boat Harbour or the Northumberland Strait. All that the people of Pictou Landing First Nation knew beforehand was what they had been told by the government people, provincial and federal. The Elder says they were told that Boat Harbour was going to stay clean, the water would be fine, and they would see no change except that money would be pouring in from the mill.

"The mistake that my people make, and they're still doing it, is we're trusting one hundred percent," says the Elder. "That's because that's part of our upbringing ... so even if it's somebody who has never told us a single truth in their life, because it's our upbringing we put the same trust on that individual." Because they trusted the government officials who promised them there would be no harm done to Boat Harbour and the fish, they gave their consent for its use for mill effluent. She tells me signing that contract was the biggest mistake the Mi'kmaq ever made.

It may have been a very big mistake, but it was not one of Mi'kmaq making. Federal and provincial bureaucrats had been instructed to get the Pictou Landing First Nation to sign off on an agreement that would allow the mill to pipe its industrial and chemical waste into Boat Harbour.

The groundwork was laid in 1963, when the provincial government appointed a board of commissioners that constituted the Nova Scotia Water Authority, to which it handed absolute authority for implementing the 1919 Water Act.[63]

That meant these appointed commissioners were in charge of water use and water bodies throughout the province, and, in theory, would also be responsible for protecting water bodies from pollution.

The first chair appointed to head the Nova Scotia Water Authority was an interesting choice, or perhaps a strategic one – none other than Dr. John Seaman Bates, who had originally worked with Scott to find the location for the mill that would afford it good access to plenty of fresh water and trees.[64] Bates was a chemist from the pulp industry who had been involved with mills across the country. He had also made the initial connection with Stora, the Swedish company that came to the province in 1961.[65] He was acutely aware of the high toxicity of effluent from mills such as the one at Abercrombie Point, which he knew carried "solids, solubles and toxic substances, often in quantity and condition too staggering for polite conversation."[66]

Bates is an enigma. On one hand, he made strident public pleas for the protection of water, which he described as the "most wonderful substance on earth."[67] He expressed concern about water pollution caused by toxic and acidic industrial discharges, which could diminish oxygen content in water and result in what he called "unnatural conditions." "Companies sometimes hesitate to go along," he wrote, but they "always appreciate the technical help offered by government agencies and in the end say how much better it was to control properly than to pile up more pollution."[68]

And yet it was Bates who devised the plan to dump the mill's industrial effluent into Boat Harbour, a body of water that he said had been "doing nothing."[69] Bates envisaged Boat Harbour as a treatment centre for mill and industry waste, as well as for municipal sewage systems for the towns of Pictou, Trenton, and New Glasgow. There had been some consideration of using Pictou Harbour for the waste disposal, but officials didn't want to discharge the effluent into that "picturesque" harbour.[70] And Boat Harbour also had the political advantage of being invisible to everyone except residents of Pictou Landing. Even today, very few people in Nova Scotia have ever seen Boat Harbour; it is not easily accessed by the public.

Bates foresaw that the causeway he had conceived would impound 100 million Imperial gallons (about 455 million litres) of fresh water every day, of which a quarter would be used by the mill. A slightly smaller volume of effluent would be pumped out of the mill every day, then piped under the mouth of the East River for "nature's purification" in Boat Harbour, before it would overflow to the open ocean.[71] This, Bates said, meant pollution of Pictou Harbour could be avoided, creating "perhaps the best natural treatment facilities in the country, and certainly the Scott pulp mill the finest of its kind in Eastern Canada ..."[72] The plan to direct the waste to Boat Harbour became known as "Bates' scheme." Scott agreed to it and in July 1965 the Water Authority began working hard to get it set up.

But there was a hitch. Someone had to get permission from the Pictou Landing First Nation for the use of Boat Harbour, as this was a federal issue involving the Department of Indian Affairs. In July 1965, W.S.K. Jones, Nova Scotia's Minister under the Water Act with responsibility for the Water Authority, wrote to the federal Minister of Citizenship and Immigration, John R. Nicholson, about the possibility of using the estuary for "waste water treatment." Jones assured Minister Nicholson that "the appearance of the harbour would in fact be improved" and that the project could be carried out "without creating any nuisance for residents of the area."[73]

The general manager of the Water Authority, Armand F. Wigglesworth, held a meeting with officials of the Indian Affairs branch and members of the Pictou Landing Band on August 25, 1965. He assured those present there would be no odour, except perhaps when the ice broke up in the spring, and there would still be fresh water in the lagoon after it was dammed up, although salt-water species would die. The Pictou Landing Band members said they were not willing to let Boat Harbour be used by the Water Authority. At the end of the meeting, Wigglesworth asked if they would withhold any publicity until after the Water Authority could study the matter further. They did not offer him this assurance.[74]

Federal Minister John Nicholson, whose responsibilities also included the Indian Affairs branch, then wrote back to Nova Scotia's minister in charge of the Water Authority, W.S.K. Jones, citing the six objections the Mi'kmaq had raised at the meeting. "1. Fishing as a source of food would be lost forever. 2. Continued high water level and contamination would ruin feeding ground for game birds such as ducks and geese which are an important source of food. 3. The harbour would be lost as a safe haven for fishing boats. 4. The waters could no longer be used for swimming and recreation. 5. Odours would at times be blowing off the waters onto the residential area of the Reserve which is less than a quarter mile away in some cases. 6. Loss of possible building lots on Boat Harbour shoreline."[75]

One of the oldest members of the band, Michael Denny, was always dead set against the scheme, and had warned about it, telling people that this idea to put the pollution into Boat Harbour was "craziness," that it would be no good for the First Nation community.[76] And there's no ambiguity in the letter from the federal minister to his provincial colleague reiterating the Mi'kmaq objections to the plan. Not only did the Mi'kmaq strongly oppose Bates' scheme but both levels of government were made aware of it.

What happened next was "almost criminal," in the words of Daniel Paul, Mi'kmaq Elder, scholar, and author, who himself had once worked for the federal Department of Indian and Northern Affairs.[77] On the weekend of October 10, 1965, the Water Authority bureaucrats, Wigglesworth and Bates, quietly invited the chief of the Pictou Landing Band and a band councillor to New Brunswick. There they were told they would be able to see for themselves how a similar waste treatment system worked.

There is a remarkable interview with John Bates done in 1988 when he was ninety-nine years old. It was for an episode of the CBC television program *Land and Sea* that looked at how Boat Harbour became the sewer for the pulp mill. At one point, journalist Claude Vickery asks Bates what he remembers about the weekend he took the chief and councillor from Pictou Landing to New Brunswick and showed them the water treatment facility.

Bates says he remembers inviting them, that it was only fair to "let them see ...," and here he pauses and pulls at the collar of his white shirt, rubbing at his neck as if he's developed a tic. Then an odd smile appears on his face and he continues, describing what they went to see as "a pollution pond in practice quietly purifying the sewage. When you walk around it you can't even smell it."

Vickery persists. "Did you smell anything that day?"

Bates chuckles, then nearly shouts, "No!" He maintains there was sewage going into the pond and there was no smell. They walked all around it, until the chief said to him, "Now you have convinced me."

Truth be told – as it wasn't being back then – Bates and Wigglesworth didn't take Chief Louis Francis or Councillor Martin Sapier to a pulp mill in New Brunswick. Rather, it seems they took them on a tour of a domestic sewage disposal lagoon in Renforth,[78] a suburban area northeast of Saint John that has since become part of the town of Rothesay. It appears the facility they visited was not even operational, and the water they walked around was coming from a spring-fed brook.[79] It's no surprise, then, that in an interview he did in 1969 for an episode of the CBC program *Country Calendar*, Chief Francis tells reporter Peter Brock that there was "no discolouration in the water, no odour or anything coming out of that pulp mill up there."[80]

In the *Land and Sea* program in 1988, Vickery asks Councillor Sapier for his recollections of the trip. Sapier says they weren't paid to go to New Brunswick, and all they got out of it was a good supper and a good sleep. He recalls "the old gent" – Bates – suggested to them that if they didn't know it was a sewer they could drink from it. Sapier smiles when he says this, and his reply is difficult to understand. It sounds as if he was saying he didn't know whether that was true. But then he assures Vickery he trusted Bates.

Vickery asks him if they were being pressured to make a decision. Sapier replies that over breakfast the next morning, Bates and Wigglesworth asked them if they would agree to the Boat Harbour deal, and they said they would if the Band received $65,000, which Wigglesworth said he would vouch for.

"The deal was done?" asks Vickery.

"The deal was done," says Sapier.

Wigglesworth wrote up a two-page agreement, which Chief Francis and Councillor Sapier signed, with himself as witness, dated October 10, 1965, and the rights to Boat Harbour were sold for $65,000.

In his 1988 interview with Bates, Vickery asks whether he was concerned that the scheme to use Boat Harbour for the mill's effluent meant it would be so close to the First Nation Reserve. "They weren't living in the water," Bates replies. "They were living in sight of the water." After a pause, he adds, "And so what?"

A week after that trip to New Brunswick, Wigglesworth appeared at a public meeting at a Pictou Landing school and told a room packed with fishers, cottagers, and non-native residents of the area that after the trip to Saint John, the chief had given approval "in principle" for the use of Boat Harbour.[81] He said there would be compensation for the Mi'kmaq for the loss of fishing privileges and told the audience he would not go along with anything unfair to the First Nation, that he had taken the chief to Saint John to see a lagoon waste disposal system in operation.[82]

He assured them the mill effluent would not pollute Boat Harbour. He maintained it would become a freshwater lake that could be used for skating and boating, if not for swimming. Wigglesworth also said aerators could be installed to replenish oxygen supplies in the water to prevent it from dying and to reduce bad odours.[83] He added that a skidway would be constructed that would allow boaters to continue to get into the "lake" where they could still moor their vessels. By the end of the meeting, Wigglesworth seems to have had people more or less on side. Previously sceptical cottage owners said they were satisfied their interests would be looked after, and a committee of citizens was elected to work with the Water Authority.

In April 1966, Premier Stanfield, acting as Minister under the Water Act, put his signature on a report to the Executive Council (the cabinet), which authorized "the Nova Scotia Water Authority to provide for the disposal of effluent from the Scott Maritimes Pulp Limited mill into Boat Harbour" and gave it the go-ahead to acquire all the land it needed around the estuary, stipulating that the provincial Minister of Finance and Economics would pick up the tab for the waste disposal facility.[84]

It wasn't until September, however, that the Governor General in Council, on the recommendation of the federal Minister of Northern Affairs and Natural Resources, officially transferred the riparian rights in Boat Harbour to the province of Nova Scotia.[85] In return, the province would compensate the Pictou Landing Band by paying $60,000 into the federal treasury for the use of Boat Harbour as a waste treatment area for the mill's effluent, with an additional $5,000 for renovations on the Band's church.[86] It would also build a skidway for boats, and take "remedial action should a septic condition detrimental to the Pictou Landing Band develop in Boat Harbour."[87]

The federal government, which was legally obliged to help protect the band by providing independent expert advice on how the mill's effluent would affect Boat Harbour, had failed to do so.[88] Instead, it hid information from the Band and ignored advice from the departments of Justice and of Indian Affairs that the scheme would be detrimental to the Band and to the Crown itself. Elders in Pictou Landing said they had agreed to the scheme only reluctantly, and they did so not just because of the lies they were told but also because they feared if they didn't there would be backlash from the Department of Indian Affairs and from the people of Pictou County, so many of whom were welcoming Scott Paper as their economic saviour.

In his interview with Peter Brock for CBC's *Country Calendar* in 1969, Chief Francis recalls that the superintendent of Indian Affairs came to see him and warned him he should let them have Boat Harbour; otherwise the government would step in and expropriate it.[89]

"So, 'expropriate' is a big word for us down here," Chief Francis says to Brock. "Ever since the first white man landed here that's all that's been happening to us is expropriating. All we ever had was a little bit of land left over for us." He explains he agreed to the deal only because he figured if they were going to lose Boat Harbour anyway, it would be best to get some money out of the agreement so they would have something to fall back on once the harbour had been expropriated.

Then he says it was only later they found out the superintendent had lied, that no one had the right to expropriate Boat Harbour from the First Nation Band. But by then, he says, it was too late. After that he adds, "Anyway, what I sold, it wasn't Boat Harbour I sold, it was the water rights, the fishing rights for the Indians."

In April 1966, just as Premier Stanfield was signing off on the Boat Harbour deal, Armand Wigglesworth left his position as general manager of the Water Authority and also as chair of the Pictou Area Water Commission, to take a job as regional director of the Canada Emergency Measures Organization in Nova Scotia.[90] Three months later, John Seaman Bates also left the Authority, and then Minister under the Water Act I.W. Akerley appointed E.L.L. Rowe to replace him. Bates remained a consultant to the Nova Scotia Water Authority, and continued to head similar authorities in New Brunswick and Prince Edward Island.[91] He would go down in history as an "environmentalist." He had been awarded honorary doctorates from the University of Ottawa, the University of New Brunswick, and Dalhousie University, and was named to the Order of Canada.[92]

Wigglesworth went on to a career with the federal civil service before he retired and returned to his home on the South Shore of Nova Scotia in 1983, after which he too received the Order of Canada and was remembered as a "distinguished Nova Scotian."[93]

Whether by design or by a stroke of incredibly good luck, they both got out just in the nick of time, before the deal they'd pushed through went sour, the waste went into the water, the fish died, the beaches were destroyed, and Boat Harbour turned into a "living hell."[94]

5

The first wave of dissent (1964-1970)

Just look around you. You will see that the movement we need has sprung up all over the world, in small communities fighting for their futures.

– Linda Pannozzo[95]

Even before the mill opened, there were already stirrings of citizen dissent and discontent in and around Pictou Landing, both on and off the Reserve. One of the early contentious issues for non-First Nations citizens was the government's expropriation of land they owned around Boat Harbour.

Many had no interest in giving up their family land. Robert Christie's family was one of those. In the 1830s when his ancestors settled in Pictou Landing, they obtained an entire section of land that stretched all the way from Pictou Harbour overland to Boat Harbour, and then continued on the other side of the estuary as far as Little Harbour. By the 1960s, the family's land holding was greatly reduced. Over the years Christie's father, Jack, had happily sold or given away small parcels for next to nothing to friends or people in need, deals made on the back of an Export A cigarette package and sealed with a handshake. But that didn't mean Jack Christie was about to extend the same generosity to the Water Authority officials who went house to house in Pictou Landing to try to get residents with land bordering Boat Harbour to hand it over to the government.

Christie remembers the day the man from the Water Authority came calling, although he can't recall his name. It was a beautiful sunny morning, he says, when a heavyset older man drove up and came to the door, asking for Christie's father. As is the way in rural Nova Scotia, they invited him in and then gathered around the kitchen table while the visitor explained that a water treatment facility was going to be built at Boat Harbour. The man said the bottom line was they needed two parcels of the family land, one on each side of Boat Harbour.

"Dad would sit and listen to anybody, drunk or sober," says Christie. He was just a young man then and much of what the man from the Water Authority was saying didn't make sense to him. Apparently it didn't to his father, either, who said so. At that point the official said if they didn't accept the offer, their land would be taken anyway. Christie's father was the kind of person who was generally relaxed about things, a man in the habit of giving away family land. But he didn't like ultimatums from strangers. So he asked the man to leave, saying, "There's no deal to be made here."

In the end, the family land bordering Boat Harbour was expropriated for $15 an acre, wood and all, says Christie, when the actual value even back then would have been ten or fifteen times that amount. Like the Christies, many families refused the offers and watched in dismay as farms that had been in their families for generations were taken from them.

The Sproull family is one of those. Their roots in the area date back to 1824 when the family bought a farm that bordered Boat Harbour. Like other landowners around the estuary, they were forced to give up their land in 1966 when the government expropriated it in advance of turning Boat Harbour into what Jane Sproull Thomson calls a "cesspool" and a "circle of hell." The government offered just $4 an acre, and then failed to pay anything at all. The Sproull family took the matter to court and won, but wound up losing money because the legal costs were higher than the amount they were paid for the land.

That was just one part of it. In addition to the family farm, in 1939 her father had also purchased a piece of waterfront property in Moodie Cove, a lovely stretch of coastline in the lee of Lighthouse Beach, a stone's throw from the Pictou Landing Reserve and Boat Harbour. A medical doctor, he had then divided the property into cottage lots and sold them to his friends, mostly fellow doctors, and the cove became a summer paradise for a dozen families.

Now, five decades later, we are sitting at the kitchen table in the Moodie Cove home of Jane Sproull Thomson. The glass doors afford us an idyllic vista – the still waters of the small cove, then Lighthouse Beach and after that, the wide-open waters of the Northumberland Strait. Although it's summer, there is no one out there swimming, not a person to be seen on the beach. This part of the coast has long since become a no-swim zone. Even five and a half kilometres from the mill as the foul odour flies, inside the house the sulphuric smell insinuates itself around us. Paradise that has now been lost.

Sproull Thomson and her husband, Callum Thomson, have just made the difficult decision to give up their waterfront property where she has spent summers since she was a child, and move to British Columbia. This was not the original plan. A few years ago they winterized their cottage in Moodie Cove and planned to retire here. They gave it a try for five years. No more. The pollution in the air and water in the area provoke her husband's asthma, making it impossible for him to sleep at night. Whenever they are on Vancouver Island, where they will now be living permanently, his asthma disappears. It is only since they returned two weeks ago to pack up their things for the move that he has had to start using his puffer again.

It's an emotional time for them; the issue of the mill and the years they have spent as part of successive environmental groups fighting its pollution are clearly taking their toll on the family. Sproull Thomson's sister Barbara Sproull Seplaki, who has joined us for the discussion, fights back tears as she tries to express her frustration about the decades they have struggled to try to get one government after another to force the mill owners to clean it up. Now one sister is leaving, and the other, Sproull Seplaki, will stay behind, even though her own grown children are reluctant to come home to visit because of the stench.

My presence and questions just seem to make them sad, reminding them of how much they've given up over the years. If I hadn't showed up today, Sproull Thomson says, she would have tossed all the files that document the work she and her fellow citizens have done over the years. Instead, she hands them over to me, along with a great raft of electronic files.

"Mentally, it's just that you get exhausted," Sproull Thomson says. "And that's what they count on." Government and mill officials are paid for their time. Citizens are not. "Everything that we have done over the last fifty years has been unpaid, on our own time, taking time away from our families," she says. "They're people with families who don't get paid for all of the hours that we put in trying to get these issues addressed. And these people who work for the mill have the nerve to speak to us, to call us 'environmentalists,' with a sneer in their tone."

The two sisters have powerful and poignant childhood memories of life before the mill, of summers spent picking mayflowers in the fragrant woods around Boat Harbour, and swimming across the cove to Lighthouse Beach, much loved because of its beauty and warm water. A fresh spring provided crystal clear water to the twelve cottages in Moodie Cove.

"It was a wonderful place to grow up," says Sproull Thomson. "We used to go down to the beach and dig clams and have big clambakes." Then came the announcement in 1964 that a mill would be built at Abercrombie Point. Sproull Thomson says her father was upset from the start because he knew what a pulp mill was going to bring. He and several others in the area held the very first public meetings to discuss the mill and Boat Harbour, a core group that would eventually evolve into an organized association protesting the pollution.

"Fortunately, he never had to see it," she says. He died in 1965, even before the family's land around Boat Harbour was expropriated.

The murky and divisive way that the Nova Scotia Water Authority and the government handled the Boat Harbour deal – how it obtained the rights for the water from the Pictou Landing First Nation and expropriated the land around it from other residents – led to unhealthy misunderstandings and hard feelings in the area.

According to Mi'kmaq scholar Daniel Paul, what some non-First Nations residents of Pictou Landing were paid for their properties was "far in excess" of the $60,000 paid to the Band to compensate them for their rights to the waters of all of Boat Harbour.[96] At the same time, some non-First Nations residents of Pictou Landing complained they were paid amounts equivalent to the "price of a shoe,"[97] between $10 and $15 per acre, while the price paid for the area of Boat Harbour itself worked out to nearly six times that much.[98]

In truth, both groups were treated very, very badly. Whether it was intentional or not, the government did divide the people of Pictou Landing so it was able to conquer and secure rights over Boat Harbour from the Mi'kmaq and seize surrounding lands from the non-First Nations residents.

And all the while, the authorities were sticking to the official line that no harm would come of the scheme. The Nova Scotia Water Authority under E.L.L. Rowe continued to try to assure a sceptical public that all would be well, that "the effluent will be completely pure when it comes into the Strait after being processed in Boat Harbor."[99] And if it had a coffee colour, that would be "quickly dispersed with the tides, and it is understood that there is no chance that it will cause any damage to fish or to any people who want to swim in the area."

Rowe was making these claims three years before a serious scientific study was done to determine whether in fact the Northumberland Strait could handle the effluent. Such a study, undertaken in 1969 by the federal Bedford Institute of Oceanography in Dartmouth, Nova Scotia, found it couldn't, concluding that "the flushing capacity of the area is inadequate to dilute the effluent below the proposed water quality standard of 1% and a new location for the effluent outfall is suggested."[100] This, of course, is very much what people in the area had been worrying about from the beginning.

There were dissenting voices, like that of Mi'kmaq Elder Michael Denny who spoke out early on, saying it wouldn't be good to allow effluent into Boat Harbour. There was also Dr. Joe B. MacDonald, who owned a cottage at the outlet of Boat Harbour. MacDonald was a family physician in the nearby town of Stellarton, who shared a medical practice with a young man by the name of Dr. John F. Hamm, who would go on to become premier of the province in 1999 and, later, chair of the board of the company that owned the mill.

But back in March 1966, Hamm was just a name on the letterhead of the medical practice that he shared with MacDonald, who was busy writing opinion pieces to newspapers and no-holds-barred letters to Premier Stanfield to express his concerns about the claims being made by Bates and Wigglesworth. In one letter dated March 19, 1966, MacDonald takes issue with the suggestion that damming Boat Harbour would make it a beautiful freshwater lake that could be used for everything but fishing and swimming. "This is exactly like taking a man who has two good legs and removing one – and then saying to him, 'You are better off with one,'" he writes to the premier. "'It will be less bother and you can do everything except, (1) walk well and (2) all those other pursuits that require two legs.'"

Not one to curb his extraordinary gift of laying out his position in droll prose, MacDonald continues, "This claim of theirs – that Boat Harbour will be improved by damming – would be much more reasonable if they were going to dam Boat Harbour and use it for the storage and propagation of sharks. The presence of sharks would only be a relative contraindication to the use of the place for swimming and fishing."

Even as Dr. MacDonald was penning his pointed letters, plans were being finalized for the fibreglass pipeline that would be laid from the mill to carry its waste under the East River and then back onshore and overland to Boat Harbour.[101] By November 1966, tenders were out for two dams, one to impound a swampy area above Boat Harbour and a second at the outlet to the Northumberland Strait. The blanket expropriation in the area was being pushed through to permit the contractor to get on with the work, and landowners were being encouraged to "come in and talk business."[102]

Municipal Councillor Henry Ferguson took the case to court, saying the Minister of Lands and Forests had no right to expropriate his land that abutted Boat Harbour. The court ruled against his claim, awarding him just $10 per acre, plus another hundred dollars for his loss of access to Boat Harbour and another small sum for compulsory taking, for a grand total of $385.[103]

Ferguson continued mobilizing residents in the area. In 1966, he organized yet another meeting in Pictou Landing, and as he had before, he invited the Water Authority, politicians from all levels of government, and Scott Paper. Only the new head of the Authority, E.L.L. Rowe, and one Member of the Legislative Assembly (MLA) of Nova Scotia showed up to respond to public questions. The citizens present expressed concerns about the effect the waste would have on one of the finest beach areas in Canada and on the Northumberland Strait, one of the world's most important Atlantic lobster fishing grounds. Secretary of the citizens' group, Lloyd MacKay, said that the residents had sent someone to Ottawa to see the federal Minister of Fisheries to express their concerns, only to be told the department couldn't do anything until the "contamination was a fact."[104]

A young teacher named Ferguson MacKay asked Rowe about the cost of the aerators, which Wigglesworth had assured concerned citizens would be installed in Boat Harbour to reduce odours. Rowe replied there wouldn't be any aerators because he was a "cost man." Tempers flared and the meeting lasted four hours. Lloyd MacKay was angry, saying that the residents knew less at the end of the meeting than they did at the beginning. Neither side was backing down.

Rowe said he was "surprised at the hue and cry," and while he tried to assure the people of Pictou Landing that the mill's waste disposal system would not harm the fisheries, he also said industrial progress was greatly needed in the province, so people had to accept that there would be some effect on fish, wildlife, and game.[105]

The war of words and wills between the authorities and Pictou County residents concerned about the effects the mill would have on their water and air had begun. The residents would eventually organize themselves into the Northumberland Strait Pollution Control Committee, and continue locking horns with Rowe, the provincial minister in charge of the Water Act, and Walter Miller of Scott.

But first came 1967, Canada's centennial. In September of that year, Premier Stanfield resigned to become the leader of the federal Progressive Conservative Party and then, a year later, unsuccessfully contest the federal election against Pierre Elliot Trudeau. Stanfield's deputy, G.I. Smith, took over.

Two months later, the pulp mill held a grandiose formal opening, but Premier Smith was not able to attend. He was otherwise occupied with a slew of simmering crises he had inherited. One of these was the trouble-plagued Deuterium of Canada Ltd.'s heavy water plant. The province had plowed $100 million into it and it had not produced a single heavy water molecule two years after its planned start. Another was the Dominion Steel and Coal Corporation in Sydney, which was losing money and threatening to close down, which would throw 3,000 out of work. A third was Clairtone, the company belonging to furniture designer David Gilmour, and to Peter Munk, the entrepreneur and engineer who would later become immensely wealthy after founding the world's largest gold mining company. Industrial Estates had brought Clairtone to the province with $10 million in bonds and preferred stocks, but it was failing and the province eventually took it over before it went belly up.[106] [107]

So Premier Smith had his hands full and it was Highways Minister Stephen Pyke who officiated at the launch of the new Scott mill. A long list of dignitaries attended the celebrations, including the chair of Scott's board of directors, Thomas B. McCabe of Philadelphia, Nova Scotia's Lieutenant Governor H.P. McKeen, and many municipal, provincial, and federal politicians. Guests were treated to a luncheon and a tour of the mill.

It's probably just as well the tour didn't include Boat Harbour. The VIPs might have suffered indigestion – or worse – if they'd had to see and smell the mess. The mill had already been operating for two months, and what had happened to the once-beautiful estuary and coastline was very much what many in Pictou Landing had predicted. As the Mi'kmaq Elder had told me, the fish began to die en masse just days after the waste began to flow. In 1988, Elder Michael Denny told CBC's Claude Vickery, "They killed every fish out there, all along the shore, dead smelts and seals and everything all around. They killed them right away ... three or four days after the plant started."[108]

At first, there was speculation in the press about whether the problem was that the Water Authority was understaffed for the extensive job entrusted to it, of which Boat Harbour was only a small part. Then came promises from the authority that it would apply "the best technical and scientific knowledge which can be obtained" to the pollution problem.[109] But the jet-black colour of the water, the rotten smell it gave off that could "knock you over," the fibre-laden foam that was floating on Boat Harbour and then flowing through the dam onto the beaches and shoreline of Pictou Landing, and the stench of the mill itself were too much. Earlier ripples of discontent turned into a wave. Residents and cottage owners and fishers of Pictou Landing, many who had once agreed to work with the Water Authority, turned on it. Articles began appearing in the local newspapers about how the air and water pollution and the smell of the pulp mill might adversely affect the tourist industry.[110] Fishermen said their lobster catches in the area were down.

Government officials chose to deal with the public protest by downplaying or obfuscating the issues. At a meeting of fisheries officers in early 1968 in the town of New Glasgow, a biologist with the Department of Fisheries said he was not very concerned about the effluent in the Boat Harbour area and the dark brown colour of the effluent did not necessarily mean it was toxic.[111] E.L.L. Rowe stuck to his story that the effluent from Boat Harbour was not polluting the Strait and he didn't know why people were complaining so much.[112]

Incensed citizens countered in letters to their local papers, saying the water at the outlet was so dark and murky you couldn't see the bottom even when it was only six inches deep, and it was also blackening the sand.[113] Residents of Pictou Landing complained that the foul air from Boat Harbour was discolouring the paint on houses, and that living in the area had become unbearable. The situation was so bad, they said, that citizens were now uniting to try to get the Water Authority to do something. In the fall of 1968, a group of property owners collected a thousand signatures on a petition that outlined the problems with the mill's waste facility. Municipal Councillor Henry Ferguson said the government "ignored" their petition, that they'd been "slapped in the face."[114]

Donald R. MacLeod, Minister in charge of the province's

Water Act and the Water Authority, then waded into the increasingly toxic discourse. In November 1968, he said people had to be "prepared to make sacrifices" if they wanted new industry and jobs in the region. And as for the citizens who were upset about the pollution, "There are a lot of people talking," he said. "And they don't know what they're talking about."[115] He did concede that the government was concerned about the situation in Boat Harbour, and said there were plans to extend 700 feet of pipeline from the outlet out into the Strait to try to reduce the pollution and discoloration of water along the shoreline. The citizens of the area were not impressed.

In December 1968, Councillor Henry Ferguson called yet another public meeting at the Pictou Landing school – the fourth in just two years – to discuss the pollution of Boat Harbour and adjoining waters, to which he also invited members of the provincial legislature, the fisheries department, the Water Authority, and Scott Paper. Once again, Rowe – now head of the Water Resources Commission that had supplanted the Water Authority – was quizzed at length by citizens sceptical of the province's methods of dealing with the mill's effluent, which he told them had already cost $2.25 million. The media were starting to take notice of the growing protest; three newspapers, one radio station, and CBC television sent reporters to cover the event.

Rowe again said a new pipeline would be extended out into the Strait, but because of the cost, that would now be just 170 feet long rather than the 700 promised earlier. His audience was having none of it. Lobster fishers argued the waste was damaging the fishery and a pipeline should extend into the Strait for at least half a mile. Once again, Rowe showed himself to be a "cost man," countering that each foot would cost $200 and thus a longer pipeline would be too expensive.

It was a raucous meeting. Rowe argued that the effluent was held for four days before it went into the Strait, long enough to eliminate toxicity so there was no danger of it poisoning lobster larvae. "Who's going to say it's held four days?"

someone shouted back. Rowe then said it was held forty days, and when he was again challenged, he said it was all a question of "semantics." He said the reason paint on houses was turning black was because people were using lead-based paint, and the sulphides in the air would discolour it. "Are we going to have to buy paint to suit the pulp mill?" asked one man. Rowe then retorted that anyone who bought lead-based paint was "crazy."[116]

Representatives from the federal fisheries department claimed they had undertaken research that showed the effluent would not hurt lobster larvae or adult lobsters, despite fishers' own accounts of dramatically lower catches since the mill went into operation.

The meeting resolved absolutely nothing. Dissatisfied with the response they were getting from Rowe, sixteen lobster fishers gathered a few days later in a hotel in New Glasgow where they agreed to try to seek an interview with Premier G.I. Smith and the federal Department of Fisheries office in Halifax. Chair of the meeting and president of the Northumberland Fishermen's Association George Reid had taken a sample of water near the Boat Harbour outlet and sent it to a laboratory in Montreal for analysis. The lab results indicated that more than 150 tons of suspected solids were flowing into the Northumberland Strait every day, at a concentration ten times – 1,000 percent – higher than levels permitted by the Quebec Water Control Board.[117] Fred Tasker, a spokesperson for Scott, took to the podium at a Rotary Club meeting to defend the mill's industrial waste treatment, which he said was "second to none."[118]

Even if the government wasn't exactly caving in to the concerned citizens on the demands to end the pollution of Boat Harbour, it looks as if their activism was not going completely unheeded. In early 1969, Premier Smith's government announced it was creating a cabinet committee to fight pollution in Nova Scotia, which would comprise four ministers, including Donald MacLeod, responsible for the Water Act.

The committee would "counteract the growing water pollution problem" in the province.[119] Although opposition leader
Gerald Regan welcomed the cabinet committee, there's no record of it ever taking the "strong action" he said was needed if
the province was to avoid recreating situations like the one in
Pictou County with the effluent from the pulp mill creating a
problem for fishermen.[120]

But then came the Delaney Report, and the standoff over
the mill and its waste intensified, the cabinet committee to
fight pollution faded from sight and mind, and a whole set of
new players joined the fray.

6

A war of will and words (1960s-1970s)

We the people of this generation, have no right to destroy and leave a dead world for those who come after us."
— Executive and Members,
United Steelworkers of America
Local 1231[121]

Ferguson (Fergie) MacKay had just begun teaching when he became an early recruit to the ranks of concerned citizens coming together to protest the way the mill's effluent was handled. By the late 1960s, that group, led by Councillor Henry Ferguson, the erudite, letter-writing Dr. Joe MacDonald, and George Reid, a fisherman and a warden, had developed into the Northumberland Strait Pollution Control Committee.[122] MacKay, author of a book about the history of Pictou Landing, grew up next door to Robert Christie.[123] His family's land around Boat Harbour was also expropriated by the Water Authority.

MacKay admits that when they began, the group lacked expertise in the chemistry and biology of pulp mills and their effluent. They knew they needed to engage experts if they were going to be able to make their case to the authorities and dispute their claims that the pollution was not causing undue harm.

"They were trying to outwit us," he recalls during an interview in the summer of 2016. "And it went on and on, and so they would react, you can see by the newspapers, we would react, and there was this wearing down of people as well. And they had money, we actually didn't have any money to employ solicitors ... whereas the government could sit back and throw a bombshell in as need be."

In 1969, the Committee engaged the services of a Montreal-based consulting firm, J.A. Delaney and Associates, to study the effects of the mill effluent on Boat Harbour and the Strait. Delaney, an engineer, found the discoloured water from Boat Harbour was affecting twelve kilometres of coastline and clearly visible from the air as it fanned out into the Strait as far as Pictou Island, almost fifteen kilometres away.[124] The report confirmed what fishers had observed, that there had been a 30 percent drop in lobster catches between 1967 and 1968. It also noted that swimmers at beaches in the area emerged covered by a brown, sticky substance, and there was toxic buildup in coves and inlets along the shore.

Delaney proposed that to solve the pollution problem, Scott start to pre-treat the effluent before it left the plant, using clarifiers and aerators to remove toxins and solids; he'd visited a mill in Quebec that did this. He recommended that the treated effluent, along with treated municipal sewage and waste from other industries in the area, be piped to the mouth of Pictou Harbour where the three rivers emptied into the Strait, and that it should not be released from Boat Harbour, where there was insufficient mixing with the salt water and tidal currents.[125]

In November 1969, Delaney presented his findings to the Northumberland Strait Pollution Control Committee and members of the public in the historic Norfolk Hotel in New Glasgow. He said the study included input from a McGill University biology team and he also introduced Dr. J. Gordon Ogden, a professor of biology from Dalhousie University, who had developed an interest in the issue.

"Boat Harbor is a biological desert," Ogden told the audience. "It's dead like nothing I have ever seen. It's one of the most appalling situations I've seen anywhere."[126] The next day, Delaney presented his findings to Premier G.I. Smith.

E.L.L. Rowe was not to be cowed. He described the effect of the mill's effluent as mostly "aesthetic" and said he had a nervous feeling that they were approaching "hysteria" when talking of pollution.[127] Dr. Ogden fired back in a letter to the media, saying the pollution warranted hysteria. He said there was no oxygen left in the water of Boat Harbour, so the biological processes available to degrade the pulp mill waste were anaerobic, and these produce methane gas and if sulphur is present, also hydrogen sulphide. The latter, he pointed out, has a nauseating smell like rotten eggs and is highly toxic. Further, the water entering the Strait from Boat Harbour had such a high biochemical oxygen demand that it was killing fish at a distance of more than a quarter of a mile from the outlet.[128]

Then the general manager of the mill, Walter Miller, chimed in. He wrote a letter to Scott workers, saying that while he declined to participate in a "newspaper debate" with J.A. Delaney, he did want to give his employees some of the "facts and background" on Scott Maritimes' position.[129] Miller reminded employees the province of Nova Scotia had agreed to take charge of the mill's effluent, so the province both owned and operated the effluent facility. He also said the federal Department of Fisheries in New Brunswick had given the facility a "clean bill of health" from the standpoint of marine protection. "Any precipitous actions, any uneconomical and wild schemes," he wrote, "will add nothing to the solution of the pollution problem except to place restrictive financial burdens on various companies and citizens within a community."

His letter was printed in local newspapers and immediately became part of the heated debate that was raging in and around Pictou. A few weeks earlier Miller had told *The Chron-*

icle Herald there was no technology available for a reasonable cost that would allow Scott to change the colour of its effluent and that Scott was "in no position to undertake vast expendi-·tures of money on an experimental basis."[130]

The indefatigable Dr. MacDonald shot back, taking particular issue with Miller's suggestion that to deal with the pollution problem was too costly. This statement, wrote MacDonald, exhibited "a new and sinister kind of arithmetic, whereby a wealthy company, which in a very short time has acquired huge land holdings in Nova Scotia (by various means – tax sales, ordinary purchases, but chiefly Crown grants at very nominal figures) can state that it is not able to afford proper disposal methods or depollution for its polluting effluent."[131] He accused Miller of merely coming to the rescue of the Nova Scotia Water Authority, which had "dealt so handsomely with his company at the expense of the citizens of Pictou County."

Towards the very end of 1969, yet another back-and-forth erupted in the newspapers between concerned citizens and fishermen on one side, and members of the Progressive Conservative government of Premier Smith on the other. At a party meeting in the small community of River John, the Minister of Agriculture and Progressive Conservative MLA from Pictou West, Harvey Veniot, had harsh words for the people protesting the pollution of Boat Harbour. He derided them as "calamity howlers" who wanted to revert back to the hungry times of the Dirty Thirties in the county. He said they had all been "duly warned" long beforehand that the lagoon had been selected as a collection pond for the waste from Scott Paper.[132] He said neither Boat Harbour nor the area of the Strait around its outlet were breeding grounds or living places for lobsters, and there were very few bona fide lobster fishers in the area. He dismissed the complaints as politically motivated.

Two days later, George Reid spoke up on behalf of the fishers in the area who were up in arms over Veniot's words. He said he'd fished the area for thirty years, it had been one of the best lobster fisheries in the Northumberland Strait, and that everything Veniot had said was "completely false."[133]

The controversy continued to rage into 1970, an election year in Nova Scotia. The Northumberland Strait Pollution Control Committee accused the government authorities of whitewashing the problems with the mill's effluent and also warned that its emissions, together with those from the power plant and Hawker Siddeley steel works in nearby Trenton, were causing dangerous air pollution.[134] They continued to direct most of their ire at E.L.L. Rowe and Donald MacLeod, the Minister responsible for the Water Authority.

Dr. Joe MacDonald, now secretary of the Pollution Control Committee and also chair of the public health committee of the Nova Scotia Medical Society, was not about to give in or up. In 1970, he once again captured the controversy in one of his classic letters: "... the foul odour from the lagoons indicates that they are 'dead' – that no oxygen is available to carry out the necessary degrading. Mr. R.M. Billings of Neenah, Wisconsin, then vice-president of the Kimberley-Clark Corporation advised Dr. John Bates in 1965-66 that this could happen and said that if it did, that the addition of 1:1,000,000 parts of oxygen would largely correct the odoriferous condition."

And he continued, "Mr. Armand Wigglesworth, then chairman of the Nova Scotia Water Authority definitely undertook to have aerators installed. This commitment on his part was taken at a meeting of a citizens committee, Federal Building, New Glasgow in February, 1966. The Chairman of what is now called the Nova Scotia Water Resources Commission, at a meeting of citizens, at Pictou Landing in the autumn of 1966, Mr. E.L.L. Rowe, disclaimed any responsibility whatsoever, for any previous commitments made by Mr. Wigglesworth and stated the aerators would not be installed because he said it would cost too much money, and to quote himself 'he was a cost man.' To date no attempt has been made to add oxygen." Then, for good measure, MacDonald added, "We more than agree with Mr. Rowe that he is a 'cost man.' He has cost our county a great deal."[135]

MacDonald also continued to decry the high concentration of sulphur dioxide in the air over the area, which was forty-five times higher than the level deemed safe. Walter Miller denied this, saying that all tests and reports had refuted any claims that the mill's effluent was harming the fishery or that dangerous smoke pollution was pouring from its stacks.[136]

But the work of the citizens' Pollution Control Committee and the Delaney Report seem finally to have had some impact on Rowe at the Water Resources Commission. In early 1970, he announced he had given the consulting company, Rust Associates of Montreal, "practically a blank cheque" to undertake a "completely independent" study of the treatment system, although he still said the effluent was non-toxic and thus was not harming fish in the Northumberland Strait.[137] And as a final stage of the Rust study, he said the consultants would meet with concerned citizens and take submissions from them at a public hearing organized at the Norfolk Hotel in New Glasgow.

It's unlikely that E.L.L. Rowe or the men from Rust had any idea what they were in for when the doors opened for the public hearing. Thirty briefs – representing the requests and opinions of over 8,500 county residents – were presented in just seven hours.[138] Rowe acted as "guide" for the day's proceedings, and Ferguson MacKay from the Pollution Control Committee acted as chair for those presenting briefs, while fourteen members of the Committee picketed outside the hotel. Inside, tempers flared.

The briefs documented the effect the mill's effluent was having on livelihoods, property values, and the environment in the area; the situation was described as "intolerable" and "alarming."[139] The New Glasgow Jaycees, a young men's service and leadership training club that is not generally associated with public protest, said it was incredible that the Nova Scotia Water Resources Commission should be one of the largest polluters in the province while simultaneously being responsible for administering the province's Water Control Act.

The Maritimes Packers Division of National Sea Products said they were very worried about pollution in the area, where lobster catches had decreased by 26.7 percent in 1968 and by 42.2 percent in 1969. Many spoke of how the toxic air darkened laundry hung outside on clotheslines to dry, and how they had to keep their windows closed to keep out the stench coming from the mill and Boat Harbour, complaining they'd been bulldozed into accepting the scheme. Cameron MacKay, who owned a lobster bar in Pictou Landing, recalled the days before the mill when it was common to see 2,000 people flock to the beaches in the area on a Sunday afternoon. Now because of the air and contaminated water, his business was floundering. A United Church minister said a church camp was threatened by the pollution. The New Glasgow Lions' Club bemoaned the loss of once-great tourist attractions and recreation areas around Lighthouse Beach and the deplorable environmental conditions on the Pictou Landing Reserve.

Mill workers also joined the chorus. Local 440 of the International Brotherhood of Pulp, Sulphite and Paper Mill Workers expressed their concern about the mill's pollution, which it said was having "devastating ecological effects." In its submission, the union blew the whistle on Scott, saying the equipment that should have been controlling the acidity of the effluent by adding lime water had "lain idle since the plant start-up period," and "Much of it has never been checked to see whether or not it would operate. The pH monitoring units functioned for a time but eventually became inoperative, owing to the corrosive nature of the plant's atmosphere."[140]

None of this went down well with Rowe, but he took particular exception to two presentations. Delphine McLellan, a biologist from McGill University, said she had tested water in the area and found dead or dying zooplankton and phytoplankton, which she said would hurt lobster larvae and fish populations in the area. Rowe didn't accept her findings. But his biggest clash was with Delaney, author of the report that said the effluent should no longer be stored in and emptied from Boat Harbour. Rowe demanded the engineer divulge the name of the mill in Quebec that his report claimed was far cleaner than the one on Abercrombie Point. Delaney said he had agreed not to reveal its name, and suggested that Rowe should consider going to lots of different mills. Rowe then insisted Delaney explain the circumstances surrounding his visit to the mysterious mill in Quebec. Delaney again refused, and a rude remark from the audience led Rowe to use his gavel on the table.[141] The discussions ended quite literally with a bang.

After that Rowe suspended public submissions until Rust delivered its report. While everyone waited for it to appear, the skirmishes in the media escalated. Pictou County doctors entered the fray, joining the Medical Society of Nova Scotia in urging the government to "hasten its efforts in the matter of air and water pollution abatement and control."[142] Then the Pictou Local of the province's teachers' union lent their voice to the cause, publishing a resolution that denounced the "devastating effluent" from Scott Maritimes that had "completely ruined the 350-acre Boat Harbor tidal lagoon," endangered the fishing industry, despoiled one of the Northumberland Strait's best swimming areas, and made real estate values plummet. They sent their motion to Premier Smith.[143]

As all this was happening, the Pollution Control Committee got wind of and took up another environmental issue. Since late 1968, work had been underway to construct the plant for Canso Chemicals just beside the pulp mill. Canso Chemicals was owned and managed by Scott Maritimes, Nova Scotia Pulp Ltd. in Port Hawkesbury, and Canadian Industries Ltd. (CIL). Scott's general manager Walter Miller was on its board of directors.

It would cost $8 million to build and would produce the chemicals – caustic soda, chlorine, and sodium chloride – needed for the two pulp mills. A CBC television program had just sounded the alarm on mercury poisoning in Japan, bringing the story about the devastating effects it had on human health, causing brain damage and ataxia, a lack of muscular coordination – a neurological syndrome that came to be known as Minamata disease after the bay that had been polluted with mercury.

Despite attempts by governments and corporations to suppress research and findings about the immense dangers that mercury posed to human and animal health, word was emerging that chlor-alkali plants like the one being constructed by Canso Chemicals used a lot of mercury, and lost about ten percent of it each year both in waste water produced by its chemical processes and in exhaust gases.[144] A Dow Chemical plant in Sarnia, Ontario, had been releasing mercury that had been accumulating in and contaminating fish in Lake St. Clair. In March 1970, six plants in Ontario using mercury were ordered to "virtually eliminate mercury losses" through waste water. This included Dryden Chemicals that served the Reed Paper Company and dumped its waste into the Wabigoon River, and two CIL sister plants to the one being built at Abercrombie.[145]

This news deeply concerned people in Pictou County, and on April 24, 1970, the Pollution Control Committee sent a telegram to the federal Minister of Fisheries, Jack Davis, requesting that Canso Chemicals not be permitted to open until the matter of mercury had been attended to. Canso Chemicals' Jack Pink assured the public that his company had not come to poison anyone, just to "employ people and perform a useful service."[146]

E.L.L. Rowe countered that it was not possible for total containment in all cases, but that Canso Chemicals must demonstrate satisfactory treatment to ensure negligible mercury loss. Four months later, Donald MacLeod, Minister under the Water Act, gave the company the approval to go into production, following the installation of equipment that was said to "have pollution abatement measures comparable to any chlor-alkali plant in the world."[147] Just what that really meant was not clear then, nor would it be later when tons of mercury went missing. But that was all in the future. An official opening ceremony for Canso Chemicals was set for October 1970, and even before that happened the plant was already expanding.[148]

Meanwhile, throughout the spring and summer of 1970, people in Pictou waited impatiently for the Rust Report about Boat Harbour. In early June, the media reported it had been delivered to the Nova Scotia government, but there was speculation that it was "weak." Ferguson MacKay, who had now become president of the Northumberland Strait Pollution Control Committee, warned that his group would not accept the report unless it contained concrete recommendations.[149] Two weeks later, Minister Donald MacLeod was still mum about the report, refusing to say when or if it would be made public.[150]

The Pollution Control Committee held an executive meeting to discuss the lack of transparency, and MacKay told the media, "We are extremely disappointed that the government has chosen to shroud the Rust Report in a cloak of mystery."[151] A month later the provincial New Democratic Party (NDP) went further, accusing the Progressive Conservative government of suppressing the report to avoid genuine discussion of the mill's pollution.[152] There was suspicion that the government didn't like the interim report, and that it was being amended to satisfy them.

When it was published at the end of July, the Rust Report – 88 pages long with an Appendix of 103 pages – came as a "crushing blow" to those who wanted to see the pollution problems tackled. It echoed suggestions that Rowe and Minister MacLeod had made many times that the pollution in Boat Harbour was mostly "aesthetic" and that the mill was doing a good job of treating its waste, meeting all the regulatory requirements.[153] However, Rust did recommend improvements that would involve at least some treatment of the effluent and cost $4 million. Rowe responded that even if all the recommendations were implemented he would have a hard time convincing himself "that there would be much material difference" and he thought the money would be better spent elsewhere in the province.

Ferguson MacKay said the Pollution Control Committee was extremely unhappy that the group had not been provided with a copy of the report, and was outraged with the comments Rowe had made at the press conference when the findings of the report were summarized for the public.[154] The NDP called for the resignation of Minister MacLeod and E.L.L. Rowe, and sharply criticized Conservative MLA Harvey Veniot for his insulting description of the concerned citizens fighting the pollution as "calamity howlers."[155]

The leader of the provincial Liberal party, Gerald Regan, then chastised Rowe, a civil servant, for expressing his opinion about where money should be spent in the province. "I take issue with Mr. Rowe's reaction in that he doesn't seem to recognize that the Nova Scotia Government has a special responsibility to Pictou County in regards to combating pollution because of the fact that they bungled it to begin with."[156] And just in case anyone had forgotten, Regan reminded the public that it had been a Progressive Conservative government that invited Scott to Pictou and then agreed to take responsibility for all its effluent.

The Director of the Bedford Institute of Oceanography and biology professor at Dalhousie University, Dr. J.G. Riley, said he didn't agree with the Rust Report at all, that it looked to him like a "whitewash job."[157] He said the pollution problems could hardly be described as just aesthetic, and criticized the report for not addressing air pollution, which damaged trees and farms around Boat Harbour. J.A. Delaney met with the press and denounced the Rust Report as "a deliberately conceived vehicle compiled with the knowledge of the N.S. Water Authority and the N.S. Government to induce complacency and to block all further avenues of technical approach to the N.S. Government to clean up the mess at Boat Harbor."[158]

Walter Miller said Scott Maritimes was already taking action to reduce the discharge of bark and wood fibres.[159] He also complained that his company's public image had been "tarnished" by all the controversy about its effluent, and any decisions about changes to its treatment were the responsibility of Rowe's Water Resources Commission.[160]

Emotions were – to say the least – running very high. The Jaycees put together a float for a parade in New Glasgow that depicted the hanging of the Minister in charge of the Water Act, Donald R. MacLeod, whose effigy they placed in a barrel with a rope around his neck. They plastered the float with signs saying "Help Donald R. Fight Pollution – Drink Up Boat Harbour" and "Support Your Local MLA – Swim in Boat Harbour."[161]

Then the clergy got in on the act. Reverend D.H. Gass of the Sharon-St. John Church in Stellarton broke with his own habit of steering clear of such controversy and wrote a letter of protest to Premier G.I. Smith. In it, he said he was deeply concerned not just by the pollution in Boat Harbour, but also by the attitude of representatives of Smith's government, and Reverend Gass described himself as a lifelong supporter of the Progressive Conservative Party. He took umbrage at the belittling attitudes of Rowe and Minister MacLeod, the way they disparaged concerned citizens by calling them "complainers" and dismissing their protests as "emotional nonsense."[162]

He received a lengthy response from Rowe, who once again described the mill's effluent disposal processes as "the best available at the present time" and repeated claims that the effluent was not toxic, and that he personally didn't find the odour offensive. But he assured the reverend the Water Resources Commission had "manifest" regard for the public.[163]

The Pollution Control Committee met in the Pictou Landing school to decide on their next move. The seventy-five members present decided that if the government did not start treating the effluent, they would take legal action against Scott Maritimes and the Water Resources Commission. A bottle of the dark effluent from Boat Harbour was put on the table for all to see, while mosquitoes that were proliferating in the polluted waters filled the schoolroom. The anger was palpable; the only one of the three MLAs for Pictou in attendance took a great deal of heat on behalf of his Progressive Conservative Party and government. Dr. Joe MacDonald capped off the evening with another of his quips, regretting that Scott's manager, Walter Miller, was more concerned over Scott's image than the "rape of Pictou County."[164]

A week later the Committee postponed any legal action, pending a meeting they'd been promised with Walter Miller and Premier Smith. Money was also an issue; the group relied heavily on its original core members to fund its activities and was still paying Delaney and Associates $11,000 for the studies it had undertaken. Ferguson MacKay said Miller had also told him the mill was already working on a program of air and water improvements.[165] In September, the group met with Miller and emerged feeling optimistic, reassured that the company was installing pollution controls in the plant.

Miller announced that Scott would spend two years and $1.5 million on a new on-site environmental control program to deal with odour, solid wastes in its effluent, and stack emissions.[166]

At the same time, Minister MacLeod went public with the news that the Water Resources Commission would start a detailed design for an aeration system in Boat Harbour for oxidation of the lagoon and reduction of its odour.[167] However, he said there were no plans to put in a clarifier and other recommended measures; dredging of the settling pond would be part of "a general program aimed at improving the appearance of these works." And after this, more studies would be undertaken before any decisions would be made on further measures, such as piping the effluent further out into the Strait.

Ferguson MacKay was not encouraged by vague statements about programs that would be undertaken over a period of time, and said studies were needed on how and where the waste should be treated and disposed of.[168]

Just after that, in October 1970, MacKay was chosen as a Liberal candidate in the upcoming provincial election slated for the second week of October.[169] Although he wasn't elected, the Liberal party was, and Gerald Regan took over from G.I. Smith as premier. Members of the Pollution Control Committee invited the newly elected Liberal MLA for Pictou East, Lloyd MacDonald, to accompany them on a tour of a kraft pulp mill in Woodland, Maine. The comparison with the mill in Pictou was striking. According to MacDonald, the mill in Maine was able to reduce discoloration of its effluent by about 90 percent, something that would make a great difference were it installed in Pictou. They also learned the mill in the U.S. was paying $22 for a cord of wood, while the Scott mill in Nova Scotia was paying just $18.50. Further, the American mill did selective harvesting of trees, while Scott did only clear cutting.[170] More grist for the critics of the mill.

On February 1, 1971, Ferguson MacKay was appointed to the Water Resources Commission. A year later, Conservative MLA Harvey Veniot learned of the appointment and went to the media, saying, "It is now understandable why the Northumberland Pollution Committee has been so silent since."[171] MacKay responded, saying it was his commitment to the Pollution Control Committee that had earned him the post. He said that to maintain confidence in the Committee, he had resigned as president and ceased being its chief spokesman.[172]

It is many years later – in September 2016 – when Ferguson MacKay invites me into the dining corner of the kitchen in his home in Trenton, to recall those turbulent days of protest and then his decision to join the Water Resources Commission that he had once criticized so strenuously. He tells me his appointment was "a bit of appeasement," "probably a political thing," and possibly intended to "quiet him down," although he says it didn't. He was on the Commission for a few years, but says he was never a "happy camper" there. Nevertheless, there are signs that he had a positive influence from within. A pamphlet on the importance of fighting pollution published by the Water Commission in 1972 highlights the "serious hazard of pollution," and notes, "Large plants like Scott Maritimes Pulp Ltd., in Pictou County, consume as much as 25,000,000 gallons of water daily. Effluent from this plant is as great as that of a city of 75,000 people."[173]

As for what citizens concerned about pollution could do, the Water Commission brochure seems to encourage citizen activism, and echoed the views that MacKay had been espousing for years with the Pollution Control Committee: "Public minded citizens willing to support the anti-pollution cause have formed themselves into pollution abatement committees all over the province – and indeed, all over the industrial world." And surprisingly, given Rowe's earlier hostility to the Pollution Control Committee led by Ferguson MacKay, the Commission then praises such groups: "The time to support anti-pollution programs, both those of the citizens committees and those of the Nova Scotia Water Resources Commission, is now – before the cost gets any higher. Clean water is no longer a God-given right. It's a hard won benefit."

Ironically, by the time this pamphlet came out, the Northumberland Strait Pollution Control Committee was already fading away, appearing less and less often in the media. While it hadn't managed to get the flow of effluent stopped, it had fought long and hard and made its mark, pushed the government and the mill until both came up with plans and promises to reconfigure the effluent facility in Boat Harbour.

7

(More) Citizens against pollution (1970s-mid 1990s)

The effluent has hovered like a ghost over the community for decades causing odours and health concerns.
— Pictou Landing Band Council[174]

In 1974, Scott said it was completing its own $2-million pollution abatement program, and the province had reportedly spent $2.5 million to rebuild the settling ponds and install the aerators to help reduce odour.[175] For a time, this seemed to appease the public and there was a brief lull in the media coverage of the mill's pollution.

Then, in 1976, *The 4th Estate* newspaper broke the story that the pipeline carrying the effluent to the settling ponds, which had cost the province $300,000, had broken and cracked, so the effluent from the mill was not going into the primary settling pond at all, but collecting in a small lagoon at the harbour's edge. The Department of Environment had known about the faulty pipeline for a year already, and was planning to replace it with a new pipeline for $650,000, a sum it would "attempt to recover" from the contractor that installed the original pipeline.[176] The department refused to divulge who that was, or how much Scott was paying for the use of Boat Harbour now, saying only that the province had spent $3.5 million to construct the pollution control system at the mill.[177]

A year later, there was more bad news from Abercrombie Point, this time from Canso Chemicals that supplied the pulp mill. A Canadian Press (CP) report spoke of "mysterious losses of large amounts of mercury" from the plant.[178] It said the province's environment department had ordered Canso Chemicals to take steps to sharply reduce the losses of mercury, which had averaged several tons annually since the company started reporting to the federal environmental department in 1972. "For several years federal and provincial environmental officials have expressed uneasiness about high levels of unaccountable mercury losses from the Canso chlor-alkali plant," said the CP story, adding that government testing had not been able to find where the mercury was going.

The amounts were not insignificant, reaching a high of five tonnes that had gone missing in 1975, the third highest loss from a chlor-alkali plant in Canada that year, and then one tonne in 1976, with the same expected in 1977. The engineering staff from Canso Chemicals and a Montreal firm had done a study a year earlier that showed 51 percent of the mercury that Canso Chemicals used was "unaccounted for in recovery or lost in the process."[179] The province's environment minister, Vince MacLean, a Liberal MLA from Cape Breton, had earlier threatened to close the plant if it didn't improve its performance, saying it was "totally unacceptable" that mercury was going into the environment.

Even today, three decades later, the sad tale of mercury contamination from a pulp mill and its horrific effects on health among the First Nations people at two Ojibway communities in northwest Ontario is still ongoing in Ontario.[180] A former mill worker claimed that barrels with mercury had been buried "haphazardly" behind the mill, then owned by

Reed Paper, and soil samples taken in the area by volunteers from the group Earthroots and by reporters from *The Toronto Star* showed "significantly elevated" mercury levels. Later, Ontario's environment minister said the government had done its own study and found nothing. However, the fact remains that during the 1960s, the Reed Paper mill and its chemical plant dumped ten tonnes of mercury into the Wabigoon River, about 100 kilometres upstream from Grassy Narrows. It contaminated the walleye in the river, which in turn sickened the First Nations people who consumed them.[181]

The controversy has not gone away; mercury levels remain high and there is suspicion it is still making people sick. In February 2017, the government of Premier Kathleen Wynne pledged to find the source of the mercury contamination and to have it cleaned up, acknowledging the profound impact it has had on the people of Grassy Narrows First Nation and Wabaseemoong Independent Nations.[182] But that is Ontario. To this day, there has been no public accounting of the missing mercury from the site of the Canso Chemicals plant on Abercrombie Point in Nova Scotia.

By late 1978, the Nova Scotia government wasn't issuing warnings to Canso Chemicals; it was offering it a generous handout. In December that year, Walter Miller, still president of Scott Maritimes and also a member of the board of Canso Chemicals, said that hikes in power rates made continued operation of the plant unviable, so it would be closing in March 1979.[183] The province, now with a new Progressive Conservative premier, John Buchanan, immediately offered a grant of a million dollars to keep the company going. Canso Chemicals declined, saying it was looking for a long-term agreement.

Although he would not win the seat in the upcoming 1979 federal election, at the time Lloyd MacKay, the Liberal candidate for the riding, said he was confident the federal government under Prime Minister Pierre Trudeau would get involved to help save Canso Chemicals. But that didn't stop him from expressing his suspicion that both Scott and Canso Chemicals were throwing their weight around to intimidate the government and gain financial and environmental concessions from them.[184] "These two multi-national companies are known to use shock treatment to all governments and the citizens in general," he said, presciently précising the thesis of Naomi Klein's 2007 book, *The Shock Doctrine: The Rise of Disaster Capitalism*. MacKay cited as examples of this the recent issue of – and the powerful citizen backlash against – aerial spraying of insecticides on forests in Nova Scotia to tackle an epidemic of spruce budworm, and the threat of possible layoffs by the pulp companies until permission was granted for the spraying.[185] He concluded, "It is also a well known fact both these corporations have made use of millions of dollars of free taxpayers' dollars directly or indirectly."[186]

Premier John Buchanan agreed to underwrite Canso Chemicals until 1984 to the tune of $4 million, one million of which was to be made available immediately, just in time for Christmas.[187]

Four years later, it was the pulp mill's turn to benefit from government beneficence. In September 1982, the federal and provincial governments announced they would contribute $7 million to Scott Maritimes as part of the Canada-Nova Scotia pulp and paper subsidiary agreement.[188] This, plus $44 million that the president of Scott Maritimes and general manager of the mill, Alec Glen, said the company was investing to modernize the mill, would improve productivity, upgrade its operations, reduce energy costs, and lastly, cut boiler emissions.

A few days later, on September 10, 1982, mill workers walked off the job in the third legal strike in the mill's history. The strike dragged on into the next year, paralyzing the forest industry in the province. In February 1983, president of Local 440 of the Canadian Paperworkers Union, Blanchard Fralic, told the media relations between labour and management had deteriorated in the past year and a half since the mill's management changed and then failed to live up to pledges made

by its predecessors.[189] "They have to realize they are not negotiating with their workers in Alabama," he said at a press
conference.

In April 1983, dozens of pulpwood contractors, truck
drivers and forestry workers delivered a petition with 10,000
signatures to Premier John Buchanan, asking the government
to step in and help end the strike. They pointed out that Scott
Maritimes was "the only game in town" and that businesses
and contractors that depended on it could not make a living
while the strike lasted.[190] On May 15, Scott announced it was
cancelling its plan to invest the $51 million to modernize the
plant.[191] Two weeks later, the mill workers voted to accept an
agreement negotiated by a commission chaired by a Quebec
judge, Allan Gold, and ended their eight-month strike.[192] Shortly after that, Alec Glen pledged to try to improve relations with
both workers and with the public. He hired Jack Kyte as public
affairs manager to help do this.[193]

The détente with the public, if indeed there was one, was
somewhat shaky. In 1984, a petition with a thousand signatures was presented to the Pictou Municipal Council protesting the continued pollution from the mill. The Council was not
particularly receptive; one councillor said the petition should
be used for toilet paper.[194] Scott, however, arranged a meeting
with citizens and told them that in 1985 the company would
be spending close to $17 million on projects that would affect
plant emissions.

But sometimes, the more officials claimed that things
were changing, the more it looked as if stasis had set in. Three
years later citizens began to mobilize to fight the pollution and
protest rippled through the community once again. By then,
the mill had been operating for twenty-one years and a dozen
government studies had been done on how to reduce its pollution.[195] But the pollution hadn't gone away and it still rankled.

This time, the citizen action began with a demonstration
on the Harvey A. Veniot Causeway, named after the Progressive Conservative MLA who had hotly contested the actions

of the "calamity howling" Northumberland Strait Pollution Control Committee, and the same causeway that the province had constructed as part of the package it offered Scott in 1965. While a couple of hundred citizens marched across the causeway, fishers moved along beside them in their boats in the waters of Pictou Harbour. With the mill belching smoke from its cluster of stacks as a backdrop, the visuals were impressive and the story made the national news.

Mary Gorman was one of the organizers of that protest. In a feature that CBC TV's *fifth estate* did on the pollution in Boat Harbour in the fall of 1988, Gorman shows herself to be a formidable opponent to any government official trying to convince concerned citizens that the Boat Harbour treatment facility is doing a good job.[196] First, the audience hears from Dennis Ryan of Nova Scotia's Department of Environment, who suggests there is no genuine reason for the public outcry about Boat Harbour. He says the system at Boat Harbour is "an excellent treatment facility" that is doing the job it's supposed to be doing.

"Nova Scotia has thousands and thousands of miles of coastline and many very scenic tourist attractions and places of interest," he tells the CBC's Sheila MacVicar. "And Boat Harbour is not one of them. The colour of the water is about the colour of weak tea, I would suggest. Would you agree with that?" he asks MacVicar. She doesn't seem convinced, so he proposes that it's more like "strong tea." Then he goes on to inform her that, "We have in Nova Scotia brownish waters naturally. It's called good Nova Scotian bog water."

MacVicar, who at this point in the documentary has already taken viewers on a very descriptive tour of Boat Harbour and been unequivocal about the horrific smell of the waste, points out in her narration that the brown liquid in Boat Harbour is "not bog water." This piece of her script is followed by a fascinating clip taken during the recent election campaign, and an interaction at Boat Harbour between Donald Cameron, Progressive Conservative MLA for the area and

Nova Scotia's Minister of Industry, Trade and Technology, and citizens concerned about the pollution. Cameron tries to assuage their concerns with assurances that he had committed half a million dollars to improving Boat Harbour. He refers to various studies that are being done.

The citizens around him are not having it. One man shows Cameron a handful of dark and smelly soil that he says is not fit to hold in his hand because it's full of toxic substances such as dioxins. Asked what the government is doing about the pollution in Boat Harbour, Cameron responds that the money committed to the problem is to get an expert to give recommendations on what can be done to improve the situation.

Cameron's reassurances don't impress Mary Gorman, who is standing next to him with her arms full of research papers and studies that have already been done on Boat Harbour. "Quite frankly," she says, "we don't really trust your government studies, Mr. Cameron, if you can come up ..."

He interrupts her and they speak over each other for a few seconds before Cameron turns on Gorman: "All we can hear is your mouth going, nothing else." Cameron later tries to rationalize the encounter to MacVicar. "It's an emotional issue," he says. "And all you have to do is take one look at Boat Harbour and it's very difficult to get people to listen to facts."

Gorman, however, is adamant that government is not giving people the facts. "Forgive my cynicism," she says to MacVicar. "But as far as I'm concerned the government is totally accountable to industry at the expense of the people, and I just don't believe them."

Shortly after that interview, in September 1988, Donald Cameron was re-elected Progressive Conservative MLA for Pictou East, and Premier John Buchanan began his fourth term at the helm of the province. Two years later, Buchanan suddenly resigned following allegations of government patronage and corruption, some of which led "right to the premier's office" and to the RCMP announcing they would launch an investigation.[197] The politician who had earned the nickname

"Teflon John" for what journalist Dean Jobb describes as "his ability for steering clear of previous scandals" moved to Ottawa to take up Prime Minister Brian Mulroney's offer of a seat in Canada's Senate.

In February 1991, Donald Cameron won the leadership of the Progressive Conservative party, although very narrowly, and became premier of Nova Scotia. Cameron was a vociferous and aggressive defender of the Westray Coal mine in Pictou County, and he was premier of the province when, in May 1992, the poorly inspected and faulty mine exploded and killed twenty-six men. It was a tragedy that deeply scarred people in the county, the province, and even the country, and it damaged the political careers of the mine's proponents.[198] The voters of Pictou East would not renew Cameron's mandate in the 1993 election. He would also be remembered, and not always fondly, as the premier who privatized Nova Scotia's power corporation.[199]

As for Boat Harbour, however, his tenure as premier would come and go and nothing would change. The site would, as Gorman predicted, remain a toxic mess. Mary Gorman would go on to become a lifelong campaigner for clean water – in Boat Harbour, the Northumberland Strait, and in the Gulf of Saint Lawrence as a whole, which is a crucial spawning ground, nursery, and migratory area for fish, and also where her husband fished for thirty-five years.

On an overcast, muggy day in June 2016, Mary Gorman and I meet up in Pictou, seeking a place to speak that is reasonably quiet and not too smelly. In the end, we decide to sit in the car in the parking lot of the Pictou Fisheries Training Pool. Outside the car, the air is rank from the mill, a bit like breathing through a mildewed woollen blanket.

Born and raised in Pictou County, Gorman was a founding member of the 1980s protest group Citizens Against Pollution, which took to the causeway to stage the demonstration. She says this was the largest environmental protest to date in

Nova Scotia. She traces her activism to two incidents that profoundly marked her, both related to pollution from the mill. One happened when she was thirteen years old; Scott had just begun to operate and as she had her whole life, Gorman went swimming at Lighthouse Beach in front of her family's cottage. It had always been a magical place for her, and she had "the most wonderful summers there that any human being could ever hope to have."

But on that day, she went down to the shore and found it full of black foamy effluent splashing ashore on the waves. This experience tainted her feelings about her home province, which she decided was "for sale to the highest bidder." When she was old enough to leave she did, spending many years in Toronto and after that, New York. She says she had no intention of ever moving back home, but did return on occasion to visit her parents. One warm summer day in 1988 during one of those visits, lured by fond memories of Lighthouse Beach, Gorman ventured back there, wanting just to sit and reflect. Instead, she says, the foamy effluent she found breaking on the shore in stinking waves made her go "ballistic."

She linked up with other concerned citizens, including fisher Kirk Munro, to organize the causeway protest. Two weeks later, 250 people assembled at the former CNR employees' club in Pictou Landing to quiz candidates for the upcoming provincial election on what they would do to clean up the mess.[200] It was a mixture of festive and feisty, with two fiddlers and someone singing, "The sea is dirty, Boat Harbour is dead."[201] The public wanted to know why government was not forcing industry to clean up after itself, and asked about leaks of mercury. Dr. Gordon Ogden, the same biology professor who had been accused of "hysteria" two decades earlier when the Northumberland Strait Pollution Committee was calling for a clean-up, told participants at the meeting that he was now working for the Department of Environment to study how the harbour could be rehabilitated, as part of a project costing half a million dollars.

After the meeting, Gorman decided to stay on in Nova Scotia, becoming an active member of the new group, Citizens Against Pollution (CAP), along with interim chair Bruce MacIntosh, and some other founding members such as Kirk Munro, and his sister Ishbel Munro. By 1989, Robert Fraser, a United Church minister, had become chair of CAP and Robert Christie had come on board as head of the group's Technical Research Committee and authored a detailed report in December 1988 proposing an "integrated ecotoxicological approach" to waste treatment in Boat Harbour.[202] At its peak at the end of the 1980s and into the mid-1990s, Christie says the group had a paid membership of 400.[203]

Its own leaflets to members urged them to write letters to both provincial and federal politicians, demanding that the province not renew its contract with Scott to continue handling mill effluent when it expired in 1995, that Scott be responsible for its own treatment facility using the best methods and modern technology, and that it also pay for its operation, demanding that "the Nova Scotia Government get out of the pollution business."[204] In its 1990 newsletter, CAP highlighted the 1989 paper by Dr. Dan Reid, suggesting a link between the emissions from the mill's stacks and high rates of illness in Pictou County, and bemoaned two decades of broken promises from Scott that it was reducing its pollution. The group worked hard to draw media and public attention to the plight of people living around Boat Harbour, particularly those on the Pictou Landing First Nation Reserve, for whom "Boat Harbour does not smell of money, but of racism, paternalism and social injustice."[205]

CAP also worked hard to get politicians on board and in 1989, at the behest of Elmer MacKay, Progressive Conservative Member of Parliament (MP) for the area and federal minister in charge of the Atlantic Canada Opportunities Agency (ACOA), Environment Canada announced it would be directing an in-depth study of the pollution in the Northumberland Strait and Pictou Harbour.[206] The study would cost $150,000 and last two to three years, funded by three federal agencies – ACOA, the Pictou County Economic Development Fund, and the federal Department of Fisheries and Oceans.[207]

Throughout it all, however, the effluent problems persisted. In June 1989, pollution from Boat Harbour led to the closure of the beach at Chance Harbour several kilometres away.[208] In October that year, Rob Porter of the Department of Environment announced that mercury had been found in sediment samples in Boat Harbour. However, he maintained that this "should be no cause for alarm."[209]

In 1990, there was a massive fish kill near the outlet of Boat Harbour and *The Evening News* reported that "tens of thousands of dead and dying smelts, sticklebacks, and silversides washed up on shore, apparently killed by a lack of oxygen in the water."[210] Environment Canada recommended that the Nova Scotia Department of Environment should be charged under the federal Fisheries Act for the fish kill.[211] But in the spring of 1991, the federal Department of Justice overruled Environment Canada and recommended against charges, a decision Robert Christie attributed to "political interference."[212] "It's just good old Tory politics," he told reporter Campbell Morrison of *The Daily News*. "Let's hide everything and do nothing ... their credibility is absolutely nil."[213]

The Citizens Against Pollution kept up their pressure. Scott's public affairs manager, Jack Kyte, said that the treatment facility was well run and that in 1987 the treated effluent was second best in Canada for suspended solids. Nearly thirty years later, when Kyte had become head of the Pictou Chamber of Commerce, he would repeat a similar claim about Boat Harbour during an interview on CBC radio, saying, "Boat Harbour treats wastewater extremely well."[214]

The tug-of-war of words was a never-ending story. Even back in the late 1980s, CAP wasn't accepting such claims about the effluent treatment. Its membership was questioning the validity of an investigation into the fish kill that was being done by the provincial Department of Environment, which was also running the treatment facility suspected of causing it.[215]

Nevertheless, by 1989, it was starting to look as if their activism – those endless hours that the group's members had spent doing research and building files and raising public awareness and challenging officials – was making inroads, if small ones. Scott Maritimes began to publish annual environmental management plans.

In the first of these in 1989, its president and general manager, Gerry Byrne, prefaced his message this way: "In recent months there has been a good deal of discussion in the media and throughout our local communities about environmental matters relative to Scott's operation in Pictou County."[216] He went on to say that in June that year, Scott had announced an air emission improvement program worth $2 million, that it had committed another $1 million for "other environmental improvements," while $600,000 had been spent on the prevention of spills into Pictou Harbour. He said the provincial government was installing a new aeration system in Boat Harbour and the mill would do a trial to see if chlorine dioxide could replace chlorine in the bleaching process.[217]

In September 1989, Rob Porter of the province's Department of Environment said the department was taking a "hard look" at getting out of running the facility altogether, as CAP was demanding. He said the government would spend $700,000 to improve the facility with new aerators, air systems, and the addition of phosphates and nitrates, all of which would "improve the quality of the effluent."[218] Then Industry Minister Don Cameron echoed the call for Scott to build and run its own treatment facility.[219] Scott wasn't leaping at this offer that would cost it a great deal of money, arguing that between 1982 and 1988, the net profit at the mill after taxes was considerably less than the capital investment of $100 million that it claimed it had made.

CAP countered that the Abercrombie mill was Scott's most profitable one in North America. A leaked federal study in 1988 showed that the forest industry was enjoying record-high profits, and that during the boom in 1987, only 5 percent of the $2.5 billion of capital investment by the pulp and paper industry in Canada was spent on pollution control.[220] That same year the Economic Council of Canada reported that the industry had the lowest marginal effective tax rate in the manufacturing sector, and the highest share of regional development grants, of which very small percentages went to pollution abatement.[221]

The fact remained, however, that the mill's effluent belonged not to Scott but to the people of Nova Scotia, so it would be up to the province to come up with a solution for Boat Harbour. And it would be up to the federal government to monitor what went into the Northumberland Strait, using legislation from 1970 that had made some amendments to the century-old Fisheries Act to regulate industrial effluent going into the country's waters.

The trouble was that no one seemed to know what toxins were going into Boat Harbour. They knew of some, of course, but did not know their effects on the environment and human health. Swedish researchers had shown twenty years earlier that kraft pulp mills that used chlorine produced waste full of organochlorides, including dioxins and furans, two of the most toxic chemicals known to science. As a result, Swedish mills had extremely tight regulations on the use of chlorine in pulp-making and made the transition to a pulping process called oxygen delignification that used no chlorine.[222] Not so in Nova Scotia and the rest of Canada. When asked about what effects the organochlorides in Boat Harbour might have on people and fish and the environment, the president and CEO of Scott Maritimes, Gerry Byrne, said, "Who knows? Who knows?"[223]

After the fish kill of 1990, the province commissioned a study by H.A. Simons, to be co-funded by the province, Scott, and the Atlantic Canada Opportunities Agency, to seek alternative waste treatment for the mill.[224] The findings of the study, released in November 1991, proposed four options for

Scott's effluent; two included modifications to Boat Harbour and two involved an on-site treatment facility on Scott's land, a system that was used in other Scott mills. CAP was cautiously optimistic, but concerned that it had not been involved in consultations.[225] There were also worries that Scott was experimenting with a membrane system to filter out the dark colour from their effluent, and then burning the material they filtered out in their own electrical generating plant. A CAP newsletter stated, "Scott cannot meet the high temperatures required to totally destroy dioxins, and thus dioxins will go up the stack and escape into the air. This is a serious problem for us."[226] The board of CAP passed a resolution calling on the province to enforce a moratorium on all new incineration projects in Pictou County.

CAP, meanwhile, was growing. In 1992, Jane Sproull Thomson contacted Citizens Against Pollution on behalf of the Moodie Cove Residents Co-op, many of whom had been fighting the Boat Harbour arrangement even before the mill began to operate. The Moodie Cove Co-op joined forces with and became an organizational member of CAP.[227] The group was becoming increasingly concerned that the government was delaying any action on the Simons Report. They were also trying to arrange meetings with the provincial Minister of the Environment, John Leefe, to ensure CAP was consulted on future changes to the mill and its effluent disposal.[228]

The government seemed to be favouring one of the options outlined in the Simons Report, which would involve a $17-million upgrade to the Boat Harbour facility and a long pipeline to carry the mill's effluent about two kilometres out into the Northumberland Strait.[229] This, in turn, sparked a range of reactions, with some members of CAP saying the plan might be an improvement, while others, including Mary Gorman, opposed the plan, saying it was time Scott built its own facility on-site so that the fisheries in the Strait would not be harmed by the mill's effluent. "People don't want that crap going into the Strait," she told *The Chronicle Herald*.[230] And the federal fisheries minister, Brian Tobin, said the provincial government would not be allowed to pipe the effluent into the Strait if it posed a threat to fish habitat, and that no decision could be made without a full environmental assessment and full consultation with fishermen. The Scott boss, Gerry Byrne, wrote a letter to his employees, saying that while a new treatment plant for the mill was technologically possible, it would cost between $60 million and $80 million and the treated effluent would still have to be released into the Strait. "Even a new system would be hard pressed to surpass the Boat Harbour results," he wrote, "which have always met regulations".[231]

At the same time, the Citizens Against Pollution successfully lobbied to have the provincial government seek a third legal opinion on whether it could terminate its agreement with Scott on waste treatment after two earlier ones had said it was unbreakable.[232] The existing agreement would expire in 1995, and CAP hoped there could be a new agreement that would see Scott treating its own waste in its own modern facility before then. In April 1991, the law firm Patterson Kitz informed the province that the contract obliging it to treat Scott's waste was indeed breakable.[233] But it wouldn't be until 1995 that the government – a new Liberal one headed by Premier John Savage – would decide what it would do about the mill's waste. And when the decision came, it would not be what the citizens' group had asked for.

By then, though, the momentum and energy of Citizens Against Pollution were starting to wane, even if many individual members would continue their campaign with letters to government and to newspaper editors for many years to come. Gorman recalls that people felt frustrated and started to ask themselves why they were meeting, why put out another press release when the media weren't picking it up, and they were feeling discouraged that nobody was listening. It also had to do with "exhaustion," according to Ishbel Munro, sister of Kirk Munro, who had been one of the founders of CAP.

Munro tells me about her own experiences and memories of CAP when I visit her at her home on the outskirts of Tatamagouche in the summer of 2016. With her precocious and curious grandson perched on her lap and adding his own toddler's two cents' worth from time to time, she reflects on her life and how the mill has shaped it.

Her father grew up on a homestead in Pictou County, a direct descendant of John Munro, who came from Scotland on the Ship *Hector* in 1773, the replica of which now sits on the Pictou waterfront. As the family lore goes, her grandfather owned a store in Stellarton. But when the Great Depression struck, Munro's grandfather took up bartering rather than charging his customers cash, and the family store went bankrupt. She laughs and says her grandmother found the basement full of potatoes when better times came; her grandfather had given away all the food and milk in exchange for potatoes that everyone grew in their yards.

She recalls her father's stories about taking the train to Pictou Landing and spending time on the beaches along the shore there. He called Pictou County "the most beautiful place in the world." Her aunt and uncle owned a waterfront property in Moodie Cove, and Munro has rich memories of summers spent swimming there and on Lighthouse Beach, when it was "stunningly pristine" before the mill was built.

As a young woman, Munro moved west and lived for a time in Oregon, which is where she was when her brother Kirk helped organize the demonstration across the causeway in 1988. She had just had surgery and had a young child, and decided to move back to Nova Scotia where she would have some support from her brothers. Years later, Kirk told her he figured if he got her involved in the cause of stopping the pollution from the mill, she would agree to stay in the province. He was right.

She and her two-year-old daughter moved to Pictou, and Munro became active with Citizens Against Pollution. When her daughter was five, she took her back to Oregon for a visit.

While there, her daughter became ill. "I went to see a doctor who did an x-ray of her lungs," she says. The doctor told her that Pictou air had not been good for her daughter, whose lungs were like those of an eighty-year-old woman. When she returned to Nova Scotia, Munro decided she would not allow her daughter to continue to breathe the air in the town of Pictou. She got some wind charts to help her identify a place less affected by the mill's emissions, and moved to Blue Mountain about thirty kilometres southeast of Abercrombie Point. But she still remembers how, one evening at twilight, her daughter looked up at the first star that appeared in the sky, and began to sing, "Twinkle, twinkle little star, I wish with all my might that Scott Paper would disappear."

Munro got involved in setting up the First Nations Environmental Network, which would help connect indigenous peoples across the country, and she brought prominent First Nations' activist Milton Born with a Tooth to Pictou Landing in 1990. She had been involved in research on First Nations communities before returning to Nova Scotia, and had found that the vast majority of pulp mills in the late 1960s and early 1970s were placed next to First Nations' communities, which led to growing awareness of and concern about environmental racism in the country.[234]

She suggests the demise of CAP in the mid-1990s may have a lot to do with the involvement of the federal government. Munro says the government sent a consultant to the area to work on the issue and to placate CAP and the Pictou Landing Band, and then hired yet another consultant to do yet another study of Boat Harbour, urging the concerned citizens to stay out of the media while everyone was working on the issue. "Down in Halifax, they held this giant meeting in a huge ballroom," she says. "And they flew in a phenomenal amount of people from Health Canada, [Departments of] Fisheries, Environment, you name it, they were all there."

Following that, the federal government came up with a list of pollution hot spots in Canada, two of which were in

Nova Scotia – the Sydney tar ponds and Boat Harbour – as part of Environment Canada's Coastal Action Program. Then Ottawa came up with $50,000 for a group to tackle pollution in the area, and in 1995, the Pictou Harbour Environmental Protection Project (PHEPP) was born, headed by Robert Christie. Unlike the Citizens Against Pollution group, PHEPP had funding, an office, and salaried employment.

Christie resigned as chair of CAP's board in 1991, although he said he would continue to be an active member.[235] He saw the advent of the PHEPP as a positive sign, and as its head, he began to make amends with and defend the same industry that he had been criticizing for years. Between 1995 and 2010, Northern Pulp (the name of the mill's owner starting in 2008) said it had "partnered on 29 projects with PHEPP, contributing funding, equipment and services."[236] In 2010, Jack Kyte, who had handled public affairs and communications for the mill for many years under different owners, is identified as the PHEPP president, with Christie still its executive director.[237] That same year, Northern Pulp announced it had "reaffirmed its commitment to environmental stewardship through an Environmental Stewardship Partners Program (ESPP) agreement with the Pictou Harbour Environment Protection Project (PHEPP)."[238]

For some former members of Citizens Against Pollution, PHEPP was seen as a deliberate effort to confuse and divide the membership, and they believe the formation of a new, government-funded group in the area helped sink the unfunded campaign run by concerned citizens volunteering their time for environmental protection. Ishbel Munro says CAP members were burned out and felt tricked by the federal consultant who had come to work in the community and set about defusing their protest with big promises.

"We did initially have some hope that the Pictou Harbour group [PHEPP] that had been set up was actually going to make some changes," she tells me. After all, they had an office and the Citizens Against Pollution group had nothing. But she thinks they were more effective when they were independent protesters, expressing their views in the media and calling out the government and the mill on what they were doing, than when they agreed to work with them.

So was all the hard work of Citizens Against Pollution worth it? Ishbel Munro points out that the research they had done on dioxins and furans, and the exposure about the toxic mess in Boat Harbour, led to greater awareness of the problem. For five years, Scott did publish an annual Environmental Management Plan, and worked hard to convince the community of its social and environmental responsibility. In 1992, it stated that in the last twenty-one years, Scott's environmental capital expenditures totalled $38.1 million.[239] The same year, Scott said it was investing $6 million to phase out the use of chlorine in the bleaching process, and replace it with chlorine dioxide, which would not produce measurable amounts of dioxins and furans as waste.[240] Its upgrade of the chlorine dioxide generator allowed the mill to produce chlorine-free pulp.[241] "We now meet stringent new federal regulations for the release of effluent containing chlorinated dioxins and furans," said Scott's 1993 environmental management plan.

That year, tests showed "trace amounts" of dioxins and furans at the mill.[242] This had not been made public before. It could be that Scott was simply responding to three new sets of federal regulations governing industrial effluent that would come into effect in 1994. While its decision to go chlorine-free seemed, initially, to be a response to citizen concerns, it turned out these were not local ones in Pictou or even Canada. Rather, it was all about pleasing markets in Europe. When he announced the mill would be producing chlorine-free pulp, Scott general manager and president Gerry Byrne said this would "allow Scott to regain important European customers lost as a result of consumer demand for products made without molecular chlorine."[243]

The change from chlorine to chlorine dioxide in the pulping process would mean the loss of thirty jobs at Canso Chemicals, although the company would reportedly continue to "carry out water treatment and environmental monitoring."[244] Canso Chemicals ceased operations in 1992, and decommissioning of the site began after that. In 2000, a final report on that decommissioning was completed and submitted to its general manager, Dan Currie.[245]

It detailed the results of an "ecological and human health risk assessment" on an area with "residual mercury" that had not met the objectives of a 1993 clean-up and remediation plan. The mercury had migrated into the bedrock on the site, about five metres below the water table, according to the report, which meant there was "potential for it to dissolve into groundwater and migrate towards" and "discharge into Pictou Harbour in the future."[246] The risk to the ecological system, however, was said to be "negligible" because of how slowly the mercury would migrate and how much the harbour would dilute it. Still, the consultants recommended a monitoring program for the mercury. Marc Theriault, inspection specialist in the area with the Department of Environment, told me in a phone conversation on March 8, 2017, that such a monitoring program was ongoing.

Not all CAP members were convinced they'd achieved anything. Mary Gorman says that while she doesn't regret spending thirty years of her life being an unpaid activist, she does feel it has all been for naught. "What I regret," she says, "is my apparent idealism and naiveté in thinking I could make a genuine difference. I've seen governments get worse, not better." She thinks the governments have been "conned" to protect industry instead of their own people, and they get away with this because their tactics work. "The government has been very successful at dividing and conquering," she says. "People have been very reluctant [to speak up] because number one, they think it will make absolutely no difference if they do, and number two, because they don't want to be estranged from their neighbours. And it's not the [mill] workers' fault. I don't blame the workers, not one bit."

Instead, Gorman faults politicians who, she says, fail to look out for the people who elect them and fail to protect sustainable and viable local industries such as inshore fishing and tourism, while supporting unsustainable and polluting industries such as pulp and paper, which harm the environment and "treat this province like we are a Third World country."

8

A First Nation's ultimatum, a court case, and a settlement (1980s-2005)

When the last tree is cut, the last fish is caught, and the last river is polluted, when to breathe the air is sickening, you will realize, too late, that wealth is not in bank accounts and that you can't eat money.

– Alanis Obomsawin[247]

From the day the mill began to discharge its effluent into Boat Harbour, there was simmering discontent among the people of Pictou Landing First Nation, deep resentment about the trickery that had been used against them, and sadness – even trauma – about the sorry fate of their once-bountiful estuary and the immense loss for the community and its culture. In 1970, Chief Louis Francis, who had been deceived into signing the deal for the use of Boat Harbour, was quoted in *The Mysterious East* magazine, "If they gave me another chance to sell Boat Harbour again, I wouldn't let them have it for six million dollars."[248]

Just a couple of weeks before the provincial election of 1970, the frustration and hurt had boiled over, this time not just in Pictou Landing but among Mi'kmaq leaders from all over the province. A few days after the government and Scott made headlines with their promises to take measures to reduce the mill's pollution, the members of the Union of Nova Scotia Indians decided they'd had enough.

In late September, the Union organized a two-day conference to look at solutions for the mess in Boat Harbour. In attendance were Chief George Manuel, president of the National Indian Brotherhood, Chief Noel Doucette who was president of the Union of Nova Scotia Indians, James O'Reilly who was national legal council on treaty and Indian rights, Ferguson MacKay of the Pollution Control Committee, and Pictou Landing Band Chief Raymond Francis.

Chief Manuel said the federal Department of Indian Affairs had made "a real blunder" in how it had aided the province to obtain rights for Boat Harbour, and said it had "sold the Indian down the river."[249] "To an Indian, water, air and land provides life," said Chief Manuel. "This has been destroyed with pollution. Indians should hold the premier of Nova Scotia and his government responsible for the destruction."

Chief Doucette said he couldn't see anyone in their right mind going near Boat Harbour and not complaining, while Chief Francis said, "If it causes such harm to the area's growth, and water which is so evident, and if paint can be destroyed on the buildings in the area, then what is it doing to the human body?"[250]

The delegation then went to Boat Harbour and ceremoniously blocked the large ditch that carried the reeking effluent across 300 metres of Reserve land to the Boat Harbour waste treatment area. They said if something was not done to close off the stream in one month, they would come back with bulldozers.[251]

On the same day, they sent a telegram to Prime Minister Pierre Trudeau, Minister of Indian Affairs and Northern Development Jean Chrétien, the premier of Nova Scotia G.I. Smith, the minister in charge of the Water Act Donald MacLeod, and

E.L.L. Rowe. In it, they informed the federal and provincial governments they were contesting the validity of the agreement that transferred rights for Boat Harbour to the province, and demanding immediate remedial action to get rid of the ditch and the "septic condition" of the Harbour.[252]

In early October, James O'Reilly, speaking on behalf of the Band, followed the telegram up with a letter to Chrétien saying, "the Government of Canada should oblige the Provincial Government to carry out its obligations under the contract."[253] This correspondence seems to have lit a small blaze under the backsides of some high-level politicians.

In early November, federal Minister Jean Chrétien sent a reply to O'Reilly, in which he said he had sent a telegram to the premier of Nova Scotia "requesting that immediate remedial action be taken to correct the septic condition in Boat Harbour and also advising him that we have no record of an application to use Reserve land for a ditch to carry effluent to the harbour."[254] A week later, representatives from the Departments of Indian Affairs and Northern Development and of National Health and Welfare, the Union of Nova Scotia Indians, and the Pictou Landing Band met to discuss the situation. They decided to request a meeting with the new Liberal government of Premier Gerald Regan to find out what it was planning to do about Boat Harbour.

The first thing it intended to do, as it happened, was to commission more engineering surveys and studies. It was a stalling tactic that had worked well before, and for a time it seemed to be quelling some of the dissent; citizens in the area seemed willing to wait and see. In early 1972, the Minister in charge of the Water Act, Glen Bagnell, announced the government was hiring two engineering firms to design new treatment facilities in Boat Harbour. This would include rerouting the pipeline to the mill to skirt the Reserve land, draining and eventually abandoning the existing settling pond, and building two new ones so that one could be functioning while one was drained and the sludge sediment removed every six months.[255]

The federal government would contribute up to $150,000 to the project and the province would put in as much as $2 million.[256] After years of delaying, the government also agreed to put aerators into Boat Harbour, and by 1973 ten "big Mixmasters" had been put in place.

Reporters from *The Evening News* who went to see the aerators in action observed large amounts of foam and a considerable smell coming from the still-dark waters of the harbour, and noted that despite the improvements, it was still "unlikely to become a picnic area." A year later, as part of its two-year anti-pollution program, Scott installed a black liquid oxidizer at the plant to halve the amount of hydrogen sulphide it emitted into the atmosphere. It would remain to be seen how it all worked, if the situation really improved. Seventeen years later, it seemed it hadn't.

In 1990, there was the big fish kill, and Environment Canada's decision not to charge the government of Nova Scotia for the damage to the fishery. Perhaps in an effort to defuse anger over this decision and to make a show of doing something about Boat Harbour, in April 1991, the provincial Department of Environment started piling rock across the outlet of the harbour. The idea seemed to be this would prevent fish from getting into the shallow inlet where many thousands of them had died from lack of oxygen. Four truckloads had been dumped at the site before the people of Pictou Landing First Nation reacted. Led by Chief Rod Francis, about twenty people set up a blockade and staged a peaceful protest, effectively stopping any more infilling, which they said would merely worsen the situation by creating another small lagoon.[257]

"It's time this Band did something," said Chief Rod Francis. "We're not going to take it anymore." It was neither the first – nor would it be the last – time that a Pictou Landing chief would declare such a thing.

The stench from the polluted lagoon and the emissions coming from the mill had driven many people away from Pictou Landing, and there had also reportedly been a dramatic rise in the suicide rate on the Reserve.[258]

For many years, Chief Raymond Francis, who had succeeded Chief Louis Francis, had looked for legal recourse to get the government of Nova Scotia and Scott to do something about the toxic mess in their backyard, relying on advice from the Department of Indian Affairs and the Union of Nova Scotia Indians.[259] This led nowhere. In 1981, Chief Raymond Francis went to see Daniel Paul, who had recently been appointed District Superintendent of Lands, Revenues and Trusts by the Department of Indian Affairs and Northern Development.

Paul advised Chief Francis that he and the Band had been chasing after the wrong party, that the legal action should be taken against the federal government itself for its dereliction of duties back when it failed to block the Boat Harbour deal. It took some time, but in 1986, with the involvement of Daniel Paul, four members of the Pictou Landing First Nation filed a ten-page statement of claim on behalf of the Band to the Federal Court.[260]

Today, Daniel Paul, a Mi'kmaq Elder, is the holder of numerous honorary doctorates, a prolific writer and speaker on indigenous affairs and rights, and author of the landmark First Nations history book, *We Were Not the Savages*. He is also a member of the Order of Nova Scotia and the Order of Canada. To find out more about the case, I go to see him in his home in late 2016. He has just finished treatment for cancer and although he looks much younger than his seventy-eight years, he says, "I'm on my way out." It certainly doesn't look that way to me, or even as if he is slowing down; he has written a novel that is to be published in a few months, as is a biography written by Halifax journalist and author Jon Tattrie. Paul's basement seems to double as a rec room and office, with his computer on a desk and tables piled high with books and papers, although he says his main activity these days is to concentrate on recovering from the cancer and its treatment. My impression of him is that of an extraordinary thinker, writer, and doer, a very busy, gracious, and fully engaged man.

He says he got involved with Boat Harbour for one big reason: he had been to the estuary when he was young and seen it in its pristine state, and he wanted to see it cleaned up. When Chief Raymond Francis took him back there in 1981, shortly after he'd become Chief Superintendent of Lands for the federal government, Paul was appalled by the stink and the foam.

"I was totally pissed off, to be honest with you, when I reviewed the files and looked at the harbour," he tells me. But he was in an awkward position. He had been summoned to a meeting by his boss in Amherst, Nova Scotia, and instructed to make the Pictou Landing Band Council a settlement offer of $250,000 for Boat Harbour. He did as he was told. He arranged a meeting with the Band Council and put the federal government's offer on the table, and then told them to meet him again later in the day when he was "off duty." At that second meeting, he told them to tell the federal government to "shove it." Even if this meant he was officially going against the explicit orders of his employers in the federal government, Paul says he was in fact doing his job, which was to look out for the best interests of the Mi'kmaq.

At first, he says, the Band Council was not very interested in turning on the Department of Indian Affairs, which had convinced them that any legal action they took should be against the province. But in 1983, Paul got hold of a memo written by an official in Ottawa to a lawyer meant to be working in a partnership with the department and the Band. It instructed the lawyer in Nova Scotia not to share information or be open with the Band Council. When the Band saw the memo, they decided it was time to pursue action against the Crown. Paul then went looking for a lawyer to represent Pictou Landing

First Nation. The head of the Nova Scotia Human Rights Commission recommended Esbon Anthony Ross, a lawyer with a great deal of legal experience in Canada and the Caribbean, and, as Paul tells me, with the added advantage of also being an environmental engineer.

Led now by Chief Roderick Francis, in July 1986 the Band filed its notice of action against the Crown in the Federal Court in Halifax. Their intention was to sue the federal government for having failed to protect them when the deal was signed with the provincial government for their rights to Boat Harbour.[261] The claim stated that "Boat Harbour has become seriously polluted. As a result, members of the Band have suffered and continue to suffer damage to their health and the enjoyment of the amenities of their reserve lands."[262]

In August that year, the Deputy Attorney General of Canada, "on behalf of Her Majesty the Queen" issued a statement of defence, denying "all allegations of damage suffered by the plaintiffs of the Pictou Landing Band."[263] It also stated that although Boat Harbour had gone septic after the installation of the effluent disposal system, in 1971 and 1972 the government of Nova Scotia had built a new dam and settling ponds, and installed aerators and a new pipeline. "This action by the Province of Nova Scotia," it claimed, "cured the septic condition of Boat Harbour and no pollution or septic condition has existed in Boat Harbour since that time."[264]

Ross went to work mounting the case. He had the Federal Court issue an order that forced the province to hand over thousands of documents relating to Boat Harbour. During a discovery hearing, he got Armand Wigglesworth to admit under oath that his job had been to "get the easement rights across the lands and for the use [of Boat Harbour], not to tell the Mi'kmaq that the system wouldn't function properly, and that he had indeed once responded to criticism of this plot with the words, 'So, they're only Indians.'"[265] Daniel Paul tells me they found out that the facility to which Wigglesworth and Bates had taken the chief and Band councillor in 1965 didn't start functioning for another two years. During discovery, Paul says, Wigglesworth admitted he had taken a drink of the water, pretending this would be just like the water in Boat Harbour once the effluent was treated.

Ross mounted what Paul tells me was an "iron-clad" case, which he believes would have been won "hands down" had it gone to court. But, and this he regrets enormously to this day, the case didn't go to court. In July 1993, Paul, Ross, and the representatives of the Band met with federal officials at a hotel in Halifax, and told them if they didn't want to negotiate, they would happily take the Crown to court. The federal government decided it could not afford the embarrassment that such a case could engender, and agreed to negotiate.

"They reacted very quickly," says Paul. "It was mind-boggling how quickly they agreed to the $35 million," which is the amount the federal government agreed to award the Pictou Landing First Nation in an out-of-court settlement. The Band itself would administer the money in a trust fund in the Bank of Montreal, and the Canadian Parliament passed the Pictou Landing Indian Band Agreement Act in 1995 that stipulated it would fall outside the terms of the Indian Act.[266] Some of the funds were given to Band members, while the rest was held in trust funds. According to a letter to the Band membership from the Band Council in 2002, the Band had been "fully compensated for all the impacts of 'Boat Harbour' except for unforeseen health problems when Canada paid $20,000,000 as specific compensation with a further $15,000,000 provided so that if necessary, or even desirable, we could relocate our Reserve to an area (or areas) not impacted by the Boat Harbour treatment system."[267]

The offer reportedly divided the Band, with some members unhappy with the amount Ottawa was offering, and others fearful that such a settlement would not protect them from future pollution.[268] Sandy Denny told *The Chronicle Herald* he thought they were being "fleeced" by men like those who betrayed his uncle, the late Chief Louis Joe Francis, when they tricked him into signing the Boat Harbour agreement.[269] He called the settlement a "bad deal, very, very rotten." Others were concerned that the closure of Boat Harbour was not part of the agreement, but in the end members voted 141 to 25 in favour of it.[270] The future of the former estuary remained unresolved. "We could have got a schedule for the closing of Boat Harbour," says Paul.

Shortly after the out-of-court agreement was signed, the Mi'kmaq Warrior Society from Pictou Landing set up a protest barricade at the site where the dam separates Boat Harbour from the Strait. Jonathan Beadle of the Pictou Landing First Nation has clear memories of that protest.

It's early summer in 2016, and the late afternoon sun bathes us in its golden light as we sit on the porch of Beadle's home on the Reserve, a stone's throw from the Northumberland Strait on one side and Boat Harbour on the other. He has so much to tell me – about the harbour and its troubled history, the settlement in 1993 and the resulting trust fund, and how the whole issue has affected his community. He says he has suffered enormously over the years because of the presence of the mill, the pollution in Boat Harbour, and the injustice and racism in Canada towards First Nations' communities. While two of his children play in the yard beside the porch, his wife, a teacher at a middle school in Trenton, prepares dinner on the BBQ and generously serves an additional plate for me, with delicious fresh haddock and vegetables.

Beadle's passion and energy seem limitless. He tells me he coaches different sports and tries very hard to impart health and wellness, and when he's not doing that, he's working as a photographer. His eldest daughter has become a mother, he says, and now that he's a grandfather he is determined to keep his latent anger at bay, because to be an Elder is to be someone who is not angry. "But how to achieve that in the face of gross injustice?" he asks. He is profoundly concerned about our responsibility to Mother Earth, and he remembers well that protest back in 1993 when he joined thirty or forty Mi'kmaq Warriors for the blockade.

He was just a teenager at the time, but he recalls the protest began in the morning and continued all day. There was drumming, and it made him feel good. But as the sun set, the numbers dwindled as others left to get coffee and by the time night had fallen, he found himself alone at the site.

"The area has spiritual powers," he tells me. "It's haunting. After a while I was distracted by this, and I forgot what I was there for. I thought the others were going for coffee and coming back with one for me. Then I realized they weren't coming." The next morning he walked home, a changed person, reflecting that he had an obligation to take up the issue of Boat Harbour and the environment. "My whole thing is wellness," he tells me. He has not given up hope that one day things will improve. "If they can fly a man to the moon," he says, "they can clean up Boat Harbour."

Two years after the out-of-court settlement with the Pictou Landing First Nation, the mill changed hands. In July 1995, Kimberly-Clark, a giant American pulp and paper company and maker of Kleenex tissues and Huggies diapers, agreed to buy the entire Scott Corporation for about $7 billion.[271] The annual revenue of the newly merged company would be about $11 billion. Scott's chairman and chief executive, Albert Dunlap, did very nicely from the merger, making between $90 million and $100 million when Kimberly-Clark took over all of Scott's assets, including its Canadian mills and land holdings. The deal netted him between $20 million and $30 million more than the estimated cost at the time of a new and effective treatment facility for the mill in Pictou.[272]

This was the same year the original agreement obliging the province to look after the mill's effluent was expiring. In December 1995, the provincial government under Liberal Premier John Savage signed a new Memorandum of Understanding giving Scott Maritimes, owned now by Kimberly-Clark, permission to continue to use Boat Harbour as its effluent treatment facility.[273] It transferred the responsibility for operating a planned "reconfigured facility" for the mill's effluent treatment from the province to Scott (Kimberly-Clark), which the Minister of Supply and Services said would save the province a million dollars a year.

The government also agreed to continue providing the mill with more than 100 million litres of fresh water per day for the next twenty-five years. For the next ten years the rate for the water would be $18.53 per million gallons, or about $170,000 per year for 9.1 trillion Imperial gallons (41.5 trillion litres).[274] Starting on April 1, 1996, the fee for water for the next five years would be an annual base charge of $157,124 in addition to a charge of $64.84 per million Imperial gallons, for about $592,000 per year. But the government then turned around and offered Scott an "annual environmental improvement credit" of up to $100,000 on the water charges. And the province would continue to treat 87 million litres of waste each day for an almost token charge of $100,000 a year.[275]

The province would still be responsible for system improvements and clean-up activities that had begun in 1994.[276] Then the provincial government made a fateful decision that has huge repercussions even today and possibly for many years to come. On New Year's Eve in 1995, it signed a separate indemnity agreement to ensure the mill's owners could never be held accountable in any way for the treatment facility.[277] A separate lease agreement was signed the same day that gave the mill the right to use Boat Harbour for another ten years, until 2005.[278]

In return, Kimberly-Clark agreed to close down Boat Harbour within ten years, prompting Nova Scotia's Minister for Supply and Services, Gerald O'Malley, to announce that there was finally "an end in sight for Boat Harbour."[279] As part of the deal with the new owners, the province agreed to build a water-flow control system that would lower the water level in Boat Harbour to recover Band land, and it said it would restore Boat Harbour to its original state after Kimberly-Clark stopped using it in 2005. O'Malley said the new contract "absolutely" ensured that Boat Harbour would close by the end of 2005. The mill's manager, Gerry Byrne, assured the public that eventually, an on-site treatment system would permit the discharge of treated effluent into Pictou Harbour.

On hearing the company's pledge that it would stop dumping waste into Boat Harbour in 2005, Jonathan Beadle reacted this way: "I've seen this before. What are you going to do – fool us again?"[280] His prescience was remarkable. All the promises made over the years about an improved treatment facility and clean-up of Boat Harbour were, to say the least, premature, if not disingenuous.

As the ten-year deadline for the lease of Boat Harbour grew closer after the new millennium dawned, the provincial government, now headed by Progressive Conservative Premier John Hamm, looked again at opening Boat Harbour to the Strait and piping the effluent further offshore, allowing tides and currents to disperse it. It engaged the services of a consulting firm that had done a number of reports on waste treatment options, Jacques Whitford, to prepare detailed studies of the tidal flushing option so it would pass federal environmental regulations.[281] Later assessments, however, indicated that the plan might cause still more environmental problems when the waste washed ashore and back into Boat Harbour with the tides. After Kimberly-Clark spun off its Canadian pulp operations to Neenah Paper in 2004, it engaged ENSR, an American consulting firm, to look at the proposed effluent treatment plans. It predicted that this could cause eutrophication in Boat Harbour, and this, according to the mill's public affairs manager Jack Kyte, would result in an algae buildup and even more smell.[282] And so the project, like previous plans, was abandoned.

Meanwhile, Kimberly-Clark and the province had entered into new negotiations with the Pictou Landing First Nation. In 2001, Kimberly-Clark had proposed an arrangement with the Band that would allow it to continue to operate the aerated stabilization basin at the top of Boat Harbour with a pipeline buried underneath it that would discharge the effluent into the Northumberland Strait. In exchange for this arrangement that gave the mill the use of the aeration ponds, the company would pay the Band $950,000 immediately, and then $200,000 annually for the next five years, increasing the amount by $20,000 every five years until 2030.[283] Kimberly-Clark also committed to transferring to the Band 4,000 acres of land in northern Nova Scotia, and to putting in a pipeline that would bypass the stabilization basin, permitting the Band and the province to look at other options for its use.

The Band voted to accept the agreement. Following this, the province signed a lease with Kimberly-Clark in 2002 that extended the use of the treatment facility until 2030. This was hailed by the Progressive Conservative government's Minister of Transportation and Public Works, Ron Russell, as "a tremendous announcement for the future of Pictou County."[284] "Now that issues around the lease are resolved," he said, "it's time to roll up our sleeves to make sure all the proper water and air tests continue, and that the information is made available to the public." President and general manager of Kimberly-Clark, Jim Piedmonte, said, "Our employees and the system operators have set very high standards of performance for our waste water treatment."[285]

But there were still complications; this extended lease was predicated on the Memorandum of Understanding with the Pictou Landing Band that the Boat Harbour lagoon would no longer be required as part of the treatment system, and that it would be restored as a tidal estuary.[286] And as noted earlier, that plan would soon be nixed, when studies done for the mill suggested such a system would not pass an environmental assessment.

When journalism students at the University of King's College investigated, wrote about, and exposed the full extent of the toxic mess and legacy of Boat Harbour in their investiga-

tive project in 2009, they calculated that five different provincial governments had promised to close and clean up Boat
Harbour, and that so far, not one had kept that promise.[287]

In July 2016, I head to Pictou Landing for a second meeting with Jonathan Beadle. Our first one lasted hours, while he
poured out his heart and the history of Boat Harbour and its
effect on the people of Pictou Landing First Nation and on him
personally. This time, he is taking me on a late-afternoon walk
around the treatment site and the settlement ponds. We approach the facility on a path through mowed fields, which have
a park-like feel, groomed as if it were a campground or even a
rustic golf course. That illusion is quickly shattered when we
reach the outlet where the mill effluent surfaces from below
ground into a canal, which funnels it towards the two settling
ponds. And I wonder how it can be that after all these years
and so many studies and so much protest and so much government money poured into the facility, so little seems to have
changed.

The effluent still reeks, fouling the air with its stench. Further on, a few of the aerators are still churning up the foamy
liquid in a separate lagoon, and discoloured water into which
tablets are being added is still flowing into the main stabilization basin, from which the dark and smelly water still feeds
into the Northumberland Strait. We stand at the edge of it for
a while, looking out over the deceptively attractive landscape,
with the early evening sun sparkling on the surface of the lagoon, which is surrounded by woods. But something in the air
is making my throat burn, and the odour seems to have lodged
itself in my sinuses.

Beadle advises me to buy some headache tablets on my
way home that evening, saying that headaches are the inevitable outcome of a visit to Boat Harbour.

9

A lonely struggle

For miles downwind, as with every pulp and paper mill, a miasma of attar-of-rotten eggs; the clinging, tongue-coating presence of hydrogen sulphide gas is inescapable.
— Warner Troyer[288]

Although photos and footage of Boat Harbour have featured in many media reports over the years, not many people have had occasion to visit the facility and experience the sights and smells first-hand. It's not open to the general public, and it's tucked away behind woodlands and set well back from Highway 348. This is the Pictou Landing Road that winds its way from the town of Trenton out to the Northumberland Strait, through the Reserve and then further east past Chance Harbour, until it takes a sharp turn inland at Little Harbour and becomes Logan Road. The only glimpse of Boat Harbour on that entire circuit is just to the east of the Reserve, where a bridge crosses over its former outlet, now a dam where the effluent is released into the Strait.

From the bridge only a small part of the stabilizing lagoon is visible. From this narrow perspective, it would be easy to believe the picturesque body of water is healthy. The relative invisibility of Boat Harbour is convenient for those who would like to maintain the status quo. It's extremely inconvenient for the residents of Pictou Landing, who have to live with the smell and the no-go toxic area around Boat Harbour.

According to Barbara Sproull Seplaki, the fact that so few have ever seen the treatment facility has not helped people of the area who have struggled for decades to get Boat Harbour closed and restored to its original state. Some years back, she showed a photo of its murky froth to someone from Little Harbour, a village just a few kilometres east of Pictou Landing, and the woman said she didn't believe that was Boat Harbour; she thought it had been closed for years.

Although the smell of the mill's emissions is often powerful along this road, you can drive all the way from the town of Trenton to the Reserve on the Pictou Landing Road without knowing that one of Canada's most egregious pollution hot spots is just a hundred metres or so behind the trees and the houses on the eastern side of the road. To the west are the lanes and roads that lead down to properties along the shoreline of Pictou Harbour. Everyone who lives in Pictou Landing – both First Nation and non-native – is affected by the smell of the emissions and effluent from the mill.

Over the years, several families tried to get the provincial government to compensate them for the land their families lost through expropriation, and for the damage caused by the pollution in Boat Harbour and along the Northumberland Strait. In 1994, the grandson of Councillor Henry Ferguson sought a million dollars in compensation for the land the family lost, but the government still refused to pay more than the $635 that was offered for the land back in the 1960s.[289]

In March 2000, another Pictou Landing resident, Bruce Cristison, filed an unsuccessful lawsuit against Kimberly-Clark and the provincial attorney general's office seeking compensation for damages caused by the pollution and also the expropriation of his father's land around Boat Harbour.[290]

Pictou Landing residents Barbara Sproull Seplaki and

John McKay also engaged lawyers to look at possible legal recourse for the problems those living in the vicinity of the pulp mill experienced. This followed a near-fatal illness in the Sproull Seplaki family caused when a family member swam in Moodie Cove after a breach in Lighthouse Beach allowed effluent and water contaminated with sewage into the cove. Without informing residents, the federal government had put in a sewage disposal plant just beyond the beach so that when it was breached, Moodie Cove was contaminated.[291] The lawyers' report did not go as far as saying that the affected residents did not have a basis to seek legal recourse, but said their preliminary investigation indicated that the risks of being unsuccessful were "substantial."[292]

After new agreements about the use of the harbour were reached between the mill's owners and the Pictou Landing Band in the early 2000s, a "Boat Harbour Committee" was established, which for years would hold regular meetings at the health centre on the Reserve. On the Committee were representatives of the federal and provincial governments, a law firm, Band members, and the consulting firm, Jacques Whitford.[293] Excluded from the committee, says Jane Sproull Thomson, were the other concerned citizens of Pictou Landing. In this way, she says, the mill and government officials deeply divided the community in and around Pictou Landing.

One resident of the area who was profoundly and irrevocably marked by the situation, Alexander James MacKenzie, gave up on more accepted ways of seeking compensation in the courts or in meetings and launched his own unorthodox campaign.

On an unseasonably warm day in the autumn of 2016, I take a left off Pictou Landing Road onto one of the roads leading down to Pictou Harbour where MacKenzie stays. He ushers me through the kitchen and out onto a porch on the back of the house that affords a panoramic view of the town of Pictou across the harbour. It also overlooks one of MacKenzie's creations, a cement boat, and beyond that a few trees and then the blue waters of the harbour glinting in the afternoon sun. Despite the heat, he is wearing a heavy plaid shirt and a woollen cap in the blues and yellows of Nova Scotia's tartan. With his full white beard, he cuts a striking figure. And he's made a reputation for himself as a very colourful personality with a bent for highly original public protests. In 2014, fed up with the smell of the emissions from Northern Pulp, MacKenzie devised a homemade mock cannon that he mounted on his small schooner, called it his "pirate ship," and shot fireworks out of the cannon. He told Steve Goodwin of *The Advocate* that it was "a little stress relief" because he'd tried every other form of protest about the mill's pollution that he could think of.[294]

Alexander MacKenzie is the younger brother of Donald MacKenzie, the engineer who helped build the pulp mill in 1965, with whom I had spoken just a few weeks earlier. The younger MacKenzie brother is no fan of pulp mills, and hasn't been since he was eight years old. He tells me that during a road trip to Ontario to visit relatives in 1957, there was one thing that struck – and stuck with – him. They would be driving along country roads, he says, past nice houses and prosperous–looking villages, and suddenly there would be a terrible smell in the air that made him wonder how anyone could live in such a place.

"And I remember very clearly my father pointed to a sign," he says, "a big sign, and it read, 'Pulp Mill,' employing X number of people and the world-is-great type of thing." Then the mill would come into view and his father would point to the smokestacks that were emitting the noxious odour. "And I couldn't believe it that something could be so horrible as that rotten egg smell," he tells me.

So when word came in the 1960s that a pulp mill was going to be built in Pictou County and that Boat Harbour was going to be dammed off, MacKenzie saw it as bad news. Although he was a teenager at the time, he was one of many in the community very upset by the plans. He attended the meetings chaired by the early critics of the mill, including Councillor Henry Ferguson. But when the young MacKenzie stood up to speak of his own memories of how the pulp mills in Ontario stank to high heavens, he was told by the government representatives and proponents of the new mill to sit down and be quiet; this mill, they said, would be a modern one and there would be no smell.

Of course this turned out to be rather far from the truth, and the community came together as the Northumberland Strait Pollution Control Committee and later as CAP to fight the pollution. While things improved slightly with the addition of the aerators and settling ponds, the pollution continued in Boat Harbour, and continues to this day. There were also repeated breaks in the pipeline, which permitted raw effluent from the mill to escape into Pictou Harbour and onto the land around Boat Harbour. [295] Despite these community efforts to hold the government and mill accountable, says MacKenzie, "We were just beat, and beat, and beat."

Then came the federal government's out-of-court settlement with the Pictou Landing First Nation in 1993, and the awarding of $35 million for the Crown's "flagrant disregard" and "careless indifference" to the rights of the Band when Boat Harbour was transformed into a toxic sump.[296] MacKenzie says the settlement proved that the people of Pictou Landing had indeed "had something to complain about all those years," and it showed that the protestors "weren't crazy after all."

At this point in our conversation, tears form in his eyes and his voice falters. We sit quietly for a few minutes. To defuse things a little, distract him from what is obviously a painful and sensitive memory, I mention casually that the sulphuric odour from the mill is bad this afternoon. He seems surprised. "To me, the air's nice today," he says. "I didn't know it was bad." This in turn surprises me; the smell is so strong it has given me a headache. I wonder how strong it has to be before someone who lives here, whose olfactory sense has been assaulted and deadened by it for decades, notices the offensive odour.

Then he resumes his tale. What hurts him most, he says,

is the fact that the government refused to consider any compensation for the entire population of the area for the suffering and hardship the pollution caused. He says he's grateful to the Mi'kmaq for setting the precedent and pushing the government to admit its wrongdoing. His beef is that the federal government chose to offer the Band an out-of-court settlement. In his view, this meant the government avoided a case it would probably lose, which would have set a legal precedent and paved the way for the rest of the population to launch a lawsuit.

Incensed by what he saw as government injustice, in 1998 MacKenzie began the fight of his life, demanding that the governments – of Canada and of Nova Scotia – do something about Boat Harbour and about the suffering it caused everyone in the area. In the past three decades, he has run in seven elections. He was a candidate for municipal councillor five times, and he spent six years on County Council. He has run as an independent candidate in both a provincial and federal election.

He has also spent thirty-eight days under house arrest, eighty days and eighty nights behind bars, and five and a half years staging a peaceful one-man protest on roadsides in Pictou County with a sign demanding "Equal rights for all Canadians."

"I was ignored," he says. "I would spend an hour every day in front of a government building with my sign. I crossed Canada at my own expense looking up Members of Parliament and telling them the story and trying to get something done." When that failed, he decided to go a step farther, earning himself headlines and the nickname Ballot Box Bandit.[297] He would later print this on the gas tank of his motorcycle.[298]

"I was given a hundred hours community service the first time I took a ballot box and threw it in the harbour protesting government without representation," he tells me. He says he has put his own freedom on the line for the cause, spent time in jail, and done mandatory community service. He decided his protest should qualify as community service, and headed to Ottawa where he stood in front of Parliament for seven days, from before dawn until after dusk. Then, back home in Pictou County for the 2000 federal election, he stole not one but two ballot boxes and put them in the gutter. The judge gave him twelve months probation rather than assign him more community service. "They were afraid I'd go back to Ottawa," he says.

With tears in his eyes, MacKenzie says he is deeply hurt that his protests and willingness to sacrifice his own freedom for the cause are often passed off as "a joke." He tells me over and over again that his grievance is with the governments of Canada and of Nova Scotia, which, from the beginning, were not up front with the people of Pictou Landing about the effect the effluent would have on Boat Harbour and the pollution would have on their lives and livelihoods. Nor does he blame the mill for his woes.

"The pulp mill is a business," he says. "They have their shareholders, they have to make money for their shareholders, they have to push the envelope and the more they do, the more money they make, that's their job, they're doing their job. The politicians are not doing their job."

10

And then there were the forests

On the whole, man has been the worst enemy of Nova Scotia's forests.

– Ralph S. Johnson[299]

The controversy over the pulp mill doesn't end with the air and water pollution and a string of broken promises from successive governments that they would make the mill clean up its environmental act. There is something far more wide-reaching to consider, namely the source of all that pulp. I am reminded of this as I drive along highways looking at the spindly mess of trees that now pass for woodlands in so much of the province. And I think about it every time I am on Highway 106, watching the steady stream of heavy trucks piled high with tree stems, many nothing more than skinny little poles, making the turn onto the Abercrombie Road and heading to the mill to satisfy its voracious appetite for fibre and tree biomass to fuel its pulping operations. Those trucks and the chewed-up landscapes following a clearcut raise a whole slew of questions. Which and whose forests are being felled for the mill? How are the trees being harvested? Who is running the show in the woodlands of Nova Scotia? And how much has the pulp industry remade the forests and forestry policies of this province in its own interest?

It would take another entire book to answer those questions, but the influence of the pulp mill and the pulp industry in Nova Scotia still warrants a few chapters in this one. And to start, it's worthwhile taking a short meander back in time to find out what the original forests in the region looked like and what the woodlands look like today. Of course the changes to the forests of Nova Scotia didn't begin in the 1960s with the arrival of Scott and Stora, or even with Mersey back in 1929. Nova Scotia has the longest period of logging history in North America, and by the time the big pulp mills went into operation, the Acadian forests in the province had already suffered more than two centuries of exploitation, even abuse.[300]

A mature Acadian forest is a rich and diverse mixture of hardwood and softwood species, most long-lived and deep-rooted trees.[301] Although there is little old-growth forest left in eastern Canada, there are pockets of it, which forester, author, and lawyer Jamie Simpson says, "will stop you in your tracks, invite your gaze upward, and fill you with the wonder of centuries-old hemlock, pine, spruce, cedar, sugar maple, and yellow birch."[302]

This kind of healthy forest protects soil and watersheds, and stores a great deal of carbon, vital in combating climate change and helping human populations deal with its negative effects. The diversity of trees of different ages in a healthy and mature Acadian forest makes it more resistant to fire and to pests than is the more uniform boreal forest that covers so much of Canada. The recent work of Suzanne Simard at the University of British Columbia, as well as German forester Peter Wohlleben, reveal the incredibly complex and intricate ways that trees in healthy woods communicate and even cooperate with fungi and with each other through their root systems in "wood-wide webs." Their work further fuels arguments in favour of bio-diverse and mature forests.[303]

The fauna in original Maritime forests was even more diverse than the flora. The woodlands of Nova Scotia were once home to wolves and wolverine, now completely gone, and an abundance of animals now endangered or threatened, such as eastern panthers, lynx, marten, and fishers.

Early Europeans were often awed by the grandeur of the forests that greeted them when they stepped ashore on the Atlantic coast. They wrote of "vast cathedrals" and "shady groves of giants."[304] Old-growth stands were common, and they were full of massive trees that were one, two, and even up to eight centuries old.[305] In his 1877 work on the history of Pictou, George Patterson captured the first impression of settlers when they landed in 1767, and found "one unbroken forest covered the whole surface of the country to the water's edge," a forest full of the tasselled heads of the white pines, in which a pine sixty feet tall would be considered small, "not worthy of taking."[306]

But that was once upon a time, when the Mi'kmaq, Maliseet, and Passamaquoddy peoples were the ones living in and looking after the Acadian forest. After the Europeans arrived, the forests were treated more like mines than they were living, breathing organisms.[307] Any tree or kind of wood that was needed for a particular industrial purpose was targeted and the best specimens were the first to go. This kind of selective harvesting was known as "high-grading": take the best and leave the rest – the deformed, stunted, or sickly – to reproduce.

The first rush on the Acadian forest began in the 1700s, when the British went after the region's majestic and statuesque white pine, the tallest tree in the forest and ideal for ship masts. By 1887, nearly all the accessible pine and also the spruce on the eastern half of mainland Nova Scotia had been cut, and sawmills in Pictou were working instead with hemlock.[308] By the end of the nineteenth century, the province's magnificent virgin forests were all but gone, having provided the fuel for the industrialization of Nova Scotia's economy during the "golden age" of the 1800s.[309] Then, facing competition from other products and with improved national transportation networks, Nova Scotia saw-millers "turned on their forests with a vengeance" to avoid going out of business.[310]

The pulp industry was just being born. In 1844, a man named Charles Fenerty in Upper Sackville, Nova Scotia, said he had developed a groundwood process that produced paper from spruce pulp.[311] The very first exports of pulpwood from the province were to France in 1875, and in 1880 another small mill was built to grind up wood to make paper.[312]

The twentieth century would bring even more intensive exploitation of the woodlands, with loggers and sawmills high-grading timber from the woodlands, widespread felling of forests for farms, for fuelwood and construction materials, and for the growing lumber and pulp market in the United States. In the 1920s, the push for pulp started to ramp up in Nova Scotia itself, with the groundwood mill in Sheet Harbour, which would be bought by Scott half a century later.[313] At the same time, American pulp firms began to acquire vast holdings of land in the province. By 1927, the province's chief forester, Otto Schierbeck, said more than two million acres of prime forest land – nearly 15 percent of the province – were owned by American pulp and paper companies interested only in exporting pulpwood.[314]

Nova Scotia had relatively little Crown land left; most had been sold off to settlers and lumbermen.[315] In 1965, the province held only about 23 percent of Nova Scotia's forested land, 60 percent was owned by small landowners with 1,000 acres or less, and about 17 percent belonged to large owners.[316] This was a situation starkly different from most other Canadian provinces, where the bulk of the land belonged to the Crown. This left Nova Scotia forests particularly vulnerable to the influence of large landowners – often foreign-owned pulp interests.

Tree-cutting for the first half of the twentieth century was still a clumsy and relatively slow business, limited in scale by the heavy manual labour needed to fell trees using double-bitted axes and crosscut saws, transport them to mills using horses and river-power, and saw them into logs in steam mills. Even with these technological limitations, the forests were not spared serious damage. Recognition of that led, in the 1930s, to attempts to bring in legislation to clamp down on the unregulated cutting spree in the province that was being driven by the demand for pulpwood for export. Those failed. A decade later, the indiscriminate cutting in the forests led to a public outcry that the provincial government could no longer ignore. The Nova Scotia Royal Commission on Provincial Development and Rehabilitation, convened by Professor R. MacGregor Dawson in 1944, evoked an outpouring of complaints from forest workers, which revealed a "consistent theme of antagonism between independent woodlot owners selectively cutting for the sawlog industry, and the pulp and paper company clear cutting practices."[317]

In 1946, the government passed the very first law that regulated private forest land in Nova Scotia with the Small Tree Act, which restricted the cutting of spruce, hemlock, and pine less than ten inches in diameter at a height of one foot from the ground. It wasn't a perfect piece of legislation; it didn't apply to or protect Crown land, but it did help preserve quality logs otherwise destined for pulp mills and protect to some extent against clear cutting.[318] And at least on privately held forest land, it prevented the free-for-all harvesting of young trees.[319]

The destructive exploitation of the province's old-growth forests over the centuries did not happen without citizens' dissent and resistance. Environmental concerns had a long history and certainly did not begin in the 1960s or even the twentieth century. Back in 1749, the year Halifax was founded, four English woodcutters working at a new sawmill in Chebucto Bay were killed during a Mi'kmaq attack.[320] The next day, the colonial governor of Nova Scotia, Edward Cornwallis, met with his council and declared war on the Mi'kmaq, offering a bounty for scalps from men, women, and children.[321] Cornwallis believed French missionaries were inciting the Mi'kmaq to

resist British settlement. But as Paul Webster writes in his thesis on the history of resistance to forest destruction in Nova
Scotia, "There is a strong base of evidence behind the argument that the Micmacs attacked the woodcutters at Chebucto
not because the French told them to, but because they were
angry about the British assault on the Nova Scotian forest."[322]

During the 1800s, Baptist missionary Silas Rand record-
ed many accounts of Mi'kmaq history and legends, and in his
writings, quoted one Elder lamenting what they had lost: "Our
lands have been taken away, the forests have been cut down
and the moose and the bear nearly exterminated."[323]

Over the next two centuries, the First Nations' concerns
came to be shared by many settlers. In the 1870s, Captain N.M.
Becwith, a Nova Scotian sailor, shipbuilder, and shipowner
wrote an essay denouncing the abuse of Canada's forests, "We
are wasting our forests, habitually, wickedly, insanely; and at
a rate which must soon bankrupt us," and in Nova Scotia, he
said, "there was a cry that the supply of ship-timber was about
to be exhausted."[324]

Disagreements about how forests should be managed
and used go back a long, long way. In North America, during
the 1940s, views on forestry underwent an ideological divide
that persists even today. In one camp were those who viewed
forests strictly as a commodity, whom the American writer,
philosopher, forester, and early environmentalist Aldo Leopold labelled "Type A."[325] As Leopold put it, "Type A foresters
were content to grow trees like cabbages with cellulose as the
basic forest commodity. [They] feel no inhibition against vio-
lence; [their] ideology is agronomic."[326] Type A forestry drew
heavily on silviculture that promoted monocultures of trees to
serve the narrow needs of industry.

"Type B" forestry, by contrast, "takes a more holistic and
ecological approach, employing natural species and managing
the forest environment rather than creating an artificial one,
with recognition of services forests perform beyond narrow
economic returns from pulp and timber, namely wildlife habi-

tat, watersheds, wilderness areas and recreation." Type B foresters, according to Leopold, feel the "stirrings of an ecological
conscience."[327]

Lloyd Hawboldt, the forest entomologist who began
working with Nova Scotia's Department of Lands and Forests
in 1944, and who twenty years later tried to stand up to the
government of Premier Stanfield and his deputy G.I. Smith by
arguing – in vain – that the province could not afford to host
a third large pulp mill, saw some merit in both approaches to
forestry. Hawboldt wanted to develop an alternative somewhere in the middle by marrying the two.

He knew, however, that if the government were going to
find a healthier way to manage the province's forests, it needed a comprehensive inventory of Nova Scotia's woodlands.
That was done in the 1950s, and once the data were in, Hawboldt and his colleague, forester R.M. Bulmer, were assigned
the daunting job of summarizing them, looking at what they
meant economically and what message they had for those
looking to develop forest policies.

The result of their collaboration was the landmark book
The Forest Resources of Nova Scotia, published by the Department of Lands and Forests in 1958. Their findings were remarkable, especially when one considers that this was when
most logging in the province was relatively small-scale, when
there was far less mechanization, and when the province hosted just one medium-sized pulp mill, the Bowater-Mersey plant
in Brooklyn on the province's South Shore. Even so, Hawboldt
and Bulmer concluded that the harvest of logs for timber in
Nova Scotia needed to be reduced by half, and that forest
policy should ensure there was no more erosion of the forest
"capital" in the province, which would mean there should be
an annual surplus in forest production and no decline in the
growing stock.[328]

But they didn't stop there. They also recommended there
should be more use of hardwoods. If the pulp industry were to
expand, they said, the total inventory of softwood species pre-

ferred for pulp production would too, and there could be no more sawlog industry, which used tree stems to produce lumber. When small sawlog and pulp operators in the province got wind of the big pulp deals in the making, they worried that the government was giving away too many benefits, which would harm them.[329]

Their fears were not unfounded. Once the big mills got going in the 1960s, the scale of tree harvesting and the speed at which it would be done with increased mechanization would turn out to be beyond anything anyone could possibly have imagined earlier. The arrival of big pulp brought the demand for new forestry legislation that would permit the kinds of tree harvesting that would satisfy the voracious needs of the big new mills in Pictou and Port Hawkesbury. In 1965, the year the Scott Maritimes Act was proclaimed, the Small Tree Act was scrapped.[330]

For many years, Scott had been exporting custom sawn lumber to the United Kingdom from its extensive land holdings in the province. The company had picked up many of these when it took over the land owned by Hollingsworth & Whitney Ltd.[331] By the time the mill opened in 1967, Scott owned outright more than a million acres of Nova Scotia, had a long-term lease on over 230,000 acres of Crown land, and it owned another 30,000 acres in New Brunswick it had purchased from Fraser Pulp & Lumber.[332] Before that, clear cutting had been a relatively rare harvesting technique on Scott lands.

Once the pulp mill went into production, it became company policy "that if a stand were to be harvested, then it would be clear cut."[333] Although this was unpopular with the public and among foresters concerned about biodiversity and environmental health, whose leanings were towards more holistic Type B forest management, Type A forestry for pulp was ruling the day, and governments were more than willing to promote it.

The federal and provincial governments coughed up more than $21 million in grants for a Pulp and Paper Modernization Agreement to increase the production capacity of the Scott and Bowater mills.[334] Stora was also increasing its output, and by 1975 it would be producing 175,000 tons of sulphite pulp and 160,000 tons of newsprint every year, with 90 percent of it for export to the United States. Thanks to a generous half-century lease from the provincial government, it controlled about 1.5 million acres of Crown land in eastern mainland Nova Scotia and Cape Breton.[335]

Meanwhile, the Small Tree Act was replaced by the Forest Improvement Act, which aimed "to provide continuous and increasing supplies of forest products, thereby maintaining forest industries and providing continued employment; to conserve water and prevent or reduce floods; to improve conditions for wildlife, recreation and scenic values."[336] As the name of the new legislation suggested, its purpose – at least for Hawboldt, who helped develop it – was to improve the way the province's woodlands were managed and exploited.

And to listen to Premier G.I. Smith waxing lyrical at a banquet held during the 1968 annual meeting of the Nova Scotia Forest Products Association, one might have thought government had every intention of protecting the precious woodland resources from any destructive industry practices. "The forest is something that in its proper time may be harvested for our use and for its own benefit," he said. "Good management is its best assurance of survival. Bad management sets in motion a slow-moving ruin. The forest is not only trees. It is the kingdom of the wild, a reservoir of moisture, and a giver of life far beyond its borders."[337]

But such lyricism about the province's forests withered quickly under the growing influence of big pulp and its foreign owners, who wanted to get on with clear cutting, the clearest path to profits. And the government was in no hurry to challenge the pulp and paper companies they had enticed to the province by imposing forest legislation that might not please them. Passed in 1965, the Forest Improvement Act was not proclaimed until 1976, and even after that, it was never

enforced. In 1986, it was rescinded. The Act failed largely because it did not serve the interests of the big pulp companies.
Small woodlot owners could not compete against the jugger-
naut created by government cozying up to the pulp and paper
industry, its lobby group the Nova Scotia Forest Products Association,[338] and other like-minded groups such as the Canadian Institute of Forestry.

The province's first chief forester, Otto Schierbeck, had
already highlighted the relationship between a "captured
state and a powerful corporation." That was revealed back in
the 1920s when the Crown had agreed to provide a million
cords of pulpwood to the Mersey Paper Company in southern
Nova Scotia, a company backed then by Izaak W. Killam and
the Royal Securities Corporation of Montreal, which put pressure on the government to assure the mill a long-term and secure wood supply.[339]

Many concerned citizens were unhappy to see their own
government becoming increasingly beholden to big pulp. Just
as Scott faced citizen backlash for its polluting ways in Pictou
County, it also faced growing pushback over its clear cutting
and its growing control of the wood market throughout the
province. One of the earlier woodlot owners and operators
who stood up to Scott Maritimes was the late Murray Prest of
Mooseland, on Nova Scotia's Eastern Shore, who became "the
key figure in the movement amongst independent foresters in
challenging the pulpwood regime."[340]

From the 1940s onwards, Prest had been selectively and
sustainably harvesting wood to feed his sawmill. When he had
cut as much as he felt he could without harming future generations of trees on his 1,400 acres, he started doing the same
kind of ecologically sensitive cutting on Crown land in Halifax
County that he leased from the government. In 1965, the government leased this land to Scott, and Prest had to lease the
public lands not from his own government but from an American company.[341]

In 1983, Prest spoke to award-winning writer and naturalist Harry Thurston of his dismay when he first realized what the Scott Maritimes Act, which gave Scott control of 230,000 acres of prime Crown land, would mean for independent operators and the forests themselves.[342] In 1966, just a year after the Act was passed and even before the pulp mill went into operation, Scott's woodlands manager summoned Prest to Abercrombie and told him about the company's new policy for people leasing Crown lands from Scott to harvest wood, as Prest was doing at the time. They could continue to lease and work on the lands, but only if they clear cut the forest. Prest told Thurston, "... if we left a tree four inches on the butt and eight feet long, a quarter of a mile over the hill, we had to go get it – she's all coming off."[343] Prest said this was a "shocker" because they had just spent the last quarter-century trying to promote healthy woodlands management. He wasn't buying the deal, and he told the Scott woodlands manager, "Look, if Christ himself came through that door and told me to do this, I wouldn't."[344]

Rather than go along with, and make money from, the industrial pulpwood regime, Prest became a vocal opponent of it and by 1974, this had cost him his sawmill.[345] He spent three decades pushing to have the Forest Improvement Act implemented, with its small programs that would allow woodlot owners and operators to have a say in regional forest management policies. He served as president of the Nova Scotia Woodlot Owners Association and as a member of the Provincial Forest Practices Improvement Board. This board had been set up with the aim of improving forest practices and giving forest workers and operators a say in policy.

The government dragged its feet on implementing the Forest Practices Improvement Board's program, and people began to resign. Clement Comeau, who had been on the Digby County branch of the board, made it clear in his resignation letter what was wrong with the politics that he felt had taken over forest policy in Nova Scotia: "... for over seven years I feel that we have been held back from being a productive board, both by Government and big pulp companies," he wrote. "Lately their members on the Provincial and District Boards have come out and stated that the Boards should be done away with and Forestry left to [the Department of] Lands and Forests." Comeau said while this might look good, "there are still lots of people in Nova Scotia that do not trust government, and big companies even less ..."[346]

In 1983, Prest told Thurston that forest policy in the province – the scrapping of the Small Tree Act and the passing of the Forest Improvement Act that was never enforced – laid the groundwork for "a full-scale blitzkrieg – 20 years of the most destructive methods of forest harvesting in Nova Scotia's history."[347] Prest died in 2014, in the heat of a new debate about an even more destructive kind of forestry practice, namely whole-tree harvesting for biomass that the pulp and paper mills were using as a source of energy.

But well before this, in 1990, biologists were observing that the province had put all its efforts into growing "toothpicks" for the pulp and paper industry.[348] To clean up the mess, they said, the province should ensure that forests be allowed to mature, become complex and diverse as they had once been, which would bring both ecological and economic benefits.

In 1986 in his book *Forests of Nova Scotia: A History*, Ralph Johnson, the former chief forester with the Bowater Mersey Paper Company, expressed pessimism over the future of the forests, largely because of the practice of clear cutting, "taking all the trees off an area regardless of age or size of trees."[349] He recognized that in some situations, for example with stands of white spruce and balsam fir that could just blow down if partially cut, clear cutting might be the only viable option. Nevertheless, he concluded that based on evidence from other countries, the clear cutting followed by treeplanting was not ecologically sound, and that in the future, Nova Scotia "would pay for this in decreasing water quality."[350] It would later emerge that Johnson's original manuscript had been even more critical than this, and that the Department of

Lands and Forests had insisted on deleting entire chapters because they did "not conform with the province's current forest policy of clear cutting and planting."[351] And, Johnson noted in another piece of correspondence, the deleted chapters were the most important ones.[352]

In 1958, before the big pulp mills in Pictou and Port Hawkesbury went into operation, forests older than eighty years still covered about a quarter of Nova Scotia's forested land, and forests more than a century old accounted for 8 percent. Just over four decades later, years during which pulpwood became the biggest driving force of and raison d'être for much of the forest industry, forests eighty years old accounted for just 1 percent of the woodlands and those older than one hundred years just 0.15 percent.[353]

In 1986, Ralph Johnson had this to say about the abuse of Nova Scotia's woodlands: "Forests have often been harvested without regard to the future due to ignorance, poor logging techniques, and the demand for low-cost forest products. Today we are paying for the mistakes of past generations. Our children will pay more dearly than we for these past errors and for our current errors in managing natural resources."[354]

In 1992, author Mike Parker interviewed eighty-three-year-old Leonard Taylor of Antigonish County for his book *Woodchips and Beans: Life in the Early Lumber Woods of Nova Scotia*. Taylor had worked in the woods since the age of five. This was his take on the pulp industry: "They should never've had pulp mills in Nova Scotia. I don't believe in clear cutting. It's the worst thing that's ever happened. I don't know what's going to happen in Nova Scotia. They're raping it."[355]

11

Pulping the rural economy?

Wearily, let me say this for the umpteenth time. In practice, DNR [Nova Scotia Department of Natural Resources] is not a department of government but of the pulp and lumber industry. It's been that way since the 1960s.

— Ralph Surette[356]

Before the pulp industry came to dominate the market for wood products in the province, rural Nova Scotia was full of small family farms, and those farms typically had woodlots. Household income came from diverse sources: some from the woodlots, some from agricultural production, and some perhaps also from fishing or off-farm work, so there was money all year round. Woodlots also provided firewood, building supplies, game, maple syrup, wild berries and foods, even medicinal plants.[357] Those products, combined with what came off the farm itself, allowed rural dwellers to produce much of what they consumed, while income from the diverse activities on the farm and in the woodlot rounded out their livelihoods.

This is certainly the way my grandparents provided for themselves and their four children on their farm in northern

Nova Scotia's Cumberland County. My mother remembers that the farm consisted of vegetable gardens, a few strawberry fields, and there were always chickens, half a dozen cows, and several horses, which were essential in the logging operations on the woodlot. They produced much of their own food, and the farm was so productive that during the Great Depression years when people in the Canadian prairies were suffering from drought that had turned their farms into dustbowls, my grandparents were able to donate extra produce to the aid efforts, as Maritime farmers shipped food to Saskatchewan to help out.

My grandparents' income came from market gardening, selling cream for butter, furs from silver foxes they raised for a time, and in winter from logging operations on the woodlot. To learn more, I turn to my uncle, Edgar McLellan, now into his ninth decade of life, and ask him for his memories of those days of yore and his youth, when he worked with my grandfather in the woodlot, which comprised 360 acres, while the farm itself was just forty. I want to know how the logging business worked, what wood they cut and where they sold it, so that I can grasp the ways and extent to which things changed once big pulp became a major player in shaping forestry policies and wood markets in the province.

My uncle recalls that my grandfather preferred selective cutting in his woodlot, and this meant culling only trees larger than twelve inches in diameter at breast height. They did the cutting using a double-bitted axe, one side of which was for chopping and the other for limbing, a crosscut saw about six feet long that had to be sharpened daily, and a twelve-foot measuring pole. "A typical crew would consist of two men felling, limbing, and junking [cutting the log to the desired length]," he says, "and the yard man with his yarding horse dragging the logs to a log brow at the side of the logging road." Then the logs would be loaded on sleds, which would accommodate between twenty-four and thirty logs up to sixteen feet long. The cutting was always done in the winter, when the ground was frozen and preferably snow-covered to keep the logs relatively clean. "Sawmill operators were never happy when asked to process stone-infected logs," my uncle says.

Sometimes they would take the logs directly to the local sawmill just a few kilometres away on the River Philip, or they would stack them up on the banks of the river upstream from the mill, for rafting downstream once spring came. His father (my grandfather), like other woodlot owners, marketed his own lumber, and there were several buying companies to choose from, so prices could be negotiated. The sawn lumber would then go by boxcar to one of these purchasers for further distribution or export.

"The bulk of my father's income was derived from logging operations," my uncle writes in a delightfully detailed report he compiles in response to my questions. And although it was hard and often risky work harvesting and transporting the trees, such local industry – from the harvesting to the milling to the purchasing from local companies – meant for a strong rural economy, lots of employment, and a good deal of autonomy for family farmers working in their own woodlots, for millers, and for wood buyers.

The huge new pulp mills created a burgeoning new market for pulpwood. Many believed this would be a good thing for the province's 30,000 private woodlot owners, and create a great deal of wealth in rural Nova Scotia. But it soon became clear this was not happening. According to author Julia McMahon, as early as the 1970s the "growing corporate control of the resource and the use of highly mechanized woodcutting technology to move a constant supply of pulpwood from forest site to the mill" meant that in Nova Scotia this minimized employment opportunities in the woods.[358] Greater mechanization and clear cutting reduced the number of jobs available in the forestry sector, squeezed the small woodlot owners and operators out of the equation, and this in turn contributed to an exodus of people from family farms and rural areas.

What was happening in Nova Scotia was not unique.

Similar trends had already been documented in neighbouring New Brunswick. Between the end of World War II and
1960, the number of family farms in New Brunswick, which
typically included woodlots, had fallen dramatically and the
farmers who remained had come to depend even more heavily
on sales of wood from their land, which could bring in two-
thirds of their total farm income.[359] At the same time, pulp and
paper companies, and particularly K.C. Irving's, were increasingly controlling the province's forest resources. As of 1960,
pulp companies owned more than three million acres, about
a third of all privately owned land in New Brunswick, and had
fifty-year leases on five million acres of Crown land. They used
these holdings as "a lever to reduce the price of private wood,"
creating hardship for independent woodlot owners and operators trying to earn a living selling wood to the pulp industry,
which now dominated the wood market.[360]

In Nova Scotia, as in New Brunswick, pulp companies
were determining what wood to accept and what prices to pay
for it, and vast swaths of Crown land were no longer available
to many small operators, as Murray Prest had learned in Halifax County. For some rural dwellers, this meant the farm unit
was no longer viable and out-migration became the only option. The giant mills in Nova Scotia had a great deal of control
over the entire value chain. Woodcutters had no union, and
they faced low wages, poor working conditions, no long-term
security, and had to cope with seasonal work.[361]

Pulp also smothered many small lumber producers.
In 1965, there were thirty-two lumber producers in Pictou
County alone, including some that exported large amounts
of lumber overseas.[362] In 1993, the number of sawmills in the
county was down to five, and there were also value-adding en-
terprises such as furniture producers that would not survive
past the turn of the century.

By the mid-1970s, the large pulp mills had come to dominate the entire forest industry in the province. They demanded higher productivity and lower prices for wood, which,

according to Julia McMahon, meant that the "richly diversified woodlot has been reduced to a one-dimensional pulpwood yard. Woodlot owners, already confronted with the disastrous decline of the rest of the rural economy, now face a rapid and unremitting squeeze on their position as producers and sellers of wood."[363]

In Nova Scotia, a few years after Scott went into production, about 80 percent of the total harvest of trees in the province was pulpwood.[364] And, just as Lloyd Hawboldt and R.M. Bulmer had predicted would happen in their 1958 book, *The Forest Resources of Nova Scotia*, the harvest of sawlogs had fallen dramatically. Between 1951 and 1983, while sawlog harvesting had dropped 60 percent, cutting for pulpwood had increased by 500 percent.[365] In 1974, Scott began its "Continuous Woodlot Management" program with private landowners, whereby Scott would manage an individual's property under a long-term agreement in return for the wood supply from that program. By 1977 there were 8,000 acres under this program.[366]

So why were the woodlot owners not able to organize themselves into a group that could negotiate bargaining rights with the mills? The answer to that question is very long and convoluted. According to Lorne Burrows, chair of the board of the Nova Scotia Woodlot Owners and Operators Association (NSWOOA), it's not for any lack of trying on their part. Burrows has spent many years trying to defend the interests of those who own the woodlots – the "asset owners" as he calls them – in the face of competition from those who export the wealth from the forests – the "commodity traders."

We meet on a relatively mild day in January 2017 in a popular and noisy little restaurant in the town of Truro. After we've placed our orders I start hammering him with questions, aware that the forestry industry in Nova Scotia is very complex and controversial. I want to know whether he thinks many people in the province are getting wealthy from its forest resources.

"No, no," he replies. "There are pools of wealth being generated in the sawmill agents of the pulp mills, there is wealth being generated there. Other than that, there is just a living [to be made]; most people are surviving, not making wealth." He says the struggle for woodlot owners is to ensure that the woodlands of Nova Scotia are managed and exploited in ways that broaden economic activity. "We should have a very diverse forest and a value-added manufacturing pool, which leads to very diverse markets," he tells me. He points out that the cost of moving wood in the raw form is so high that processing should be done locally.

The pulp industry has successfully taken a colonial approach, not to own the land but to manage an economic sector, Burrows says. "They pretty much colonized the forest products industry in Nova Scotia," he adds, so they are exporting not wood but wealth. If the status quo is maintained, he believes that pulp interests will continue to milk what they have in Nova Scotia until the forest economy grinds to a halt. What Nova Scotians are seeing now in the forests with all the clear cutting, he says, "is nothing compared to how bare it will be then."

Although the Bowater mill is now gone, and the Port Hawkesbury mill working with a dramatically reduced workforce and limited to producing only glossy calendar paper, he doesn't see the Pictou mill scaling or closing down any time soon. The global pulp industry needs the long fibre that comes from conifers in the region to mix with poorer pulp they get from other mills around the world, and besides, he adds, "where the hell else in the world can they get the set-up they have here?"

In their 2000 book *Against The Grain: Foresters and Politics in Nova Scotia*, L. Anders Sandberg and Peter Clancy have painstakingly documented the long battle by woodlot owners to organize to get a fair deal for the wood they harvest from their land. But those efforts, according to Clancy, senior research professor at St. Francis Xavier University in Antigonish, never resulted in "what can be objectively considered a 'fair' price for that wood."[367] This is a paradoxical situation in a province where some 30,000 smallholders own over half of the forested land.[368]

Even before the advent of big pulp, the co-operative movement for local economic development that had emerged at St. Francis Xavier University in the 1920s had been angling to get co-operative groups to market forest products.[369] The push for such a co-operative movement gained traction again after the government inked the deal with Stora in 1959, which gave the Swedish corporation a lease on massive amounts of Crown land in eastern mainland Nova Scotia and Cape Breton, with the rock-bottom stumpage rate of just $1 per cord. Wood-lot owners worried this would suppress prices they could get for wood from their private woodlots and remove any incentive for improved forestry management and harvesting practices. The result was a renewed campaign to organize woodlot owners.

In 1960, the nascent movement elected an executive and developed a broad mandate that included not just pulp marketing but also extension and support for members to plan and sustainably manage their woodlots for the production of a wide range of forest products. Their campaign garnered early support from the Federation of Agriculture, and the Department of Extension at St. Francis Xavier University promoted it widely.[370]

But it would not be until 1969 that the first Nova Scotia Woodlot Owners Association (NSWOA) would be founded as a non-profit society. Its mission was "to support woodlot owners through education, demonstration, marketing, and cooperation" to help small forest landowners in the province achieve "prosperity, stewardship, and solidarity through the practice of ecologically, socially, and economically sustainable forestry."[371]

Pulpwood marketing reform was one of the key issues and earliest endeavours of the NSWOA. For a time, its leaders seemed to think it was going to be straightforward getting the government to include pulpwood under the Natural Products Marketing Act of 1933, and to set up a pulpwood marketing board that would provide them some leverage over prices. NSWOA sent a delegation to meet with Premier G.I. Smith and senior bureaucrats in the Department of Lands and Forests to request these things. Almost immediately after that meeting, "the political battle was launched."[372] The government called a meeting with representatives of the three big pulp mills and with Donald Eldridge, then executive director of the Nova Scotia Forest Products Association that functioned as a lobby for the forest industry, which in Nova Scotia was dominated by the pulp corporations.

The battle of wills continued through the end of Premier Smith's term in office and into that of the new Liberal government formed in 1970 by Premier Gerald Regan, with thousands of woodlot owners pushing for the marketing reform while industry pushed right back. The NSWOA found itself in a drawn-out fight to survive while it continued to press for pulpwood marketing rights. This meant it was largely distracted from achieving its wider goals of enabling members "to speak and act as an organized group on matters affecting the forest industry," "to formulate and promote woodlot development policies which will increase woodlot productivity and income," and "to promote the organized marketing of any forest product when its producers consider it necessary."[373]

Eventually, in 1972, the government did pass the Pulpwood Marketing Act, which involved the creation of a Pulpwood Marketing Board. NSWOA applied to the board for certification as the sole bargaining agent for pulpwood marketing and in 1974, it was approved. This did not go down well with industry, and set the stage for a showdown between the woodlot owners and Nova Scotia Forest Industries (NSFI), the Stora subsidiary that owned the mill in Port Hawkesbury, in which Scott had a minority interest.[374] NSFI refused to acknowledge NSWOA's bargaining right and took the Pulp Marketing Board to court to have it quashed. The NSWOA president at the time argued the Department of Lands and Forests was openly siding with the pulp industry.[375] It certainly didn't help dispel impressions like these when, in 1979, Donald Eldridge, who had been a strong advocate for the industry and who had headed the Forest Products Association since 1968, was named Deputy Minister of Lands and Forests.

By then the woodlot owners had already suffered an enormous setback. In 1975, Chief Justice Ian MacKeigan sided with Nova Scotia Forest Industries in the Supreme Court of Nova Scotia and decided against the Pulpwood Marketing Board, overturning the recognition of NSWOA as exclusive bargaining agent.[376] A year later NSWOA tried again to get bargaining rights, but this time the Pulpwood Marketing Board rejected their application, saying the association could not seek bargaining rights for all woodlot owners because its membership included just 10 percent of them. In 1977, the association changed its name to the Nova Scotia Woodlot Owners and Operators Association (NSWOOA).

Five years later, the government set up the Nova Scotia Royal Commission on Forestry, primarily because of concerns about a future shortage of pulpwood, and hearings were held until December 1983. When the Royal Commission report came out in 1984, it was clear whose interests it was defending. It set out guidelines for a secure market for what it called "input" industries for pulp, namely those supplying pesticides, seedlings, and fertilizers. This would help to entrench and empower industrial pulp forestry, and further discourage forest management that had always been fairly labour intensive and that depended on natural regeneration.[377] The Commission also recommended rescinding the Forest Improvement Act, which, although it had never really been implemented, still did encourage public input on forestry policy. The beneficiaries of its elimination would be the multinational pulp companies.[378]

The Royal Commission on Forestry concluded that the low prices paid for pulp were necessary for the health of the industry. And in 1986, big contractors in the province that worked directly for the mills asked the Pulpwood Marketing Board to decertify NSWOOA. This effectively opened the door for the "group venture" movement to take off, with its proliferation of government-funded co-operatives or groups that had been set up in the late 1970s and early 1980s, which ecologist David Orton believed were "totally committed to the well-being of the pulp and paper industry." Such groups, Orton claimed, "helped undermine the efforts of private woodlot owners to organize" and their main function was "to enlist private woodlot owners as suppliers of pulpwood to the industry."[379] The "venture" groups throughout the province, financed by both federal and provincial governments, Orton said, "helped to ensnare a section of the small woodlot owners through subsidized 'forest management plans,' as suppliers of cheap pulpwood to the mills."[380]

"Small woodlot owners," he concluded, "have had their attempts to *independently* [emphasis in the original] organize collectively over the years undermined by government and corporate hostility, court challenges, and the setting up of captive bargaining groups."[381] In his submission to the Royal Commission on Forestry, Orton said, "The kind of opposition to the woodlot owners parallels that of the Michelin Tire Company in preventing a union being formed at their plants in the province."[382] He believed that because the pulp and paper companies owned – or controlled through Crown leases – so much forest land in Nova Scotia, they were undercutting private woodlot owners.[383]

In 1991, Orton documented the extent of the forest holdings by pulp and paper companies. He calculated that the Swedish company Stora owned 50,000 acres but controlled another 1.7 million acres of Crown land. Scott owned over one million acres and had a lease on another 250,000. The British company Bowater owned 765,000 acres in the southwest of the province. J.D. Irving Ltd., which owned pulp and paper mills in New Brunswick but none in Nova Scotia, also owned large tracts of forest land in the province that supplied pulp-wood to its mills in the neighbouring province.[384]

In his master's thesis tracing two and a half centuries of dissent against the destruction of forests in Nova Scotia, Paul Webster concludes that from the early twentieth century on through the 1980s, the repression of dissent had emerged as "a strong theme in the history of opposition to forest destruction in the province."[385] And he concludes, "What is somewhat more surprising, and perhaps disturbing, is the extension of repression internally among competing elements in the province's forest industries, with the power of the state being used to support the dominant (foreign controlled) corporate ideologies and interests. There is something sinister about this repression." In the words of Julia McMahon, the industrial forest model promoted by pulp "required that the woodlot owners be kept in disarray and disorganization."[386]

For many years, Tom Miller has been part of the struggle by woodlot owners to organize to get better prices for their wood and to manage the province's forests sustainably. He owns and operates a woodlot near the historic little village of Earltown in Colchester County, and another around his home in the beautiful rolling hills – part woodland, part farm fields – about fifteen kilometres from the Abercrombie Mill, in a community appropriately called Greenhill. Named 2005 "Woodlot Owner of the Year," Miller's perspectives on forests, forestry, and pulp have changed dramatically since he first began working in the woods forty-six years ago. Today, he heads a local conservation group, the Friends of Redtail Society, which aims to preserve and protect forest land and ecosystems.[387] Miller believes the large pulp mills have "had a devastating effect on the forests of Nova Scotia."

He hasn't always felt this way; his has been a long career in forestry that has afforded him a wealth of first-hand knowledge of how it all works. On a glorious, hot summer day in 2016, Miller welcomes me to his home, which is tucked away out of sight of the paved road that winds its way through Greenhill. We start with a short tour of his impressive vegetable garden and stands of fruit trees. Later, when we are out of the hot sun and settled inside at the kitchen table, he tells me about his own professional evolution from a trainee at Scott Maritimes back in 1974 to a committed and outspoken defender of the Acadian forest.

Miller says he has always liked working physically and being outside. Growing up with woods in his backyard, he spent most of his Saturdays with a backpack and a packed lunch in the forest, and became "a tree guy." After his stint working as a forest harvest technician with Scott, he was promoted to power saw operator, but decided he wasn't going to make a go of that. So in 1976, he went to the Maritime Forest Ranger School at the University of New Brunswick, and came home to work for two years with Scott as the district supervisor for silviculture.

But he soon realized he wasn't "a company man," so he left and launched his long career of self-employment as a contractor, mostly doing pre-commercial thinning and silviculture. "I never was much interested in the harvesting end of things," he says. "But I liked the restoring and the bringing back. And although I didn't like what I was seeing with the clear cutting, it was my job then to plant." The planting was of softwood species needed by the pulp mill.

Although he now realizes it was "totally wrong" that the pulp mills were deciding what should be planted and what should grow in Nova Scotia's woodlands, he says for the first fifteen years as a tree-planting contractor he was fully on board. He bought a skidder for pulling trees out of the forest, moving wood to the pulp mills and wishing the environmentalists would just go home and let them get their work done.

He admits, though, that he was always a little "cranky" about the work he was doing. "We were cutting too much wood," he says. "It just didn't seem right." And over time, some of the pesky environmentalists became his friends. One of those was David Orton, the ecologist in Pictou County who headed an environmental network and wrote Green Web reports that strongly criticized clear cutting, the pulp and paper industry in Nova Scotia, and its cozy relationship with government.[388] With a chuckle, Miller tells me that one day he mentioned to a friend he thought Orton had become a lot smarter, and then realized Orton's message had not changed. The difference was Miller had started agreeing with him.

In 2006, despite his unease with the way pulp mills were handling the forest resources, Miller wound up working on a piece of Scott (by then Neenah Paper) land where he had worked in the 1980s. He was dismayed when he looked at two aerial photos of the land, one showing it a quarter-century earlier when it had a lot of standing timber, and the current one, showing only a spindly softwood plantation. He recalls a day he was called to cut a few tall hardwood trees that remained after an area had been clear cut for pulp. The remaining trees would pose a risk to the helicopter that would be spraying the cut area with herbicide to kill off hardwoods and plants that might compete with softwoods. His job was to cut down every last one of them.

Miller says there are examples of sustainable forestry in Nova Scotia, one being Windhorse Farm on the South Shore, which was owned and operated by the Drescher family when he had visited. The 100-acre woodlot had been sustainably managed and harvested for 150 years. Miller tells me that about 6 million board feet of timber had been harvested from the woodlot during that time without affecting the health of the forest standing there, which still represented about 3 million board feet. "So the joke is that they cut more wood than was there!" he says.

To visualize how much healthy forest is left in the province, Miller asks me to try and picture the print on the front page of a broadsheet newspaper as a map of Nova Scotia. "Where the periods are is where you'll find good forests," he says.

He has a lot of praise for the erstwhile extension unit in the Department of Natural Resources (formerly the Department of Lands and Forests), and the conservation and extension officers who ran conferences for woodlot owners and espoused the benefits of well-managed woodlots and the non-timber forest products that could be harvested from them. He says those parts of the Department of Natural Resources have been decimated, and that conservation officers are now very thin on the ground. He's not so complimentary about some in the upper echelons of the department.

Because the pulp mill in Pictou has so much control over the market, he says, the price that woodlot owners are paid for the wood they harvest is low. The price he receives for pulpwood from his woodlot in 2016 is exactly the same, "dollar for dollar," as it was in 1995. Which means it has dropped by nearly 50 percent, while his costs have risen dramatically.[389]

Miller continues to fight the status quo, speaking publicly on forest issues and sustainability, promoting the Friends of Redtail Society, and writing letters to editors. His is a powerful voice in challenging the Type A approach of the pulp industry to forest resources and their exploitation that prevails in the province. And he continues to work in his own woodlots to recreate a healthy and diverse forest, sometimes with his son Matt, who has picked up the forestry baton from his father.

Matt Miller began his studies at the Maritime College of Forest Technology in Fredericton, and then followed that up with a degree in forestry at the University of New Brunswick. I meet with him in June 2016, when he is still the forestry coordinator at the Ecology Action Centre,[390] and ask him how he sees the management of Nova Scotia's forests.

"Frustrating," he replies. "I'm frustrated by what I see. I worked in the woods and I went to work for my dad, and felt compelled to come and work for the Ecology Action Centre." He draws a parallel between what happened to the inshore cod fishery in Newfoundland in the 1980s where you could see the tragedy befalling the resource and its eventual collapse because of over-exploitation, and the actual situation of the forests in Nova Scotia.

"There's a sense of powerlessness, that the train is out of control," he says. The only regulations governing tree harvesting for forestry operations, Miller tells me, are those under the wildlife habitat and watercourse protection legislation laid down in 1999. "For every eight hectares [close to twenty acres] of forest that is clear cut, you must leave behind one clump of at least thirty trees that is representative of the forest that you're harvesting in," he says. "And any stream greater than fifty centimetres in diameter should have a twenty-metre buffer." This means there is no regulation to prevent the harvesting of tops and branches, or whole-tree harvesting, or maintaining levels of the deadwood that is so important for biodiversity, no rules to protect seed trees, and no mechanism to control harvesting at regional or watershed levels. "We are managing our forests to be a landscape of clumps and buffers," he says. And on Crown land, Miller adds, Scott and its subsequent owners have been operating since the 1960s, sometimes going back for a second harvest in just a few decades, with no forest management plan that is available to the public.

Like his father, Matt Miller also worries about the number of leading figures from the pulp industry who have been given high-level positions in the Department of Natural Resources. "There's a revolving door between government and pulp companies," he tells me. Two months after that interview, Matt Miller left the Ecology Action Centre and went back to work as a forester, still aiming to improve the health of Nova Scotia's forests and the well-being of the families that depend on them.

Another experienced voice in Nova Scotia's forestry landscape is that of David Sutherland, a forester who grew up in Alma, Pictou County. He never strayed too far away from home in pursuit of his profession and his passion for spending time in the woods. Like Tom Miller, Sutherland also began his career decades ago working for Scott Paper. He was fresh out of high school, and he enjoyed the job he got with Scott working on a survey team, driving about in their light-blue trucks in northern Nova Scotia. It's also the reason he went into forestry, heading off to the University of New Brunswick to get his forestry degree.

It's a frigid February day under a flawless blue sky and snowbanks dazzling in the bright sun when I head to River John to meet Sutherland in his home, nestled in a small clearing at the end of a winding driveway on the edge of his thirty-acre woodlot. Today, he heads the Association for Sustainable Forestry, a government-funded agency that serves as a conduit between the Department of Natural Resources and private landowners, to provide them with technical advice and funding for silviculture. It offers special incentives for landowners who want to do selective management of their woodlots, want their forest stands to contain diverse species of unevenly aged trees. The Association for Sustainable Forestry, he says, encourages landowners to grow higher value trees.

The association was formed back in 2000, shortly after the government set up the Registry of Buyers. The idea was that any pulp mill or saw mill that processed wood or purchased more than 1,000 cubic metres in a year would contribute something toward silviculture, which would go into a sustainable forestry fund. Over time, though, the saw mills and pulp mills decided to start or continue with their own silviculture programs with landowners, rather than contribute to the fund. So most of the silviculture in Nova Scotia is now done through the registered wood buyers' program, says Sutherland.

The Association for Sustainable Forestry was set up for those who fall through the cracks, for people who want to do the kind of silviculture work the mills aren't interested in, such as selection management. "Not every mill wants to get involved in that," he tells me. But for landowners who don't want to clear cut or do other kinds of management that industry promotes, who want instead to do selection management and harvesting to preserve the diversity of their woodlots, his association can help. "They're able to access funding through our incentive program and go into the woods with a tractor or ATV or a horse," he says, "or whatever they have available, and do this kind of work."

Before the Association for Sustainable Forestry was formed and he took over as its co-ordinator, Sutherland spent many years working with the North Colchester Forestry Co-operative in Tatamagouche, one of the eighteen "group ventures" set up throughout the province with funding from the provincial and federal governments. It was a job he loved. He came directly out of university with his forestry degree and went straight to work with the co-operative, doing everything he dreamed of – working with enthusiastic woodlot owners and helping them develop management plans, put in access roads and mark boundaries, and manage their own woodlots. When the federal government pulled its funding in 1995, the group ventures began to close, and the North Colchester Co-operative shut its doors in 2000.

Sutherland takes issue with those who call Nova Scotia a "pulpwood province," although he has heard the criticism that much of its forest management has been for pulp mills. He says many products come from the province's woodlands, including large dimension logs, stud-wood that is made into two-by-fours, and firewood, and that not everything is geared towards production of pulpwood. He tells me the Association of Sustainable Forestry doesn't offer any incentives for herbicides through its program; its silviculture involves only manual work to prune, thin, or promote the growth of preferred, high-quality trees. It's not the kind of clear cutting and spraying forest management that was favoured by the forest industry and the pulp mill in Pictou, an approach to forest stewardship that has led to a great deal of criticism over the years.

12

A boycott, a blockade, and a funeral (1980-2017)

The Scott Boycott Song
(by Judy Davis, sung to the tune of "Paradise" by John Prine)

When I was a child, I remember it well
I stood by watching, and feeling quite helpless
As over the years the green forest fell.

So Mama won't you take me down to the green forest
A beautiful place where the maples still sway?
I'm sorry, my child, you're too late in asking
The Scott Paper Company has hauled it away.

Well the Scott Paper people knew they had it easy
Cause the people were hungry and sold off the land
And they got all the Crown land without any trouble
Cause they had the politicians eating out of their hands.

Let's not let a pulp mill destroy our fine province
Let's stand up and say they can no longer take
And come along now and join in the chorus
Maybe we'll change things before it's too late.

From the beginning, the pulp industry's fondness for clear cutting provoked a lot of consternation and criticism in Nova Scotia. In the early 1970s, Scott showed signs it was ready to respond to the criticism.[391] In 1972, the company brought in a new policy of cutting 100-metre strips, which its timberland manager said would "improve natural seeding and lessen visual impact of large scale clear cutting." The strip-cutting did not significantly improve natural regeneration over the rest of the cut strip, but the purpose of the change seemed primarily to appease the public. As for whether it did, Scott's timberland manager wrote that it was "difficult to judge but the word 'rape' and the phrase 'cut and run' seemed to be used less to describe Scott's logging activities."[392] The strip-cutting policy, however, was discontinued in 1975. The clear cutting resumed and continues to this day.

The way industrial forest users and their government "associates" operated in Canada, wrote author Jamie Swift in 1983, showed that "a myopic, after-me-the-deluge attitude has always prevailed, and continues to hold sway."[393] Governments in Nova Scotia showed no interest in reverting to a rotation of a century or a century and a half to allow a diverse Acadian forest to regenerate. Rather, the aim of such industrial forestry, shaped by pulp, was to cut, plant softwoods, spray herbicides, and then reduce the rotation period as much as possible.

Herbicides were not the only chemicals the pulp mills wanted sprayed. In neighbouring New Brunswick, since the 1950s, millions of acres of woodlands had been doused in DDT and other insecticides to try to stop spruce budworm outbreaks that were harming softwood stands wanted for pulp. The outbreaks of the pest had proliferated with forest management practices promoted by pulp companies. Not only did the annual spraying not help contain the pest, but in New Brunswick it had also been shown to prolong and exacerbate the budworm outbreaks. According to Swift, the "unrestrained industrial logging" had been turning the formerly rich and diverse Acadian forest in New Brunswick into a "vast breeding ground for the budworm: a feedlot for future larval plagues."[394]

The same was happening in Cape Breton. In the mid-1970s, citizens on the island learned the province planned to approve the aerial spraying of 100,000 acres of Crown land in Cape Breton with fenitrothion, an organophosphate insecticide, to try to kill an outbreak of spruce budworm that was infesting mature and over-mature balsam fir, its prime host.[395] This was at the behest of the Swedish-owned Stora mill near Port Hawkesbury, despite the fact that aerial spraying had been banned in Sweden in 1969.[396] Scientists had described this family of insecticides as "extremely toxic to mammals" and they also had a severe impact on natural enemies of the spruce budworm.[397] This led to a grassroots campaign involving the Ecology Action Centre and other groups in Nova Scotia, spearheaded by the Cape Breton Landowners Against the Spray, which engaged doctors, woodlot owners, and respected forestry experts such as entomologist Lloyd Hawboldt to make the case against spraying for all sorts of reasons – health, economic, and biological.

A young woman by the name of Elizabeth May, now head of Canada's Green Party and Member of Parliament for Saanich-Gulf Islands in British Columbia, became, albeit reluctantly, the media's go-to and focal person for the group. Theirs was a relentless campaign to prevent the aerial spraying of fenitrothion. They linked up with doctors to draw attention to their research that linked fenitrothion to deaths of New Brunswick children with Reyes Syndrome. In response, the pulp companies proposed other dangerous insecticides. The citizens confronted an onslaught of backlash from the pulp industry and its proponents. Scott Paper's timberlands manager lashed out against the Nova Scotia Medical Society for its support of the anti-spray groups, saying if it were "as concerned with the health of Nova Scotians as it claims to be with its stand against a spray program to control spruce budworm, it should also start a campaign to ban cigarettes totally and close liquor stores ..."[398]

Then came two years of intense lobbying from the pulp companies, chemical manufacturers, sprayers, the Canadian Forestry Service, pro-pulp and pro-spray advocates in some Nova Scotian newspapers, and even some interference from New Brunswick's pro-spray Minister of Natural Resources Roland Boudreau.[399] Despite industry pressure, Nova Scotia's Liberal Premier Gerald Regan and his Minister of Lands and Forests and of the Environment, Vince MacLean, held out, heeding the voices of the Cape Breton Landowners, other experts and their constituents. In February 1977, the cabinet refused to allow the aerial spraying program, at least for the time being.[400] MacLean sent a tabulation of the letters he had received on the issue to Elizabeth May; more than 7,000 individuals and thirty-seven groups had written to oppose the spraying and just eighteen individuals and seven groups had supported it.[401]

But this was just the opening salvo in the struggle between anti-spray groups and the pulp industry. The industry continued to push for and practise intensive forest management that involved clear cutting, then replanting with a handful of softwood species, and spraying these plantations with herbicides. In 1981, Scott's Forest Management Program in Nova Scotia involved "... the use of herbicides on a minimum of 30 percent of Scott's planted acreage." And, the company said, "Scott's planting program will be substantially reduced in 1982 if permission for herbiciding is not granted."[402]

These pro-pulp forest policies were generating a groundswell of public opposition. In 1982, the Progressive Conservative government of John Buchanan gave permits to Stora's mill in Port Hawkesbury to spray herbicides on its Crown land lease to kill broad-leafed plants that might compete with softwoods planted for pulp.[403] Once again, this led to a public outcry and protests, involving Mi'kmaq chiefs and other citizens concerned about the dangers of the herbicides involved, 2,4-D and 2,4,5-T, both of which contained dioxin, a toxin that causes cancer and mutations, and for which no safe lower limit had been determined.[404] Both were components of the controversial defoliant Agent Orange used by the U.S. military in the Vietnam War.[405] [406]

Back in 1982, the government of Nova Scotia seemed unaware of the health risks of defoliants such as 2,4-D and 2,4,5-T. In reaction to the protests, Buchanan's government did temporarily ban the aerial spraying of the herbicides, but permitted ground spraying to go ahead. George Henley, Minister of Lands and Forests, called the protesters "ridiculous," said they had no interest in jobs in Cape Breton, and that the herbicides were "safe as water."[407] In response, the president of the Union of Nova Scotia Indians suggested that if Henley wanted to drink "the damn stuff" he should go ahead and "see what happens in a couple of years."[408]

Two First Nations chiefs and other concerned citizens, including Elizabeth May who was now at law school, took Nova Scotia Forest Industries to court to get an injunction to prevent the herbicide spraying. The "Herbicide Case" lasted two years, making national and international news, and it would eventually be documented in a film by Neal Livingston for the National Film Board of Canada.[409] But the temporary injunction did its job. Despite the judge's decision to allow the spraying, by the time that happened, the use of the herbicide had been prohibited in the United States. The Canadian government then followed suit, removing 2,4,5-T from its list of approved herbicides, and Dow Chemical announced it would stop producing it.[410] So despite their loss in court, the plaintiffs did win a partial victory in the long run; their campaign and court case prevented Nova Scotia's forests from being the last in North America to be sprayed with Agent Orange.[411]

The herbicide's successor came from the giant American firm Monsanto, one of the companies that had previously manufactured Agent Orange for the U.S. military. Monsanto's new herbicide was called Vision, which contained glyphosate as its active ingredient, like its agricultural herbicide Roundup, which is used widely on genetically modified "Round-up ready" crops such as corn and soybean. In 2015, the World Health Organization's research arm labelled glyphosate as a probable carcinogen.[412] And in 2017, a long-term study linked "chronic ultra-low dose" exposure to glyphosate-based herbicide with liver disease in rats.[413] The same year, documents unsealed by court order in the United States showed collusion between an official in the Environmental Protection Agency and Monsanto to falsify academic reports and stifle others to give glyphosate-based herbicides a clean bill of health.[414] In June 2017, California decided it would add glyphosate to its list of cancer-causing agents, which would require it to come with a warning label.[415]

But suspicion about the health effects of the herbicide on human, wildlife, and forest health goes back decades, and in Nova Scotia, the herbicide trial gave momentum to a growing environmental movement and increased public pressure for more sustainable forestry in the province. Members of a group called the Nova Scotia Coalition for Alternatives to Pesticides continued to oppose the spraying programs prescribed by the pulp and paper companies for the plantations, noting that these were government subsidized. "More than 25% of all forest herbicide spraying in Canada occurs in the Acadian forests and Nova Scotia and New Brunswick," wrote coalition member Charles Restino in 1993. "Sales of the herbicide Vision, manufactured by the chemical giant Monsanto, have enabled the company to take more than 15 million dollars out of the region's depressed economy over the past five years."[416]

On the mainland of Nova Scotia, Scott continued what it called its "forest site preparation and conifer release programs," silviculture programs that the company said required the use of Roundup spray.[417] "Site preparation," in Scott's lexicon, was a term for the work of preparing a cleared area for the planting of conifers by spraying a herbicide to kill off competing hardwoods, and the "conifer release program" meant spraying young plantations to achieve the same thing.

In 1986, Scott's newsletter, *Trees and People*, stated that "the long term future of our company in Nova Scotia depends on whether we have confidence in knowing we can invest and plan for our next crop of trees." Scott's timberlands manager wrote, "Hand in hand with this, forest protection is *essential*."[418] The emphasis was his.

A year later, Scott said its "herbicide season," which involved helicopters spraying over 6,097 acres, was "completed without incident, and the public was very co-operative."[419] The same would not be true in 1988. New citizens' groups were forming to protest Scott's environmental record and pulp's influence in the province. One of these was the "Boycott Scott Committee," founded in 1983 by two women from Pictou County, Judy Davis and June Daley. Davis passed away in 2010 of "cancer and a broken heart, the latter caused by witnessing the continued destruction of the ecology of the planet," according to the obituary written by David Orton. But thirty-four years after they launched the campaign to boycott Scott, Daley is still very much engaged in movements to promote healthy communities and protect the environment.

On a blustery, rainy day in early 2017, June Daley and her partner and fellow activist, Catherine Hughes, make their way to my home to tell me more about the campaign to boycott Scott. They've spent a few weeks sorting out old files and boxes of documents, and they arrive bearing envelopes full of leaflets, newspaper clippings, a video of a 1990 protest, even a "Boycott Scott" pin. Daley starts by telling me why she wanted to organize a boycott of Scott.

"I've been fighting that mill my whole life," she says. "And I would like to see it closed for good." She grew up and lived in the nearby town of Westville where her father ran a taxi business and her mother owned a hair salon. She was a child when the mill and the infrastructure around it were built, but she has clear recollections of the huge changes they brought. Her family had always spent their holidays and free time at their cottage at Abercrombie, at a place along the West River called Second Gut, close to the site where Michelin would build its tire production plant a few years later. "It was a really nice place," she says. "But then the pulp mill came along and everything changed."

The family property and cottage were in the way of the dam the province was putting up to provide the Scott mill with fresh water, and in the way of the new stretch of highway that would link up to the new causeway. The Daleys' cottage and property were expropriated.

As a young adult, she went to work for a farmer in the area, hauling logs out of his woodlot with a horse. At first, there were various markets for the wood, with some going as sawlogs for timber, some to the coal mine in Westville as pit props, and some to the pulp mill. Then, she says, she started to notice changes; the only market seemed to be for pulpwood. It was becoming impossible to sell to Scott unless you joined one of the government-supported group ventures or co-operatives that had explicit agreements to do so.

That wasn't the only thing about the pulp industry that worried Daley and Davis and other activists in the area, including ecologist David Orton's group. "People started clear cutting, and we could see it wasn't a good thing to do," Daley tells me. "It was destroying the woods, the runoff [was excessive], and you'd see sites and it would break your heart the way they were cutting and spraying."

"We just saw the pulp mill was destroying our province," she says. There was also what Daley calls the "Scott stink" and what she saw in Boat Harbour when she went there with a friend from the Pictou Landing First Nation. "We couldn't believe this was going on. To go there and just to smell it would make you sick, so to live there?" This prompted Davis and Daley to find out what products Scott made and sold around the world, and to launch a campaign to have people throughout North America boycott these until the "destructive forest practices" such as clear cutting and the use of herbicides were stopped.[420] Members of the Boycott Committee wrote letters, mailed out a lot of pamphlets, and urged consumers to avoid Scott products and to write to the mill's general manager.

"We got quite a bit of response from Americans," she says. In her extensive collection of documents she still has some of the correspondence sent by American campaigners to Scott, as well as the replies they received. These touted the 500 jobs in the mill itself, the work in the woodlands for an additional 600 others, and defended Scott's environmental record in the forests, saying the company had "worked hard in recent years to develop the best forest management practices to ensure we manage our lands in an environmentally sensitive manner."[421]

In a letter to a citizen in Washington State, Scott's public affairs manager said the annual spraying of the herbicide Vision involved 4,000 to 5,000 acres each year in Nova Scotia. "However, we are caught in somewhat of a dilemma in that we want to regrow our forests to a state whereby they can be harvested by our children," he wrote. "The only viable way to do this, given modern day forest harvesting and management techniques, is to use chemical herbicides. We found it extremely interesting last year that the Government of Nova Scotia adopted new forest spray regulations based almost entirely on the activities that Scott was already doing."[422]

David Orton had been publishing reports documenting the ways pulpwood forestry was negatively affecting Nova Scotia's forests. In 1991, his Green Web Bulletin pointed out the problem inherent when governments, which are supposed to be the watchdogs, adopt policies set by the corporations they are supposed to be regulating. "For too long," wrote Orton, "public spokespersons for the mills have told us what a great job they are doing and how their industry 'is in regulatory compliance.' While government environment officials, who have self-defined their roles to be apologists for the industry, 'confirm' such statements or keep their silence."[423]

The Boycott Scott Committee found itself overtaken by other events in 1988. By then, Davis and Daley had been living for several years near the village of Tatamagouche in Colchester County. In July that year, a notice went up on their road informing them that a recently cleared area would be sprayed with the herbicide Roundup/Vision. The residents of the road got together to oppose it, signing a petition and sending it to the Ministers of Lands and Forests and of the Environment. They also picketed for a week in front of the North Colchester Forestry Co-operative in Tatamagouche, one of the venture groups that they alleged was "working hand in hand with the government to get access to privately owned lands for the pulp industry and in turn promoting the use of herbicides in forestry."[424] They made personal pleas to the landowners and requested support from their local MLA. The residents then organized a blockade at the site starting on the morning of August 4, 1988. Supporters were advised to bring camping gear and some food.

"We had the blockade for five weeks," Daley tells me. "We blocked the road, we were in a tent, and everyone on our road except for one came to the blockade. We had meals there. We had a lot of media but they made us mad because they always wanted to talk to Judy or myself and they wouldn't talk to the other residents on the road."

The sprayers arrived early one morning at dawn, accompanied by the police, Daley says. Davis immediately began to mobilize everyone on the road. Chaos ensued. Catherine Hughes recalls approaching the vehicle of the people who had come from Quebec to do the spraying, and trying to convince the woman inside the truck that her son and her husband, who would be handling the herbicide, were exposing themselves to health risks. Just then, she recalls, Davis, Daley, and another female protester, Bernadette MacDonald, came running out of the woods.

When that happened, Hughes says the woman with the spraying team seemed to switch sides, and began shouting, "Bravo, les femmes!" in support of the women protesters.

The three women then began throwing stones at Dale

Downey, the field supervisor for the forestry co-operative, which had arranged the cutting and was now managing the spraying. One stone broke the back window in his car; another hit his foot. One press report called it "an egg- and rock-throwing melee," which led to the arrest of Davis, Daley, and MacDonald.[425] They were taken away to a police cell in Tatamagouche, before being released. Hughes recalls that the police were rough when they arrested Daley, and she shouted at them not to break her arm.

The spraying went ahead. Davis was charged with damage to property, and Daley and MacDonald were charged with assault. Two weeks later in a court hearing at the firehall in Tatamagouche, all three pled guilty. Judy Davis represented herself, describing the North Colchester Forestry Co-operative as a "government sponsored venture group" that had admitted publicly to having knowingly violated the Department of Environment spray guidelines by not informing residents of the timing of the spraying, yet no charges were being laid against them.[426] Davis was found guilty and charged $50 for damaging property; Daley and MacDonald were also found guilty, but not fined. They were all put on probation.

Dale Downey's perspective on the blockade and the spraying is very different from Daley's. In March 2017, Downey drops by my home to provide his views on the co-operative, herbicide spraying and pulp, and what happened that day. He says he never perceived the protest as being against the pulp mill, but as targeting the North Colchester Co-operative itself. Nor does he think that the philosophy behind the herbicide spraying comes from the pulp mill. Rather, he tells me, it's part of forestry. He doesn't see it as a black and white issue at all, but one of "risk management." He is aware that the spray cannot be described as "safe" but says there is a need to look at what harm it does and what good it does, and to balance the two.

He says if the protest were truly against the Scott mill, as Daley and Davis say it was, there is irony there. When the group ventures were first set up, Scott Maritimes was "hostile" to the idea, fearful it might strengthen the organization of small woodlot owners.[427] The renowned forester David Dwyer saw the system as a way to give woodlot owners the support they needed to effectively manage their own woodlots.[428] And, Downey says, North Colchester Co-operative was not using the same silviculture practices as the pulp mill. While the mill did aerial spraying, the co-operative did only ground application of the herbicide because they were working with small woodlots and had more control that way. In fact, he says, they were trying to counter the kind of large-scale industrial forestry the pulp mills practised.

So when it came to the 1988 blockade and protest, he and the co-operative were not about to back down. They saw it as a test case, he says; if they gave in, then they would have to confront protestors every time they tried to spray. On the day they decided to break the blockade and do the spraying, two police cruisers and all the co-operative's board members joined what he called "the procession" of vehicles that accompanied the spraying contractors to the site before dawn. "It was a protest, they were taking a stand," he tells me. "And they were going to stand up to us and put us down. And that's why we did it there. That's why we did it." He also believes that when the neighbours who had supported the protest saw the stone throwing, they withdrew their support.

Although they failed to stop the spraying, Daley says the anti-spray blockade was "still kind of successful. Our whole road got together, people who had never talked to each other before, and everyone got together because we were all very sure we did not want that in our neighbourhood." And she is adamant that the protest was very much directed against Scott, which, as Downey told me, provided the co-operative with a quota for selling pulpwood.

Three days after the arrests, it was Scott's turn to get itself in trouble with the law. The Crown found Scott World Wide Inc. (as Scott Canadian Timberlands was known in the province) guilty of harming trout spawning and rearing areas in Cumberland County, where it had used heavy equipment and dumped sediment into streams and brooks.[429] Sandy MacGregor, manager of Scott Timberlands, said that his company would "do whatever restorative work which needs to be done."[430]

Then in the early spring of 1990, members of the Boycott Scott Committee, the North Shore Environmental Web, and David Orton's Green Web group mobilized more than sixty people for a mock "funeral" for Spiddle Hill, set amid the beauty of the range of Cobequid Mountains that stretch across the north of the province. Daley and Hughes have a blurry digitized copy of a video from the event, which shows the clearcut, possibly a hundred or more acres, which was slated for planting and then spraying. Some of the protesters wear black armbands to signify their mourning for Spiddle Hill. Some carry flowers and some have brought signs, declaring that "Scott destroys the environment" and "Pulpwood forestry = clear cutting and pesticides." Children scamper over the stumps and the brush and chewed-up landscape left by the heavy logging equipment.

Judy Davis starts the "funeral" by strumming her guitar and singing the "Scott Boycott Song" she'd written and set to the tune of John Prine's song "Paradise," which protests strip-mining for coal in Muhlenberg County, Kentucky. Then, one after another, the activists speak about the importance of healthy forests and improved forestry policies, while a CBC cameraman moves about to capture it all on film.

One speaker, Al Flemming, a beekeeper and honey producer in the area, an engineer and a former university professor, points out that this area would have been covered by rich, diverse Acadian forest until 150 years ago, when it was settled by Highland Scots who cleared it for farm and pastures. Over time, he says, the soils would have grown poor, people moved on, and nature tried to heal itself. The first stage of this, he tells the group, is generally a dense population of white or cat spruce, a knotty tree that colonizes former pastures and is often known as the "lumberman's nightmare." White spruce had been growing here, he says, and the cut produced a few sawlogs that could be used for lumber, but these have been put into the piles of pulpwood awaiting trucking to the mill in Pictou. Further, the soil has been torn up and left exposed to erosion from winds and rains by the heavy logging equipment.

A better way to manage forests, he says, would be to let the Acadian forest regenerate. And instead of supporting pulp forestry and monocultures encouraged with chemicals, the government could invest in research to promote the growth of a healthy and diverse forest with high-value species that would produce good lumber, even food such as beechnuts, provide habitat for wildlife, and perform all kinds of environmental services. Besides, he said, pulp had never brought in much money for the landowners. Other speakers echo these themes, and then several of the protesters fan out to plant some seeds of hardwood species. This is a symbolic gesture, because later the entire clearcut will be planted with spruce for pulp, and sprayed with herbicide.

By 1993, Daley says the Scott Boycott Committee had run out of energy, time, and resources, and they decided to end the ten-year boycott, although in their message to members they said there had been no change in Scott's activities in Nova Scotia. David Orton with his Green Web continued to publish regular bulletins from his home in Salt Springs, Pictou County. Until he passed away in 2011, he never stopped criticizing the pulp industry and the industrial approach to forestry it promoted.

The campaigns didn't change the way forests were harvested and managed; the clear cutting and spraying of the herbicide Vision continued through the years, and persists today. But the government itself seemed to be aware there were imbalances in the way pulp companies were operating in the province. Following a consultant's report, in 1989, the Minister of Lands and Forests decided to increase the stumpage rates it charged Scott, from the "fire-sale" price of $2 per cord of softwood, negotiated when the Crown lease was signed in the 1960s, to $7, and with a plan to increase it to $10.49 per cord in 1991.[431]

In Scott's annual Environmental Management Plan that year, manager Gerry Byrne didn't directly address the concerns that had led to the protests over clear cutting and spraying, but he did say, "A major initiative is now underway involving Scott Canadian Timberlands staff and woodlands contractors in establishing new standards for all aspects of forest management practices."[432] Five years later, the environmental plan went further, with new practices to "ease the impact of tree harvesting on the environment." These included leaving green belts along streams, wildlife corridors, snag trees for nesting birds, deer wintering yards, and the use of "seed tree cuts" where some trees are left standing to encourage natural regeneration.[433]

While not what the environmental groups and woodlot owners had been seeking, it still looked as if their hard work had resulted in some changes in the way Scott planned to manage its own timberlands. But by then, Scott was on its way out; the even bigger American company, Kimberly-Clark, was about to swallow it up, in the first of several changes in ownership of the mill.

In 2005, when the company that owned the mill, Neenah Paper, prepared to aerial spray glyphosate-based herbicides over White Hill in Pictou County, residents once again reacted. Mark Brennan, a resident of the rural farming community, said that 90 percent of the population of 300 opposed the spraying, and that there were plans to prevent it by camping out on the site.[434] Brennan told the media that Nova Scotians living near spray sites had almost no say in the matter, and that they were "nothing but lab rats in an uncontrolled experiment."[435]

The issue was raised at a special municipal council meeting in Pictou, and several "key spokespersons" were invited to take the floor. It was an interesting selection of speakers. There was Jack Kyte, formerly the pulp company's public affairs manager and now described as its "environmental team leader."[436] Brad Skinner, district manager for the northern region of the Department of Environment and Labour's environmental monitoring and compliance division, was also present, someone who steadfastly told critics of the herbicide, "The federal government has determined it is safe to use and the medical officer as well has determined it safe to use according to the label directions."[437] Council also brought in the staunch defender of herbicide use from New Brunswick, Dr. R.A. Lautenschlager.[438] Despite the preponderance of speakers in favour of the herbicide spraying, Pictou's municipal council did take the decision, meek though it was, to have the spraying done from the ground and not by helicopter.

The controversy didn't go away. In 2009, a "Stop The Spray" group approached all the political parties for their views on herbicide spraying and launched another petition just before the provincial election that the NDP won under Darrell Dexter.[439] Although there had been no herbicide sprayed on Crown land since 2006, in 2010 the NDP announced there would be no more public funding for herbicide spraying on Crown lands or on private land.[440]

In the summer of 2016, the spray controversy erupted again when the owners of the Pictou pulp mill notified the public, as legislation required, that it had applied for a "forest management permit" from the Department of the Environment for areas in Colchester County and Halifax Regional Municipality.[441] Once again there was a flurry of letters to editors, a good deal of media attention, petitions against the spraying, and Dave Gunning, representing the Clean The Mill group, spoke at a demonstration in front of the Nova Scotia Legislature when it opened in October 2016.[442] Nevertheless, the spraying went ahead. The mill's approach to forest management didn't seem set to change, despite the fact that since 2004 the mill itself had been changing hands like a red-hot potato.

13

New landlords, new governments, new money (2000-2011)

The public's safety is the public's business. Mushrooms thrive in the dark. Societies don't.

– Warner Troyer[443]

n 2004, nine years after Kimberly-Clark took over Scott, it announced it had retained Goldman, Sachs & Co. to evaluate a potential "tax-free spin-off" of the company's Neenah Paper and Technical Paper businesses.[444] This would put the company's Canadian assets in the hands of Neenah Paper, a newly created publicly traded pulp and paper company. Neenah would thus own the pulp mills in Pictou, Nova Scotia, and Terrace Bay, Ontario, as well as owning or having access to nearly 6 million acres of timberlands in Canada, of which more than 1.2 million were in Nova Scotia.

The annual sales of the Neenah "stand alone" businesses would be worth about $650 million [US], less than 3 percent of Kimberly-Clark's annual net sales.[445] However, this mutually beneficial arrangement would mean Kimberly-Clark would assure the pulp mills a market for their fibre, and assure the mother company an almost in-house supply of fibre. The chair and chief executive officer of Kimberly-Clark, Thomas J. Falk, said he believed the spin-off would provide greater value for Kimberly-Clark shareholders. It was finalized in November that year.

This was followed by a flurry of changes in the ownership of the mill and large tracts of timberland in Nova Scotia, all of them involving players south of the Canadian border. First, in May 2006, Neenah Paper sold off 500,894 acres – about half of its land holdings in Nova Scotia – for $155 million (Cdn), or about $309 per acre.[446] The buyer was a New Hampshire corporation, Wagner Forest Management Ltd., and its Nova Scotia land holdings were under two separate corporate entities, Atlantic Star Forestry Ltd. and Nova Star Forestry Ltd.

Wagner Forest Management had been founded in the 1950s by Fred Wagner, and by 2005 it oversaw investments of twenty clients in 2.5 million acres of timberland in Vermont, Maine, New Hampshire, New York, West Virginia, Kentucky, Virginia, and also Canada.[447] CEO and president of Wagner, Tom Colgan, had joined the company in 1994, after working seventeen years for Scott in Maine, where he helped expand and also manage Scott's large timberland holdings.[448] Wagner was capitalizing on a trend, begun in the 1990s, as large and vertically integrated forest products companies started selling off land holdings. Most of the buyers were institutional investors, including pension funds, endowments, and foundations that saw timberland as a valuable new asset class in investment portfolios.[449]

A year before Wagner acquired Neenah's lands in Nova Scotia, it had bought more than a million acres from the International Paper Company in Maine. This sparked some controversy, as Wagner now controlled more land in the state than anyone else, surpassing the Irving family from New Brunswick that had until then been the largest private landholder in the state.[450] By 2005 in Maine, where several big publicly traded pulp companies had sold off their timberlands to capital management groups, more than a third of the state was now in the hands of mostly anonymous investors.[451] Wagner refused to disclose the identities of the owners they represented.[452]

Although the Wagner holdings in Nova Scotia were smaller, the pattern was the same, and, unlike what happened in Maine, there was almost no public outcry over the purchase of so much of the province. The new owners of the half-million acres – 3.7 percent of Nova Scotia – the investors that Wagner represented, were unknown.[453] This was investment for profit and the two entities holding the land for Wagner and its investors each had their own business model. Nova Star held properties that could be sold off as cottage lots and development properties. Atlantic Star was acquiring timberlands for clear cutting to feed the pulp mill; Wagner had signed an agreement to provide Neenah with fibre from its new timberlands holdings.[454]

Wagner's website says its business model involves "responsibly tended timberland investments for clients who expect solid economic performance and strong commitments to natural resource stewardship and the support of local communities."[455] For some of its tree farms in Maine, it obtained the relatively stringent certification from the Forest Stewardship Council (FSC) and the Rainforest Alliance.[456] That was not the case in Nova Scotia.[457]

Bob Bancroft is a respected and well-known wildlife biologist in Nova Scotia who worked for many years for the Department of Lands and Forests and once upon a time also for Kimberly-Clark. He has grave concerns about forest management on Wagner's land. When we meet in his home in early July 2016, he tells me that at times when Scott and Kimberly-Clark had no biologist on staff, they would call on him to assess the wildlife situation on lands they intended to cut. If he located a wintering area for deer on their land, he says, they would avoid cutting there to conserve the habitat. After the first half of the Neenah (originally Scott) land was sold, he says, everything is being cut, regardless of whether there is sensitive wildlife habitat in the area.

Two years after that land deal, Neenah went further in divesting its assets in the province. In May 2008, the media reported Neenah had agreed to pay two American firms between $15 and $20 million (US) to take over the pulp mill with all its assets, liabilities, contracts, and pension obligations, as well as its woodland operations.[458] In the end, Neenah paid the new owners approximately $10.3 million (US) to take over the mill, while incurring transaction costs of about $3.3 million (US).[459]

The new company that was formed to own the mill would be called Northern Pulp Nova Scotia Corporation, an affiliate of the private equity firm Blue Wolf Capital Management LLC of New York that had been founded in 2005, and the holding company, Atlas Holdings LLC of Greenwich, Connecticut, as well as local management as equity owners.[460] The deal did not include Neenah's remaining timberlands holdings of 475,000 acres and its lease on more than 200,000 acres of Crown land. The general manager of the mill, Keith Johnson, said this new company structure would make it "competitive in a very challenging pulp and paper business environment."[461]

Co-founder and manager of Blue Wolf, Adam Blumenthal, was later asked why his private equity firm was interested in buying assets such as the mill that "over its lifetime, under a string of different owners, fell into disrepair and accumulated a host of issues ranging from labor to environmental."[462] Blumenthal admitted there were problems with the mill, its operation costs were high, and "there were unresolved issues between the mill and the First Nations community in Canada." But, he said, these were things Blue Wolf was able to "systematically and constructively resolve."[463]

There were some rumblings in American newspapers and online about the American firms that agreed to take the mill off Neenah's hands, and questions raised about the owners of Blue Wolf Capital and their former positions in the New York City Comptroller's office, and then the firm's later contract investing New York City pensions.[464] There was also some speculation about how they had come to identify the mill in Nova Scotia as an investment, and interest in the role that the former premier, John Hamm, would come to play with the new company.[465] Hamm had stepped down as premier and leader of the Progressive Conservative Party in February 2006, and would be much decorated in the years to come.[466] A young Cape Breton teacher and fiddler, Rodney MacDonald, took his place at the helm of the Party and the province.

In March 2009, the Progressive Conservative government of Premier MacDonald loaned Northern Pulp $15 million from its Industrial Expansion Fund to cover maintenance costs and capital expenditures.[467] Wayne Gosse, chief operating officer of Northern Pulp, said the money would be used to update processing equipment and for a new effluent pipeline, which would cost between $2 and $5 million.[468] He said the government support was timely, given that demand and pricing for pulp had been falling dramatically.

In 2010, Blue Wolf and Atlas Holdings announced that Northern Pulp Nova Scotia Corporation, their "portfolio company," through another affiliate, Northern Timber Nova Scotia, would be purchasing Neenah's remaining land holdings of 475,000 acres in the province.[469] This was part of the original forest land that Scott had acquired in the previous century. Neenah cited the high Canadian dollar at the time and a shortage of wood chips as reasons to sell it.[470]

The purchase took place in March 2010 and in August that year, Blue Wolf created Northern Resources Nova Scotia Corporation, which would operate both Northern Timber Nova Scotia Corporation that owned the land, and Northern Pulp that owned the mill.[471] Although it's not clear when, exactly, John Hamm became involved with the mill's new owners, in December 2009, one media report stated that he was already one of Atlas Holdings' operating partners.[472] Blue Wolf said it brought Hamm onto its board in August 2010.[473] A press release from Atlas Holdings in March 2010 described both Hamm and Blue Wolf Capital as its partners.[474] It was announced in September 2010 that Hamm had been appointed chair of the board of the newly established Northern Resources Nova Scotia Corporation.[475]

Blue Wolf was upbeat about its environmental record. In the fall of 2010, Adam Blumenthal said that since Blue Wolf had acquired the mill it had "made an effort to become a steward of the environment."[476] It had, he maintained, "reduced the impact of the effluent treatment facility" and worked with environmental regulators "to manage the center as cleanly as possible, and to reduce its environmental footprint," although no specifics were given on what that meant. It was reported the mill's engineers "implemented a plan that reduced the area needed for the center's settling basins by almost 80 percent."[477]

In reality, things remained the same as they had been for many years. The year for a closing of Boat Harbour, 2005, had come and gone with no change, and closed-door meetings involving the government, the company, and the First Nations Band had all led to naught.[478] The licence for the use of Boat Harbour had expired in 2008 and was being negotiated from one month to the next, with no clear deadline for a closure or a clean-up.[479] During the time that Blue Wolf and Atlas had owned the mill, there had also been two ruptures of the pipeline that resulted in effluent leaks. The 2009 loan from the Rodney MacDonald government was to cover a replacement for the aging pipeline.

In 2009, *A'se'k' News*, a newsletter issued by the Pictou Landing Council, said they had been demanding the provincial government not just restore Boat Harbour to a tidal estuary by opening it up to the Northumberland Strait, but that they remove the entire treatment facility.[480] It informed its readership they were seeking a "short time line and strict terms for continued operation of the facility" and this time they would negotiate steep penalties for failure to meet the deadlines.

Although it would be years before this was made public,

a consultant determined in 2009 that the mill's power boiler scrubber had not been functioning since 2006, which meant emissions of particulate matter had been exceeding permitted levels.[481] So, not much evidence for Adam Blumenthal's claim that under the new ownership the mill had made any real effort "to become a steward of the environment."[482]

In 2009 Northern Pulp had also garnered some very strident criticism for its forestry practices. "This is the worst I've ever seen," said Jamie Simpson, then forestry coordinator at the Ecology Action Centre, of a site he visited near Upper Musqoudoboit. "It's hard to believe this is happening in Nova Scotia in the 21st century. It's an embarrassment." [483]

Simpson had been invited by concerned citizen Kathy Didowsky to a Northern Pulp clearcut in Caribou Mines, an area once known for its gold mining, now known for its "forest mining," according to Didowsky.[484] In his book, *Journeys Through Eastern Old-Growth Forests*, this is how Simpson describes the scene where about 1,700 acres had been cleared in just over two months: "I had never seen such intensity of forest destruction, on such a scale," which involved "churned earth, machine tracks and fragments of shattered trees."[485]

Simpson explains that the forestry workers who wreaked the havoc here were not employees of Northern Pulp, but contractors. And contractors, he writes, if they want to work, have to purchase expensive machinery. If they don't keep it running twenty-four hours a day, seven days a week, they may not be able to make the payments on the machines. And he notes this clearcut was done for Northern Pulp, owned at this point jointly by Atlas Holdings and Blue Wolf Capital Partners, interested in maximizing profits for investors. Writes Simpson, "Concern for the long-term health of Nova Scotia's forests, communities, or workers is not among its core values."[486]

But a contract logger who had once worked for Northern Pulp told Simpson the clear cutting problem did not lie with any one company; rather, it was caused by the lack of government regulations to stop it. And this had gone beyond clear cutting; it was whole-tree harvesting, which left the former forest floor bare and exposed to the elements, with almost no organic matter to help the soil or the forest regenerate. There were no rules against the practice.

Nine other groups in the province, as well as the Nova Scotia Woodlot Owners and Operators Association, were campaigning to try to convince the provincial government to outlaw whole-tree harvesting. As for the certification from the Sustainable Forestry Initiative (SFI) that qualified Northern Pulp's forestry operations as "green," some groups are highly critical of this industry-funded certification scheme,[487] which was set up by the American Forest and Paper Association.[488] Jamie Simpson labelled SFI's program as "greenwashing."[489]

Adam Blumenthal said it was because Blue Wolf had shown they "were good citizens," that "when the additional land that Neenah owned came up for sale the Nova Scotia government came to us."[490] Blumenthal's choice of words is interesting. However the deal was negotiated, the Nova Scotia government, now with the NDP in power under Premier Darrell Dexter, made a very generous offer to the American owners of the mill and their investment partners.[491] In 2010, the government came up with a loan of $75 million for Northern Pulp to buy the 475,000 acres of Neenah land, with a price tag of $82 million or $172.63 per acre. The loan was for thirty years, and Northern Pulp would have to pay the interest at an undisclosed rate for the first five years, after which it would have to start repayment.[492] [493]

As part of the deal, the government of Nova Scotia would immediately buy back 55,000 acres of this newly purchased land from Northern Pulp for $16.5 million, or $300 per acre, meaning that the province was gifting Blue Wolf and Atlas $7 million. The press release announcing this latest government largesse to Northern Pulp deftly sidestepped this point and resorted instead to sleight of thought.[494] It began this way: "The province is protecting jobs and the environment by partnering with one of Nova Scotia's largest employers." It also claimed that Northern Pulp "directly supported 1,700 high-paying jobs in northern and central Nova Scotia." However, at the time, the number of jobs at the mill had decreased to 240, a significant drop from the original 350 employees.[495] It also kept 400 contractors in work and was said to create 600 to 800 jobs "indirectly."[496]

The $16.5 million the government was spending to buy back the 55,000 acres of land at 1.7 times what Northern Pulp had paid per acre was described in a government press release as an investment in exceptional natural land "at an excellent price," "well below market value," which would "help us move towards our goal of protecting 12 percent of the province's land mass by 2015."[497] And the provincial loan would "allow Northern Pulp to invest $5 million to reduce odour in the community surrounding the Abercrombie Mill."[498]

Wayne Gosse, chief executive officer and chief financial officer of Northern Pulp, called the purchase of land "a win" for the mill, its employees, "the surrounding area and the people of Nova Scotia."[499] "We have been sustainably managing the resources entrusted to us for over 40 years and Northern Pulp's ownership of these lands means we can continue to do so for generations to come," he said.

In its press release, Atlas Holdings said it was grateful to the Nova Scotian government, community leaders in the province, and "our partners in Northern Pulp, Dr. John Hamm and Blue Wolf Capital Management, who helped us conceptualize and negotiate this complex transaction."[500]

When Hamm was named chair of the board of Northern Resources Nova Scotia Corporation, he said, "I joined the board of Northern Pulp to advance the goals of growing a sustainable economy and investing in assets and opportunities that enhance the rural economy."[501] "With the acquisition of 420,000 acres of forestland in Northern Nova Scotia earlier this year," he continued, "the company gained the asset base to be truly a powerful force in our community, and [sic] partnerships with employees, neighbours, governments, First Nations, contractors, community organizations and other stakeholders."

According to Percy Paris, Nova Scotia's Minister of Economic and Rural Development, the purchase of the land would not just ensure a wood supply to the pulp mill but would protect the land as a forestry asset.[502]

Not everyone was convinced. Forester Jamie Simpson saw the loan as the government "subsidizing bad forestry practices" and companies that "use clear cutting and whole-tree harvesting methods."[503] He said that such government support for the pulp and paper companies over the years meant clear cutting had become the norm. A 2008 study by the Ecology Action Centre had found that in the previous three decades, the governments of Canada and Nova Scotia had subsidized forest industries that favoured clear cutting in the province to the tune of about $650 million.

Simpson also took issue with statements from Northern Pulp that it intended to harvest just 3 percent of its managed forests annually, noting this would mean the company would be cutting its entire land base in just thirty-three years. "It doesn't sound like much," he told *The Chronicle Herald*, "but if you do the math, no forest they manage will be older than 33 years. Obviously, a lot of our native forest species aren't even mature at that age."[504] Back in 1970, Scott had said it would be operating its woodlands on a sixty-year rotation; so in just three decades the mill had halved the number of years it would give woodlands to regrow.[505] Such a short rotation, Simpson noted, would maximize fibre growth at the expense of the forest ecosystem and quality timber production.

His and others' concerns about what would happen on the land that Nova Scotians had loaned Northern Pulp the money to buy came to light again a few years later, in June 2017, when the company began clear cutting atop the picturesque mountain ridge on the western side of Wentworth Valley in northern Nova Scotia. The land in question was part of tens of thousands of acres of mostly Acadian forest, mature hardwoods mixed with some softwoods, in Cumberland County that Northern Pulp had purchased from Neenah with the loan.[506]

Residents of Wentworth called the cutting "heartbreaking" and Gregor Wilson, a director of the ski hill there, said the cutting jeopardized a plan on which he and others were working to turn the entire valley into a year-round outdoor eco-tourism destination, a little like Whistler in British Columbia.[507] Asked on CBC Halifax's *Information Morning* if government would consider trying to stop the cutting, the newly appointed Minister of Natural Resources, Margaret Miller, said that because it was on private land, there was nothing the government could do.[508] She didn't mention that the private land belonged to Northern Pulp and that it had been bought with a loan from the people of Nova Scotia.

Two years after that land deal, in January 2011, more government largesse landed on Northern Pulp. Canada's Minister of Defence, Peter MacKay, who hailed from Pictou County, announced that the federal Conservative government under Prime Minister Stephen Harper was giving $28.1 million to the company. The grant was coming from Natural Resources Canada and the Green Transformation Fund.[509]

According to Northern Pulp, the government funds went to upgrading the power boiler, to allow it to use less heavy oil and more wood waste or biomass.[510] They were also spent to increase the recovery of cooking chemicals to reduce waste to the effluent facility, which would increase the flow of black liquor – the cooking chemicals and dissolved wood products – to the recovery boiler and increase electricity production from renewable resources. And Northern Pulp said $8.7 million of the federal grant was spent on equipment on the recovery boiler to reduce sulphur compounds and collect four "odorous streams" for incineration in the recovery boiler, which it claimed, reduced "odorous compounds" by 70 percent.[511]

Four months after the federal grant and just three years since Blue Wolf and Atlas Holdings had acquired Northern Pulp, in April 2011 they sold off their Nova Scotian pulp and timber companies to yet another wealthy foreign corporation. In 2017, the Registry of Joint Stock Companies in Nova Scotia shows no fewer than eight active companies related to the corporation, four registered in 2008 and four more in 2010. John Hamm is a board member on four of them, and remains as board chair of the umbrella company in the province, Northern Resources Nova Scotia Corporation.[512]

14

New owner, new government, new favours: take two (2011-2017)

Excellence is not just our goal. It's our method of getting there.
 – Paper Excellence Group[513]

The sale of the Northern Pulp mill and its assets in 2011 attracted surprisingly little public attention in Nova Scotia, considering that during the previous two years it had received more than $90 million in loans and grants from the provincial government, and $28.1 million from the federal government.

The relative lack of media and public reaction to the mill's purchase is also surprising given the identity of the buyer. A company called Paper Excellence Canada Holdings, with its headquarters in Richmond, British Columbia, had been on a buying binge of pulp and paper mills in Canada.[514] By 2012, Paper Excellence owned five pulp mills across the country, including Meadow Lake and Prince Albert in Saskatchewan, MacKenzie Softwood and Howe Sound in British Columbia, and Northern Pulp in Nova Scotia.[515] By 2017, Paper Excellence had added two more mills to its Canadian portfolio, in

Skookumchuck and Chetwynd in British Columbia.[516]

So who owned Paper Excellence Canada Holdings that now owned the mill at Abercrombie Point? That, it turns out, is not an easy question to answer. Its deputy CEO, Pedro Chang, claimed it was owned 100 percent by Jackson Widjaja.[517] He is the son of Teguh Widjaja, chair of the giant Sinar Mas Group, which owns Asia Pulp & Paper (APP). And Teguh Widjaja, in turn, is the oldest son of the Indonesian billionaire Eka Tjipta Widjaja.

In 2015, the normally "media-shy" Paper Excellence agreed to an interview with *Business Vancouver*, and deputy CEO Chang said that while there is a family connection between his company and the Sinar Mas group and APP, Paper Excellence Canada is not a subsidiary of either company.[518] Nevertheless, an investigation done for Greenpeace in The Netherlands shows a complex corporate web of companies that does link the Widjaja family in Indonesia with Paper Excellence Canada Holdings and its pulp and paper mills in Canada.[519]

Since 2007, the APP group had been on a global shopping spree, expanding its pulp and paper interests not just in North America but also in Asia, Australia, and Europe.[520] It set up a holding company called Paper Excellence B.V. in The Netherlands, allegedly "because of the attractive Dutch tax climate," and established a family of subsidiaries that purchased mills in Canada, France, and Germany.[521] Paper Excellence also became the owner of paper marketing companies in Australia, Europe, and Japan.

Another Dutch corporate group, which includes Bentoning Holdings and two subsidiaries, in turn financed the subsidiaries of Paper Excellence to purchase the pulp mills. The authors of the study for Greenpeace, Jan Willem van Gelder and Petra Spaargaren, tried to burrow into the rabbit hole to map the complex warren of corporate ownership, but were unable to identify the owners of Bentoning. They concluded that "the ownership of Paper Excellence (B.V.) is hidden behind a string of foreign holding companies in Malaysia and the British Virgin Islands" and that it was "very likely" both were ultimately owned by the Widjaja family.[522]

They wrote that this corporate gymnastics, splitting the companies that owned the mills from the ones financing their acquisition, "makes optimal use of the favourable tax climate in The Netherlands to minimize both its total tax payments and transparency with regard to its international expansion."[523] They also say information from financial magazines confirms "that the Canadian companies which directly own the mills, including Howe Sound Pulp & Paper LP and Northern Pulp Nova Scotia Corporation, are ultimately owned by Paper Excellence B.V."[524]

Paper Excellence Canada doesn't sell its pulp on the open market; instead it sells to APP mills in Asia.[525] As a result, the company has some immunity to fluctuations in the volatile market for pulp, and this also means the market for the fibre from the company's Canadian mills is all in the Widjaja family.

Greenpeace and some media reports simply describe Paper Excellence as a "subsidiary" of APP,[526] while others call it a "Sinar Mas" company,[527] or "a subsidiary of Netherlands-based Paper Excellence, a subsidiary of Asia Pulp and Paper, which is owned by Indonesian conglomerate Sinar Mas Group."[528] That the exact relationship is so difficult to determine is problematic for those wanting to know the identity of the new owners of a mill that citizens in the province had propped up financially for years, and of extensive land holdings in the province, including a large chunk of public land.

Despite the lack of clarity on the exact nature of the relationships, it is clear that Paper Excellence is linked with APP and Sinar Mas, which is owned by the Widjaja family.[529] According to Bloomberg, in 2001, Asia Pulp & Paper set a record with the largest default by an Asian company, the "biggest missed bond obligation" to that date when it stopped payments on $13.9 billion (US) worth of bonds. "The firm became mired in legal challenges as Indonesian courts cancelled debts and creditors lost millions," said the Bloomberg report.[530]

APP's environmental record was also less than stellar. In 2004, the government of Cambodia announced it was taking legal action against one of APP's subsidiaries for illegal logging in a national park in that country.[531] According to an article in the *Asia Times (online)*, "APP's business model is a tactically aggressive one: it turns huge profits by quickly stripping forests bare, exploiting age-old forests and indigenous peoples, and leaving town before the environmental consequences are felt. By the time communities and governments lodge complaints and lawsuits, APP has divested itself of local interests and assets."[532]

In 2007, the Forest Stewardship Council, the most exacting of certification schemes available for forestry operations, disassociated itself from APP, which had still not had its certification reinstated by July 2017 although negotiations were ongoing.[533] In 2011, when Greenpeace found evidence of fibre from old-growth Indonesia forests in packaging used by Mattell, the global toy-maker announced it would no longer buy from APP.[534] A year later, APP would earn itself unflattering headlines again after reports emerged about its illegal logging activities in Indonesia, cutting down endangered tree species in forests that were habitat to the highly endangered Sumatran tiger.[535] This led three multinationals to temporarily boycott APP products, including Danone and Xerox.[536]

All of this led investigative journalist Miles Howe to write of the Northern Pulp purchase by the Widjaja family, "If you thought the Canadian pulp and paper industry was environmentally irresponsible, you were right. But the new players on the clear-cut block make them look like a bunch of patchouli-scented tree-huggers."[537] Howe also noted the "distinct lack of fanfare" from the media in Canada about the takeover of Canadian pulp mills. Greenpeace Canada issued one critical statement about APP's expansion into the country, but nothing more after that.[538]

Northern Pulp vice-president Don Breen said of the deal,

"The agreement is good news for the company's 230 employees, 400 timberlands [sic], contract employees, supplier and community and business partners." John Hamm, chair of the board of Northern Resources Nova Scotia Corporation, said the sale was "good for the local pulp mill and good for Pictou County."[539]

The next year the Northern Pulp family itself went shopping just down the road from Pictou in the village of Scotsburn. According to media reports, the Scotsburn Lumber Mill was purchased by an affiliate of Northern Pulp from Ligni Bel Ltd.[540] Today, just one person is director, president, and secretary of Scotsburn Lumber; his name is Hui-Lun Cheng and his civic address is in Hong Kong.[541] Despite the fact that the sawmill is affiliated with Northern Pulp, it is listed as a separate member of the consortium of mills called WestFor,[542] which formed to lobby the provincial government for more access to Crown land.

Among local people concerned about the mill's already spotty environmental footprint, there was no celebration about the new ownership. Jane Sproull Thomson wrote a strongly worded letter to the media, highlighting APP's environmental and financial transgressions in Asia, and requesting that the loans the people of Nova Scotia had accorded the mill in recent years be put on hold until the government could assure taxpayers "that we won't be watching more of our dollars going up in smoke along with our forests."[543]

Matt Gunning, brother to Dave, who would come to spearhead a new and powerful wave of protest about the mill's pollution in 2013, wrote to the media asking why the $90 million the government had loaned to the mill was not being used "to create an account dedicated to addressing the Boat Harbour issue, avoided for far too long?"[544]

Robert Christie, into his twenty-second year as executive director of the Pictou Harbour Environmental Control Project that worked closely with Northern Pulp, entered the fray once more. He called on the authorities to clean up Boat Harbour before it became any more costly. He said he hoped Darrell Dexter's NDP government would "sharply reduce clear cutting in the province," expressing his frustration at how government departments favoured "the economy at the expense of ecology."[545]

History seemed to be spinning round and round in circles, repeating familiar patterns for the mill. It continued to issue positive reports about itself, saying it was "progressing on the installation of the newest emissions equipment," which reportedly began following the purchase of the mill by Paper Excellence.[546]

Meanwhile, the provincial government continued to bestow its beneficence on Northern Pulp. In January of 2013, when the NDP were still in power, Deputy Minister of Natural Resources Duff Montgomerie wrote a letter to Pedro Chang, deputy CEO of Paper Excellence Canada. In it he referred to a meeting they had had four days earlier, saying, "We are very supportive of Northern Pulp," and that the Department of Natural Resources would be "working very hard to further solidify deliverables and timelines before our departure to visit you in Shanghai next Friday, February 1, 2013." He also let Chang know about the plan to purchase 550,000 acres of the former Resolute (Bowater) lands, pointing out that Northern Pulp could submit proposals under the planning process for the use of that land and previously owned Crown lands in western Nova Scotia. In the letter, he made Northern Pulp a generous offer of an additional 125,000 tonnes of fibre from Crown land, bringing its total allocation to 225,000 tonnes per year.[547]

According to the Ecology Action Centre, this letter was written before the government had even begun the public consultations on the future use of Crown lands in southwest Nova Scotia, but presumably the fibre would come in part from those woodlands.[548] A year earlier, in 2012, with a great deal of public support, the NDP government had put up $111.4

million to buy the 555,000 acres of land that had belonged to Resolute Forest Products (formerly Bowater Mersey) that had closed the pulp mill on the province's South Shore.[549] That was in addition to the rescue package of $50 million Dexter's government had given to the mill in 2011 in a desperate bid to keep it going.[550] After that failed, the province came up with another $118.4 million to cover pension and severance liabilities that the province assumed in 2012, when it bought the Bowater shares for $1 from Resolute Forest Products and partial owner, *The Washington Post*.[551]

The smaller Minas Basin Pulp and Paper Company, which employed 135, was also slated for closing in 2012. It had been a turbulent time for the pulp industry in Nova Scotia, and an expensive time for the province's citizens as the NDP government tried to keep it afloat.

The mill at Port Hawkesbury, owned at that time by New-Page, had shut down in 2011. In the words of former NDP MLA Howard Epstein, the "Premier's office went into overdrive to save that plant. It paid for keeping it from deteriorating; it sought a buyer; it negotiated the sale."[552] In all, the government spent $156 million on the mill, which Epstein breaks down this way: $12.3 million for keeping the plant in hot idle while a purchase was negotiated; a $24 million forgivable loan for improvements at the plant; a $1.5 million forgivable loan for worker training; another forgivable loan of $40 million; $19.1 million for forestry improvements on Crown land; a $1 million forgivable loan for a marketing plan; $38 million towards sustainable harvesting and land management; and $20 million to purchase 20,000 hectares (49,421 acres) of forest land.[553] The mill only resumed operations after Stern (Pacific West Commercial Corporation) bought it for $33 million, but even then that was after the government had loaned it $40 million.

The reopened plant was called Port Hawkesbury Paper – with roughly half the workers it once had.[554] In assessing the bailout, *Globe and Mail* reporter Barrie McKenna wrote that it worked out to "the equivalent of $470,000 for each of the 330 jobs saved. If those workers earn an average of $45,000 a year, Nova Scotia will essentially underwrite the mill's entire pay-roll for more than a decade."[555] And, as Howard Epstein noted, the government support meant that Stern had so little skin in the game that "[i]t would not be surprising to see the plant closed and sold off within a decade."[556]

In September 2013, the people of Nova Scotia went to the polls. After just one term, the NDP were out and the Liberals were in, led by Stephen McNeil. Although the original offer to Northern Pulp of an extra 125,000 tonnes of green fibre had been made by the Department of Natural Resources under the NDP, the Liberals decided to honour it. The new Minister of Natural Resources, Zach Churchill, said there was a "fibre shortage" in the province, which meant that some of that fibre would probably have to come from the newly acquired Crown lands. He did pledge that once a management plan had been developed for those lands, the government would do its "very best to ensure that the final management plan is as reflective of what the public wants as possible."[557] The government had had a great deal of public support for the purchase, with more than thirty groups coming together to push for the buyback of the land, hoping the government "would protect the eco-logically sensitive areas and explore options for community forests."[558]

This isn't exactly what happened. In April 2014, with the new Liberal government now in place, the outgoing Deputy Minister at the Department of Natural Resources, Duff Mont-gomerie, sent out a memo to staff announcing two key ap-pointments. One was Allan Eddy as Associate Deputy Minister of Natural Resources, who "had co-led the government's re-sponse to the Bowater Mill closure,"[559] and was a former se-nior forester with Nova Scotia Power. The other was Jonathan Porter, who would become Executive Director of the Renew-able Branch Division, and although the memo to staff didn't say so, Porter came directly from the pulp industry, having been woodlands manager at the recently closed Bowater mill in Brooklyn.[560] As investigative journalist and author Linda Pannozzo noted, they joined another former Bowater employee who had been appointed as director of forestry in the Department of Natural Resources. She called them the "company men."[561]

So perhaps it was not a huge surprise when, two years after the public purchased the Bowater lands, without public consultation, the Department of Natural Resources leased half of the newly acquired Crown lands to sixteen mills, among them Louisiana Pacific and J.D. Irving.[562] The mills later formalized their consortium, calling it WestFor Management Inc. Among the members of the consortium are Northern Pulp and its affiliated sawmill Scotsburn Lumber.

In early 2017, news emerged that the government had "quietly transferred management of 1.4 million acres of Crown land to WestFor."[563] Rumours abounded that Natural Resources Minister Lloyd Hines was extending that lease to ten years, but the minister said that talks were still underway.[564]

The Healthy Forest Coalition, an alliance of individuals and organizations that had come together to "raise public awareness of the critical state of our forests and the need for fundamental reform of forest policy" in Nova Scotia, was less than impressed by the lease to WestFor.[565] This is how they reacted to the concessions that had already been given to West-For members: "All answer to their owners or stockholders, not to the public. They are managing our crown land for *their* profit and the sustainability of *their* companies, nothing else." And, the Healthy Forest Coalition pointed out, "When a citizen sends an inquiry about planned harvests through DNR's [Department of Natural Resources] Harvest Map Viewer, a response comes back from someone who works for WestFor, not from a government employee."[566]

In early 2016, Minister of Natural Resources Hines announced the government would be dropping the Forest Stewardship Council (FSC) certification on the Medway District lands, part of the former Bowater lands.[567] The lands would still be certified with Sustainable Forestry Initiatives (SFI), a far less stringent system that permits cutting of old-growth forests, clear cutting and plantations.[568] Dropping FSC was an about-face for the Liberal government; a year earlier then Minister of Natural Resources Zach Churchill had said the province would have all Crown lands certified with FSC, which he described as the "gold standard for environmental certification systems for forestry operations."[569] But that was just one of the broken promises.

The story of the province's new natural resources strategy and its abandonment was a far bigger betrayal. In her in-depth article "Forest Tragedy" that traces the rise and the fall of that strategy for Nova Scotia, Linda Pannozzo recalls the excitement and enthusiasm that greeted the announcement in 2008 that the Progressive Conservative government of Rodney MacDonald was launching public consultations as the first phase in a process to develop a new natural resources strategy.[570]

She remembers that "citizens started gathering in droves in community halls to talk about why the natural world mattered to them" and that this was "the first time that the advice of citizens was going to shape resource policy in the province." Citizens overwhelmingly wanted less clear cutting, no whole-tree harvesting, more protection of biodiversity, restoration of diverse Acadian forests – in short, an end to the pulp forestry regime that had done so much damage to them over the past few decades.

When the NDP took over from the Conservatives in 2009, the process continued under Natural Resources Minister John MacDonell, who had long expressed concerns about the over-harvesting of the province's forests. In 2010, he agreed that clear cutting should account for no more than half of all harvesting. But there were hints that MacDonell was encountering some resistance to the policy reforms underway. That year, the Department of Natural Resources engaged the services of

Peter Woodbridge, "a consultant and advisor to several forestry companies in Canada and abroad," to look at the economic impact of reduced clear cutting on the industry. [571]

The NDP government of which MacDonell was part approved a giant new biomass plant in Port Hawkesbury that would dramatically increase the demand for fuel from the forests, and thus for clear cutting. The Department of Natural Resources had put together a voluntary steering panel to examine whether large biomass plants were going to overtax the forest resources of the province, a panel that comprised wildlife biologist Bob Bancroft and another highly respected forest biologist, Donna Crossland. The third member of the panel, however, Jonathan Porter, came from the pulp industry and in Bancroft's view, he was put there to "obstruct" the process.[572] He would write his own report that endorsed clear cutting and biomass harvesting, contradicting the report by Bancroft and Crossland.[573] As Bancroft saw it, the Departments of Energy and Natural Resources were in cahoots, and a revolving door between industry and government allowed industry a place on the inside when it came to decisions.[574]

The natural resources strategy was released in August 2011.[575] It contained some provisions that encouraged those who had hoped for a change in forest management in the province. Clear cutting was to be reduced to 50 percent of forest harvesting within five years, there would be no removing of whole trees from harvested areas, and no more public money to fund herbicide spraying. But the new strategy seemed to be encountering pushback.

A few months before its release, John MacDonell had been replaced by Charlie Parker as Minister of Natural Resources. Shortly after that, the Woodbridge Report came out with its warnings about the "cost implications to industry" of reducing the amount of clear cutting in the province.[576] This, combined with the crisis with two of the province's three big pulp mills, seems to have terrified Dexter's government. It clearly wanted to acquiesce to industry demands to try and save jobs, but didn't want to raise the ire of the many citizens who had spoken out so forcefully against clear cutting.

In the end, the Department of Natural Resources found a novel solution; it came up with a new definition of clear cutting. Officially, it decided that a clear cut would be "where less than 60 percent of the area is sufficiently occupied with trees taller than 1.3 m[etres]." This arbitrary definition, according to forester and environmental lawyer Jamie Simpson, meant that "half of all cutting can leave a moonscape; the other half can leave a scattering of low-quality trees, none necessarily higher than four feet."[577]

Then, in August 2016, the Liberal government of Stephen McNeil went much, much further; it decided to completely abandon the aspirations of the 2011 natural resources strategy that thousands of citizens had worked so hard to develop. Speaking to CBC News, Natural Resources Minister Lloyd Hines said, "In some areas, clear-cutting will not have an impact on the total health of the forest – it may even improve it. In others, clear-cutting could have a negative impact." And, "I'm very proud of the progress we've made."[578]

Gary Burrill, NDP MLA from 2009 to 2013, who was elected leader of the NDP in 2016, believes that the natural resources strategy is one of the most important things the Dexter government accomplished, and points out that it was developed not by bureaucrats behind closed doors but through intensive public consultation. In an interview in his office in March 2017, he tells me he thinks one of the "greatest tragedies" of McNeil's Liberal government is that "they threw the whole natural resource strategy in the garbage." And this, he says, didn't just set forestry in the province back a long way, but also "set democracy back in Nova Scotia."[579]

Raymond Plourde, Wilderness Coordinator at the Ecology Action Centre, sees the Liberal government's abandonment of the strategy as "borderline treasonous," the "usurping and undermining of due public process and the resulting public policy" by the senior bureaucracy in the Department of Natural Resources.[580]

In a letter to Stephen McNeil, environmentalist Geoffrey May said he had a "certain sympathy" with the premier's inability to follow decent forest policies. "The problem," he wrote, "stems from decades of UNB [University of New Brunswick]/Irving forestry school, which has trained most provincial foresters, and most forestry professionals in private and public service. These professional foresters know next to nothing about forest ecology, and have no understanding for forest structure or function. This anti-science, anti-nature forest management that has been pushed by UNB and the Irvings has resulted in reduced forest employment, reduced forest value, and destruction of non-commercial forest products."[581]

Some people familiar with the influence of industry on forest policies on government were not surprised by the Liberal decision to step away from the ideals of the natural resources strategy, which came just after the province quietly negotiated the license with the WestFor consortium to harvest the forests on the recently acquired Crown lands. And few are more familiar with industry influence on the Department of Natural Resources than wildlife biologist Bob Bancroft.

It is mid-June 2016 when I make my way to the home of Bancroft and his wife, artist Alice Reed, near the delightful Acadian village of Pomquet on the Northumberland Shore. Their home is nestled in a small clearing, surrounded by woodlands they have been nurturing back to healthy Acadian forest for many years. Today Bancroft is a well-known and passionate advocate of healthy forests and ecosystems, a popular guest on CBC's *Maritime Noon* where he fields questions about wildlife, a prolific writer of op-eds espousing wiser use of our forests, and a regular speaker at meetings about forestry. Yet for all the frustration conveyed by his words, he always manages to maintain his gentle and patient countenance.

Bancroft worked for many years as a wildlife biologist for

the Department of Natural Resources. For a time after he left government, he tells me that Kimberly-Clark picked him up, but that was a "total botch." "They offered to let me plan the management of 100,000 acres on a trial basis for them," he says. "And it all turned to nothing. It was all window-dressing." He says he wrote a comprehensive plan for the land for them, but nothing came of it and he got out of it. "All they ever did was clear cut," he says.

He has also worked as an assessor for the Forest Stewardship Council, but he believes the standards have been lowered so much that they are becoming "meaningless." Yet even these increasingly lax standards were too much for the Nova Scotia government to uphold on Crown land. Bancroft describes what is going on in the forests of Nova Scotia as a "free-for-all" and a "race to the bottom." "The nearest we can tell is that in the last twenty-five years leading up to 2014," he says, "about 42 percent of the operable forest in this province has been clear cut."

He tells me a trend that began in New Brunswick, in which the big corporations that lease Crown lands also take over their management, is now happening in Nova Scotia. And he cites the example of the WestFor consortium being given the go-ahead to cut the newly acquired Crown lands. "The main player and planners involved are from Northern Pulp," he says. "And they are planning an assault on the middle and western part of the province, 1.4 million acres of Crown land that the government is handing the management over to them."

The lands in question include the counties of Digby, Annapolis, Kings, and all along the South Shore. He quotes a high-level official in the Department of Natural Resources as saying that it would be "world-class forestry." Bancroft takes exception to such claims. "I say it's going to be clear cutting for profit," he says. "That's the last big wood basket. They've pretty well skimmed or skinned the highlands, they've skinned eastern Nova Scotia, and that's why they're trucking all the way from the west now." Bancroft believes there should be a moratorium on clear cutting and says that spraying with herbicides is "a very serious distortion of what nature wants."

"Over the past decade governments have passed out hundreds of millions of taxpayer dollars in subsidies to pulp companies that can't compete financially in declining world markets," he wrote in an opinion piece published in 2016.[582] "Unprotected public forest lands are being degraded by a feeding frenzy of biomass and pulp miners. Wildlife and ecologically healthy forests are disappearing quickly." In his view, the governments of Nova Scotia and New Brunswick are under the grip of industry people "who are using threats of jobs and power."

In late April 2017, the government of Stephen McNeil tabled its budget. In the budget speech was the announcement that the government would "appoint an independent expert to review our forestry practices to ensure we strike the right balance for our forests." And, "No future long-term timber harvesting licences will be awarded on Crown land until the work is complete."[583] Three days later, the premier dropped the writ, calling an election for the end of May.

Although the three large political parties focussed their campaigning mostly on health care and economics, citizens concerned about forestry policies and the environment did manage to get party leaders to respond to their concerns about clear cutting and to their criticism of McNeil's promise of a forestry review. They pointed out that the review was unnecessary given that under the NDP, thousands of people had contributed to the development of the natural resource strategy, and the public had expressed support for a steep reduction – even a ban – on clear cutting.[584] [585] Critics of the review and forest policy under the Liberal government also noted that even if there were to be no new long-term leases on Crown land while the review was undertaken, clear cutting continued without interruption on the province's publicly owned land, even that adjacent to highly sensitive nature reserves.[586]

Around this time, the State of the Forest (2016) report that had been due in 2013 appeared without fanfare on the Department of Natural Resources website.[587] It painted a glowing picture of the forests in the province, contradicting much of what independent experts had been finding on the ground, although it is telling that it stated that 75 percent of the province was covered by "treed vegetation," which can be something very different from a healthy forest or ecosystem.[588]

In the election on May 29, 2017, Stephen McNeil's Liberals won a second majority, albeit a slim one. In August 2017, the government appointed University of King's College president and legal scholar William Lahey to undertake the review, which was due in February 2018. So, as of this writing, it remains to be seen whether the new forestry review will result in continued clear cutting and new long-term leases on Crown land for Northern Pulp and other members of WestFor.

15

The health study that never was

If we allow this injustice without doing all we can against it, what are we worth?

– Anne Perry[589]

Regardless of who owned the mill or which political party was in power, the controversy it generated didn't go away, whether that concerned environmental health or human health or both. In the first decade of the new century, citizens concerned about the mill's environmental record – some of whom had been engaged with the issue for decades – continued to try to hold the government and the mill's owners to account. Much of the concern was about the possible effects that heavy industries in the area, including the mill and also the coal-burning Nova Scotia Power plant in Trenton, might be having on human health.

There was certainly evidence they were not good for some aquatic creatures. In 2008, a scientific study of the common blue mussel (*Mytilus edulis*) kept in cages in Pictou Harbour near untreated municipal wastewater and "bleached kraft pulp mill effluents" were found to have a "significantly greater chance of developing haemocytic leukemia" than did mussels in reference sites without these sources of contamination.[590] Haemocytic leukemia is a fatal disease that affects many kinds of molluscs.

A year later in 2009, Jonathan Beadle of the Pictou Landing First Nation linked up with an environmental group in the area concerned about the coal-burning power generating station in nearby Trenton to get some political and medical support for their environmental causes. They toured Boat Harbour and the power plant with Elizabeth May, leader of Canada's Green Party, who been a candidate the previous year in the Central Nova riding in the federal election.

Also with them was Dr. John O'Connor, who had made headlines in 2006 when he revealed high rates of bile duct cancer in the First Nations community of Fort Chipewyan in Alberta, which he believed were linked to water pollution from the oil sands. After he made his findings public and called for a study into the cancer rates and other health concerns he noted in the area, Health Canada filed misconduct complaints against him and his research was shut down.[591] The charge was dropped, but a few years later, in May 2015, Dr. O'Connor was abruptly fired – by email and without explanation – from the Nunee Health Board Society in Fort Chipewyan.[592]

After his visit to Boat Harbour in August 2009, O'Connor said the facility was "like nothing else on earth. At the very least, this ongoing pollution of these waters contravenes the [federal] Fisheries Act, and it keeps going on."[593] He said the aerators looked like a "chocolate fountain." Elizabeth May was more graphic in her description of what she saw in Boat Harbour, calling it "a sulphurous, festering pond, steaming and clotted with sludge around the edges."[594] She reiterated the call that concerned residents and doctors had been making for two decades, saying that the provincial and federal governments had an obligation to do a review of the health of residents in the area and undertake an air and water analysis.

After their tour, the group spoke at a public forum in the Pictou Landing firehall. Beadle raised the question of why there were no studies of the health situation in his community, noting that pregnant women in Pictou Landing suffered from a high incidence of medical problems. O'Connor said he had grown up in Ireland imagining Canada as a "clean, pristine" country, but then he'd seen Fort Chipewyan and Boat Harbour. "Never in a million years did I think anything like this existed," he said. "It's hell."[595]

Out of this was born another environmental group, the Pictou County Watershed Coalition, which formed just after Dr. O'Connor's visit and brought together some new activists and some who had been fighting the pollution for decades. Among them were Jane Sproull Thomson and Barbara Sproull Seplaki, who, as part of the group from Moodie Cove, had never let up the pressure on their politicians, and had even met with Premier Hamm in 2004 and 2005.

The Pictou County Watershed Coalition would devote the next five years to their campaign to have the authorities pay attention to the pollution in the area, and the effects that the contamination in Boat and Pictou harbours, and in the East, West and Middle rivers, might be having on health.[596] It got widespread support from other groups throughout the province, including the Nova Scotia Environmental Network and the Environmental Health Association of Nova Scotia.[597]

Coalition members set out, as previous groups had done, to convince government to undertake a health study in the area. And as Citizens Against Pollution had done for years, the Coalition organized meetings, wrote countless letters to politicians and to the media, met with mill management, and worked very hard to get government officials to do something about the pollution in the area. In September 2010, when they met with two officials from Northern Pulp, they were assured that $8.5 million was being spent to treat streams from the stacks, which should reduce odour by 75 percent by the fall of 2011. Such promises had been heard before, and would be heard again.

The Watershed Coalition tackled a range of environmental issues, and its spokesperson, Ron Kelly, wrote innumerable press releases and commentaries in the media, and more than a few letters to the provincial NDP Minister of Environment, Sterling Belliveau. One expressed concern about yet another leak that caused a toxic spill in East River and Pictou Harbour.[598] This was just the latest of several previous leaks in the ageing pipeline carrying effluent to Boat Harbour.[599] "While press reports indicate the mill shut down long enough to replace the pipeline," wrote Kelly, "it appears that no attempt has been made to check for leaks through the remainder of this old line where it passes overland" and residents in the area were concerned about the safety of their drinking water.[600]

Another letter informed the environment minister that the Watershed Coalition wanted "the Government of Nova Scotia and the Government of Canada to commission an independent epidemiological study of the health of all residents of Pictou County." The group noted there were many anecdotal indications that the "dirty industries" in the area were causing "the high rates of asthma, Multiple Sclerosis, and a variety of cancers associated with environmental factors in Pictou County," and this was ample evidence that an epidemiological study was urgent.[601] The letter was copied widely; it went to Prime Minister Stephen Harper, Premier Darrell Dexter, leader of the Liberal Party of Canada Michael Ignatieff, leader of the New Democratic Party of Canada Jack Layton, provincial Minister of Health Maureen MacDonald, Conservative MP for Central Nova Peter MacKay, and the three MLAs for Pictou County. The letter pointed out the health study was needed to get "an overall picture of the problems facing residents' health, their drinking water, recreational environment, air quality, and other environmental factors affecting health."[602] Such a study, Kelly wrote, had already been requested by the Pictou Landing First Nation several times.

Belliveau forwarded the letter to Maureen MacDonald, the NDP Minister of Health, who replied to Kelly that she acknowledged the Coalition's request for action "with respect to a health study in your community," and then referred him to representatives of the local district health authority that could "provide the best input and guidance on your request for support."[603] Then she added this wordy mouthful: "Community health experts may be able to provide advice in terms of what is or is not feasible regarding the information you seek about your community and, in turn, will engage the Department of Health Promotion and Protection as deemed necessary."

More than a year later, in November 2010, the Watershed Coalition had a meeting with the Pictou County Health Authority and the environment department. Its members did more than a little homework to prepare for the meeting, researching and documenting the nature of the air and water pollution from the mill, the health problems attributed to these, and compiling a list of crucial questions for which answers were needed.

In a letter to the media after the meeting, Ron Kelly wrote, "Our concerns were met with interest, and a level of surprise. It appeared that no one at the table had ever heard of these health concerns."[604] They followed this up with two more meetings, and at each they reiterated the need for a health study. What they got from the officials was less than reassuring or satisfying, causing the Coalition to write again to the provincial health minister. Their frustration is almost palpable on the page: "After several meetings, it has now become apparent to us that your local officials are simply putting up roadblocks and stalling us, in fact, it appears that the hope is that we will become tired of the process and just 'go away.'"[605]

They then issued a press release pointing out that the NDP government was investing millions of dollars of tax money in the mill even while it was "resisting" their efforts to get government to undertake an epidemiological health study on the effects of pollution from the pulp mill, a request they had been making for three years.[606]

Doctors in Pictou County had been asking for such a study for far longer than that. Even back in the 1960s, Dr. Joe MacDonald had spent a great deal of time writing letters to politicians decrying the mill's air and water pollution and the potential health effects. In 1970, the Pictou County branch of the Nova Scotia Medical Society had endorsed the provincial body's resolution deploring pollution and also expressed "grave concern at the amount of land, air and water pollution in this county particularly, and in Nova Scotia generally."[607]

The concerns about the effect of the mill's emissions on health weren't just limited to Nova Scotia. In 1989, CBC's *Maritime Magazine* program carried a story about residents of Charlottetown, Prince Edward Island, some twenty-two kilometres across the Northumberland Strait from Pictou, who were suffering from bronchitis, stomach problems, headaches, and shortness of breath that they attributed to the emissions from the pulp mill.[608] When they complained to their provincial government, they were told there was nothing it could do because the mill was in another province. Jack Kyte, who handled public relations for the mill, told the CBC reporter, Doug Huskilson, that the emissions met Nova Scotia guidelines and that the company was "spending millions" to reduce the smell.[609]

Requests from the public for answers about the health risks of the mill's emissions and effluent went back twenty years. In the late 1980s, Dr. Daniel S. Reid, a family physician in Pictou, had done a study comparing three years of data on respiratory cases in nine medium-sized hospitals in Nova Scotia.[610] He found the hospital in Pictou had a significantly higher rate of respiratory illness than other similar hospitals in the province. In his paper, published by the *Nova Scotia Medical Journal*, he said pharmacists in Pictou noticed that sales of medicines and devices for respiratory problems, such as inhalers, went down whenever the pulp mill was shut down for repairs or during strikes.

But Reid was concerned about more than just respiratory ailments. His article cited a study done in Michigan that found disproportionately high rates of some cancers among pulp mill workers.[611] He also examined figures from the Cancer Treatment and Research Foundation of Nova Scotia, which showed the highest incidence of total cancers in the province was among males in Pictou County. Excluding skin and in-situ cancers, the rate of cancer among women in the county was second highest in the province. And in his 1989 paper, Reid recommended a further epidemiological study to determine if there was a direct link between the pulp mill's emissions and the high rates of respiratory illness and cancer in Pictou. It never happened.

These days, Dr. Reid is working as a general practitioner and family physician in the Halifax Regional Municipality, more specifically, in Dartmouth. One summer day in 2016, I visit him in his office and steal a few minutes of his precious time to find out more about that paper and his experience as a doctor in Pictou. He tells me that after graduating from medical school in 1970, he went to Pictou to work with three of his classmates in what was then a new little hospital directly across the harbour from the mill. When the wind was blowing towards the town, and particularly on humid or rainy days, the putrid smell would blanket their homes and the hospital. When that happened, he noticed an increase in the number of people showing up with asthma-like symptoms.

Then in the 1974 provincial election, he ran for the Liberal party in Pictou West and won, so he spent the next four years as an MLA, before returning to medical practice in 1978. In 1995, he took another hiatus from his practice, joining the Department of Health for a few years, before picking it up again, this time as a family phyician in Dartmouth.

The study, he tells me, grew out of his concern for the health of his patients in Pictou. It didn't make him very popular with the Department of Environment or even with some people in the town. "When my paper was published," he says, "a lot of my friends and neighbours were very upset with me because they thought I was threatening their jobs." He countered that they could have jobs and clean air and water if the pulp mill were cleaned up like those in other communities, and that would result in lower health costs and improved quality of life.

Together with the local officer of health in Pictou, Reid pushed hard to get the provincial government to act. He and the health officer made presentations to the departments of Environment and Health trying to get them to undertake an in-depth health study. "Just when we thought we were going to have that happen," he says, "the government of the day turned their back on the issue." The health officer was transferred away from Pictou County, and nothing more happened.

He thinks the mill will continue to run as long as there is raw product to run it, then they'll walk away, leaving the people of Pictou and the province to clean up the "bloody mess." "It's a big mess health-wise," he says, "both Boat Harbour and a decimated forest."

Reid is feisty and apparently fearless when it comes to expressing his views on the mill, which he did in September 2014 when he took to the stage to speak at the "Clean The Air" musical concert held in Pictou to protest the mill's pollution. He began by telling an enthusiastic audience that in his twenty-five years of medical practice in Pictou he had delivered 900 Pictonians.[612] He went on to deliver a scathing assessment on the health risks posed by the chemicals in the emissions from the aging kraft mill. Forty years of health data from Pictou County, he said, showed it had among the highest rates of chronic obstructive lung disease, asthma, and kidney cancer in the province. Describing himself as a "lifelong Liberal" he still didn't hesitate to chastise all three major provincial political parties for allowing the environment department to be so weak over years. "It's time for them to buck up," he said, to loud applause. [613]

He criticized the former NDP government of Darrell Dexter, saying that in its dying days before it lost the election to the Liberals under Stephen McNeil, it had made a "sweetheart deal" with Northern Pulp, giving it until May 2015 to clean up an excessive emissions problem that had been going on for the past two and a half years. Then he went after Northern Pulp's board chair, former premier John Hamm.[614] He alleged that Hamm was contravening article seven of the code of ethics for the Canadian Medical Association, which is to "Resist any influence or interference that could undermine your professional integrity."[615] And Reid said to the audience, "Shame on Dr. Hamm for defending the pulp mill. He should resign and he should resign tomorrow."[616]

As for Liberal Premier Stephen McNeil, who had just been in China and met with the owners of Northern Pulp, Reid called on him to "tell all Nova Scotians that a new era is here now, healthy communities and healthy citizens come before foreign corporate welfare bums." And over boisterous cheers and applause, he shouted, "Get on it, Mr. McNeil!"

Dan Reid isn't the only physician deeply concerned about the health risks of pollution in Pictou. Dr. Gerry Farrell, who practised medicine for forty-five years in Pictou County, including many as Medical Director of Palliative Care for the Pictou County Health Authority, also noticed a lot of respiratory illness when he was in family practice in Pictou.

I meet with him one July morning in 2016 in the palliative care unit at the New Glasgow Hospital where, although he recently retired, he's back at work filling in for a colleague taking a short vacation. Farrell is a soft-spoken and thoughtful man, originally from Newfoundland, and there's still a lingering hint of that island's lilt in his words. He came to Nova Scotia in 1981 to join a group of family doctors in Pictou. He says the pulp mill was "certainly an issue with the medical staff." After he moved to palliative care, he saw "tremendous numbers of people with lung cancer" and the incidence seemed to be higher than in other parts of the province and country. But here he pauses and asks rhetorically, "Is that related to the mill?"

This is, of course, the multi-million-dollar question. It's impossible to give a definitive answer for the simple reason that despite all those calls over the years for an epidemiological study that would show whether it is, or isn't, no such study has been undertaken. When I ask Dr. Farrell why he thinks it hasn't, he replies, "For someone to do it independently there's not usually funding for that kind of thing so it's really, if government is concerned about the people they would be the ones funding that and doing it."

He tells me about a photo exhibit in Pictou in 2014 called Clean Air: A Basic Right.[617] The show was the brainchild of Farrell and Marianne Fraser, both of whom are photographers, and they invited people to submit photos to show their different interpretations of the effect that the pulp mill had on them and their lives. One of his photos featured in the show was also on a poster and newspaper advertisement sponsored by two groups actively pushing for change at the time – the Clean Pictou Air Group of Businesses and Clean The Mill. Farrell took the photo one day on the Pictou waterfront when the mill was producing a very bad plume and when he snapped the shutter, he captured for posterity the image of a young boy on his bicycle on the wharf, with the plume behind him looking like a doomsday cloud. He says that photo was picked up by the American environmental activist, Erin Brockovich, who put it on her Facebook page when she took up the cause of a cleaner mill in Pictou.[618] Other photos in the exhibit showed the many houses and buildings for rent or for sale in the town of Pictou, the foul mess in Boat Harbour and the tainted shoreline near its outlet, as well as the one on the cover of this book, provided by Dr. Farrell.

For medical practitioners in the area the mill was a delicate issue. "Because you know they had to support their patients who were making their livelihood at the mill," Farrell says. "But at the same time [they] had to look after them for their illnesses associated with the mill, so it was certainly a conflicted area."

One man who knows a lot about such conflicts, the health risks, and empty houses for sale in and around Pictou is Duncan.[619] His family moved to Pictou Landing when he was eleven, and he lived a couple of kilometres from Boat Harbour until he was eighteen. For his friends in the area, many of them from the First Nation community, Boat Harbour was a playground where they went to hike and bike, even though it was full of toxic waste. "At the time, as kids we knew nothing of how dangerous hydrogen sulphide gases were and there were no real barricades, so we explored," he says. Duncan swore to himself he would never work for a pulp mill, and in his twenties, he studied wastewater treatment by correspondence with a university in the United States. After that he spent some time as a millwright with Michelin Tire in Pictou County, before going back to university for a bachelor's degree.

Fate being the shape-shifting thing it can be, he then found himself working around the globe for pulp mills. "Most paper mills and in fact many pulp mills all over the world generally show a great deal of environmental stewardship these days," he says. "This is not the case for the Abercrombie mill. With the support of local government, each successive owner has seemingly done little to improve the situation without taxpayer money, and even with that the damage is already done and continues unchecked, without transparency."

He says he has no intention of ever moving back to Pictou, despite the fact that he has a lovely house sitting empty overlooking the water in Pictou Landing. Depressed property values in the area mean he's had trouble finding a buyer for it. Today Duncan makes his home in western Canada, which is where he is when we speak on Skype in late July 2016.

He tells me that in 2010, he had decided to settle back home in Pictou County with his family. At the time he figured the pulp mill would be closing down soon because the pulp market was soft and many of the mills in which he'd worked around the world had been shuttered. He says his intention had been to stay in Nova Scotia; he had grown up here and he wanted his kids to grow up here too. So he built the house overlooking the water, started a business and settled down, prepared to stay. But the pulp mill didn't close down and he figures that's because the government handed out so much money in loans.

Then, in March 2014, Duncan's youngest child, just ten months old, was diagnosed with leukemia. Mother and child spent nearly eight months at the IWK Children's Hospital in Halifax, some 170 kilometres away, until the baby's health improved and she went into remission. During that time, Duncan stayed in Pictou to look after his other two children and run his business.

Does he think pollution in the area was a factor in his daughter's leukemia?

"I have no idea, honestly," he says. "I don't know the answer to that. I do know that the government has systematically not tried to find out. They've done everything in their power not to study the issue, not to look at the effect on people. So that tells you something. What are they trying to hide, right?"

He says this was the last straw for him, and even if he still visits his family in Pictou County, it will never be to stay. "I couldn't live there where my kids were breathing this toxic waste on a daily basis, and I know what it is, what I'm doing," he tells me. "If another of my kids got sick with something, I'd never forgive myself, right?" Duncan says that when he was living in Pictou Landing, the worst of the bad air was coming from the mill, but that parts of it regularly got the smell from both the mill stacks and Boat Harbour.

In 2013, the emissions of fine particulate matter (PM 2.5) from the recovery boiler were 78 percent above permitted levels. Particulate matter, Duncan says, is a health risk, causing pulmonary heart disease. "Not to mention the long-term results from hydrogen sulphide gases, which have not been looked at, and the public has no idea of background levels of these poisonous gases from the mill that are concentrated in the flue gas stream, as there are no monitors present."

He says it is erroneous to refer to Boat Harbour as a "treatment facility." "It doesn't actually treat anything other than trying to separate the solids and strip them out, but a large part of that chemical waste goes straight through," he tells me.

He also says the monitoring stations that were set up to keep track of the emissions from the mill were placed in areas where the wind blows the least, and they are just ambient air monitoring stations that were never designed for a pulp mill. I mention to Duncan something that Andrew Younger, formerly Nova Scotia's environment minister in Premier McNeil's Liberal government, told me in an earlier interview.[620]

Younger said there is no reason the pulp mill could not have permanent 24-hour pollution monitoring on all the stacks themselves, rather than the current system which involves tests scheduled by Northern Pulp.[621] Duncan agrees. In his view, every time there is public outcry over the pollution, another "Band-Aid" is applied to keep people quiet. The strategy, as he heard it from a former member of the mill management, is what they call the "3D's: they disorganize, demoralize, and they put people on the defensive." And, he adds, they use diversionary tactics to distract critics.

He says it's a pattern in Nova Scotia, where resources are exported without value adding, aided and abetted by the government, no matter which one or which party. "It's crazy," he says. "We've done it with oil and gas, with our trees, our fishing industry." He continues, "The government is supposed to protect the people. It's the government that's not protecting the people. They just take all their information from the pulp mill verbatim and they just push it down the line and say everything is roses to everybody."

Searching through government documents for information on what comes out of the mill stacks and its effluent pipeline, and how that might affect human health, can be an extremely time-consuming exercise, with far less transparency than one might expect in a wealthy, democratic country like Canada. The federal government's National Pollutant Release Inventory shows that in 2012, Northern Pulp reported it released 1,011 tonnes of fine particulate matter (PM 2.5) into the air, an amount 337,000 percent higher than the threshold level for federal reporting.[622] These threshold levels were derived from the United States Toxic Release Inventory, and anything released above the level must be reported to Environment Canada's pollutant inventory, although Ottawa carefully avoids the issue of whether these are acceptable levels.[623] A scientific review of environmental studies on the Pictou mill determines that "Apparently, no federal or provincial standards for these emission thresholds exist, highlighting that industry standards are insufficient."[624]

Equally remarkable is that the province does not set absolute limits on what the mill can put into the atmosphere every day or every year for some of the more noxious pollutants, including total reduced sulphur or fine particulate matter. Yet in its own Air Quality Report, Environment Nova Scotia recognizes the health risks of fine particulate matter, the particles of which are less than 2.5 microns (a micron being a millionth of a metre) in diameter, so small they "can find their way past our natural defenses (nose hair and mucus) and end up deep in our lungs."[625]

The limits the province does set on sulphur dioxide and total particulate matter are based on a calculation per tonne of pulp output, which, given the mill's production limit of 330,000 tonnes per year, would allow the mill to emit 92,500 tonnes of sulphur dioxide and 165,000 tonnes of total particulate matter each year.[626] [627] The annual limit for emissions of sulphur dioxide for the entire province in 2015 was 119,070 tonnes, meaning Northern Pulp could account for 78 percent of this. In 2014, air emissions from the mill were higher – sometimes two or three times – than similar kraft pulp mills across Canada.[628]

The province's Air Quality Regulations don't cap total emissions of fine particulate matter; rather, they set a "maximum permissible ground level" concentration for a handful of pollutants.[629] And the industrial approval for the mill sets emission limits, as measured over "any 4 hour rolling average" for just two contaminants, sulphur dioxide and total particu-late matter,[630] despite the fact that Northern Pulp reports to the federal government's Pollutant Release Inventory on forty different pollutants that it releases into air or water or both. More perplexing – or worrisome – is the fact that the values reported to the National Pollution Release Inventory are "in-dustry estimates," which scientists say "raises questions about monitoring accuracy." Further, there is "widespread use of dif-ferent units of measurement" and a "lack of standardization" that make it extremely difficult for citizens to compare emis-sions from other mills, and a lack of transparency across the pulp industry.[631]

16

Politics and the power of pulp

The next premier of Nova Scotia will talk a lot about jobs, especially when he announces big "investments" in corporations from away.

– Tim Bousquet [632]

The nature and extent of the mill's pollution, how it is measured and monitored, and what effects it may have on human health are not the only areas where provincial government disclosure leaves a lot to be desired. There is also a problem with transparency when it comes to the matter of public monies. It's almost impossible to calculate the exact dollar value of all the loans, grants, tax breaks, and perquisites the citizens of Nova Scotia, via their governments, have accorded the various owners of the mill. But it's an interesting exercise to try and catalogue the largesse. Shortly after the mill opened in 1967, the owner of *The Pictou Advocate,* George Cadogan, tried to assess the value of a few of those things. [633]

First, there was the expensive infrastructure. The dam across the Middle River built to provide the mill with fresh water cost the province $2 million, and the pumping system another half a million, and these are 1960s dollars, each of which is worth about $8.35 in 2017.[634] The province also paid to acquire land for the mill's effluent facility and to relocate the railway. The causeway cost millions of dollars, and became part of the Trans-Canada Highway, so the federal government and provincial government shared those costs. The pipeline to Boat Harbour cost $2.2 million, and the province also paid to put up the dam to separate it from the Northumberland Strait.

The province provided the mill with vast quantities of fresh – and extremely inexpensive – water, and then took responsibility for the polluted water when it came out its back end. Cadogan noted that if Scott paid even three cents per 1,000 Imperial gallons for water, a common industrial rate at the time, the cost would have been $750 for 25 million gallons per day, nearly $250,000 a year rather than the $100,000 Scott was to pay. In 1988, the Department of Environment calculated that the mill produced 6.8 billion Imperial gallons – close to 31 billion litres – of effluent a year, and paid the province the equivalent of just 50 cents per tonne of pulp it produced, while the going rate in Ontario was five times that amount. Another Scott mill in Michigan was paying more than $2 million a year for effluent treatment while Nova Scotia still charged the mill just $100,000.[635]

Despite the new pressure that climate change was putting on freshwater supplies around the world, in 2016 the government of Nova Scotia backed down on big reductions it had proposed on how much fresh water the mill could take from the Middle River, allowing it to draw 92,310 cubic metres [over 92 million litres] each day.[636] This, even during extremely dry summers such as that of 2016 that led to water use restrictions all over the province.[637] And the same year, the Department of Environment eliminated an earlier requirement that the mill do a sustainability study of the Middle River watershed.[638]

And of course, the people of Nova Scotia will eventually have to pay for cleaning up the mess in Boat Harbour, and assume at least some of the costs, if not all, for an alternate treatment system for the mill. Unbeknownst to the general public at the time, in 1995, there was also the total indemnity that Premier John Savage's Liberal government provided, with legal immunity for any harm caused by the facility to all previous and subsequent owners and their respective "officers, directors, shareholders, employees, agents, consultants, advisors and their respective heirs, successors."[639] Add to that the cost of a couple of hundred consultant reports on Boat Harbour and possible ways of reducing the mill's pollution. And lastly but certainly not least, the province had given the mill's owners access to publicly owned forests on vast swaths of Crown land.

Then there was the financial support, the loans and grants given to the mill – under five separate foreign owners – by two levels of government. In 1970, the province put up a grant of $1.5 million towards a $3-million pollution abatement plan for the mill, owned then by Scott.[640] In 1981, the federal government offered Scott a grant of $364,000 to convert from fuel oil to waste wood products for energy.[641] In 1983, the federal and provincial government gave the mill $7 million under the Canada/Nova Scotia Pulp and Modernization Agreement, of which 80 percent came from Ottawa and 20 percent from Halifax.[642] This was to help Scott undertake a $51-million modernization program, which would involve a precipitator for the recovery boiler and a scrubber for the power boiler to reduce emissions of particulate matter.

In 1993, the province came up with another grant, this time for $17 million, which was to help Scott Maritimes meet new federal government pollution guidelines.[643] Then came the flurry of loans and grants starting in 2009. To recap, there was the $15 million loan to Northern Pulp, owned at the time by Blue Wolf and Atlas Holdings, from the Progressive Conservative government of Rodney MacDonald, just before it was replaced in June that year by Darrell Dexter's NDP government. In March 2010, the NDP government loaned Northern Pulp $75 million to purchase Neenah land, with a gift of $7 million when the province repurchased some of that land at a higher price.[644] In January 2011, just before the mill was sold to Paper Excellence, there was the $28.1 million from the federal government for "green transformation." In January 2013, there was the promise of 125,000 tonnes of green fibre per year from the province.

It continues. In April 2013, NDP Economic and Rural Development Minister Percy Paris announced the province would be refinancing a $5.4 million loan to Northern Pulp from 2009.[645] And it would be providing Northern Pulp with financing worth more than $20 million, of which $2.5 million was forgivable if employment targets were met, although these were not spelled out.[646] The financing included a loan of $3.6 million as well as a "capital equipment incentive of $900,000" – otherwise known as a grant.[647] This money would be used to help pay for a new branch line for Heritage Gas from its Maritime and Northeast Pipeline that carried natural gas from offshore Nova Scotia to the northeast United States, and to help Northern Pulp convert its plant to natural gas.[648] The province was also chipping in $5.2 million towards a $10.2 million chipping mill for Northern Pulp.[649]

There was also $12 million for the installation of equipment that was supposed to reduce the emissions of particulate matter by 80 percent.[650] Yet figures from the National Pollutants Release Inventory show that Northern Pulp's total particulate matter emissions between 2013 and 2014 were not reduced at all; instead, they nearly doubled, going from 1,248 to 2,255 tonnes.[651] And in 2014, Northern Pulp was allowed to emit nearly eleven times more particulate matter from its recovery boiler than was permitted for pulp mills in the United States.[652]

In all, the provincial government had financed Northern Pulp to the tune of $111.7 million in just four years.[653] Together with the federal grant of $28.1 million, Northern Pulp had received nearly $140 million tax dollars since 2009. The rationale for the provincial government support, according to Percy Paris, the NDP minister of economic and rural development, was jobs. "More than 250 families depend on the Northern Pulp mill directly, and hundreds more businesses in this community, and across the province," he said in a press release.[654]

He neglected to calculate how many jobs it cost the province. Robert Langille, president of E & R Langille Contracting in New Glasgow, owned a wood-chipping facility in Pictou County in which he had invested $5 million and where he employed eighteen people. Langille told *The Chronicle Herald* business reporter Roger Taylor that by financing a chipping plant at the mill, the government had forced his independent plant out of business.[655] Worse, he said, when he had applied for a business loan from the government a few years earlier, the government refused to grant the loan saying it would have given Langille an unfair advantage over other chip suppliers.

His was not the only small company hurt by the government's support to Northern Pulp. Another supplier to the mill, the family-run Hodgson's Chipping in Truro, went out of business, which meant the loss of seventy full-time jobs. The company said it had been hurt by the NDP policy to reduce clear cutting; this made forestry operations more expensive, but Northern Pulp had not increased prices it paid for pulpwood. Thus expired the last two independent chipping plants supplying Northern Pulp.[656]

In March 2013, the Pictou County Watershed Coalition called for an audit of the 2011 federal green transformation funding for the mill, which was supposed to have improved the power boiler performance and reduced the odour of emissions.[657] That month the NDP government issued two directives to the mill to reduce its emissions. Tests had found its sulphur and particulate matter emissions had exceeded permitted levels and Northern Pulp was given until September of that year to solve these problems related to the recovery boiler.[658] Northern Pulp's own reporting to the National Pollutant Release Inventory in 2013 showed that emissions of fine par ticulate matter, sulphur dioxide, volatile organic compounds, and carbon monoxide, had actually increased since 2012.[659] Given this performance, the Watershed Coalition found it "infuriating" and "intolerable" that the government continued to pour money into the mill. Another concerned citizen, Rita Wilson, wrote a letter to Premier Dexter and Charlie Parker, MLA for Pictou West, accusing the NDP of supporting "dinosaur" industries, and said she found it "all the more disappointing that it's an NDP government, for which many of us had high hopes."[660]

Nearly four years after this public outcry over the government support for Northern Pulp, I make my way to the home of former minister in the NDP government, Charlie Parker. He lives in the picturesque and historic community of Loch Broom, which is separated from Abercrombie Point by the broad mouth of the Middle River, now nearly completely blocked by the causeway. Parker's long career in politics is over and today he is fully occupied with his real estate business.

He ushers me up a few stairs and into the dining room. The living room windows afford a magnificent view of Lyons Brook across the ice-covered expanse of the West River. Parker grew up on a family farm in this area, before attending teachers' college, doing a science degree at Acadia University, and then becoming a teacher. A child in a staunchly Progressive Conservative family, he says he "saw the light" at university, and first ran as an NDP candidate – unsuccessfully – in the provincial election of 1974, when he was just twenty-three. In 1988, he tossed his cap into the municipal ring and spent ten years as a councillor, before switching to provincial politics in 1999. He ran and won for the NDP in Pictou West in three consecutive elections. After the NDP formed the government under Darrell Dexter in 2009, he spent nearly two years as Speaker of the House, before being given the double duties of Minister of Energy and of Natural Resources.

"It was a full plate, I can tell you," Parker says. At the time, the energy portfolio meant handling the fractious file on hydraulic fracturing ("fracking"), with growing industry pressure for and public opposition to fracking in the province. In the Department of Natural Resources there was also a lot going on, with a new and controversial definition for clear cutting, the pending closures of the pulp mills in Port Hawkesbury and Brooklyn on the South Shore, and pressure from the Pictou mill wanting to get its hands on more Crown land. The problem with air quality around the mill was also really starting to heat up. Citizens were organizing and lobbying for improvement, and Parker says he didn't disagree with them. At the same time, though, he was being lobbied hard by the CEO and management of the mill. "All three MLAs here in the county, no matter what stripe they were ... were heavily lobbied by management," he tells me. Parker says that each time the mill changed hands, first when it was acquired by Blue Wolf and Atlas in 2008, and later when it was sold to Paper Excellence, John Hamm introduced the new management team to the government and minister of the day.

Still, Parker says, he tried to listen to all sides. "I said loud and clear, and I think it caused some ripples within the Department of Natural Resources, but I stood by that, the air quality is unacceptable ... and I said a solution has to be found, and I was saying that to the mill management as well, and anybody who would listen."

I ask him if, looking back, there is anything he might have done differently about the mill.

"I wasn't always in favour of giving them a whole lot of dollars," he replies. "I just think you're buying a solution. I don't know, somehow the corporations have to take some responsibility themselves towards cleaning up their act."

Nevertheless, his government did provide Northern Pulp with "a whole lot of dollars." And some of those it gave during an election year, when yet another swell of protest over the emissions and effluent from the mill was peaking, with the formation of the Clean The Mill group that could count among its members some very prominent citizens.

The politics of the government bankrolling a polluting, foreign-owned mill came to a head in the run-up to the provincial election of 2013. Reflecting on how much of an issue it became, Parker asks, "Did it hurt me politically?" He answers himself. "Probably, somewhat. It probably did hurt me somewhat on the 2013 outcome."

Parker lost the seat he had held for twelve years, and two other NDP MLAs in Pictou County also went down to defeat in 2013. Dave Gunning of the Clean The Mill group thinks there is no doubt the government's support for the mill played a role in that result. He recalls a story that appeared just a few weeks before voting day, on the front page of the New Glasgow paper *The News*, under the headline "Balancing concerns."[661]

It reported that Parker and the two other NDP MLAs from Pictou County had met with the directors of Northern Pulp, including board chair and former premier, John Hamm. The meeting took place on a particularly bad air day, which Hamm blamed on the high humidity and wind, saying when a new precipitator was in place, there would be less particulate matter and the plume would "go up better." Parker was quoted in the story as saying the government was trying to find "a balance between protecting the environment and responsible economy" and the government would be contributing to the upgrades at the mill. Atop the article was a large photograph of the three NDP MLAs – Parker, Clarrie MacKinnon, and Ross Landry – smiling into the camera and standing directly in front of the pulp mill as its stacks belched out emissions.[662]

Dave Gunning found that photo especially galling, and in his view, the NDP support for the mill that it illustrated cost the NDP dearly in Pictou County. All three seats went to Progressive Conservative candidates, while the Liberal Party won the election and formed a new majority government under Premier Stephen McNeil.[663] Charlie Parker's Pictou West seat went to Progressive Conservative MLA Karla MacFarlane.

It's a grey, muggy morning in August 2016 when I head to Pictou to meet with Karla MacFarlane, and we settle at a small table for coffee in her lovely flat just a stone's throw from the waterfront. She tells me she grew up in Three Brooks, just outside of town, and her father worked at Canso Chemicals. She has fond memories of her childhood and says she is very grateful for growing up in a household of loving parents and siblings.

Her father, now seventy-three years old, suffered no health problems after his time at Canso Chemicals. The same was not true for her mother's father, who also worked there. He died at the age of sixty-five, she tells me. Doctors thought that he may have had multiple sclerosis in addition to high levels of mercury and lead, to which they felt the workplace may have contributed. She was a student in Maine back in 1989 when Dr. Reid published his paper calling for an epidemiological study in Pictou County, but remembers people talking about it. And she still hasn't forgotten.

She tells me that in the provincial legislature in 2015 she asked for just such a health study, putting her request to the Liberal Minister of Health. "Obviously, we've been denied," she says. "We're worthy of this, it's been requested before; I know it's expensive and not something done in a year." But, she says, there are good reasons for the study, namely the concerns about Northern Pulp and Nova Scotia Power's coal-fired plant in Trenton. "If there's no fear that nothing is hurting us from these two industries," she asks, "what's the fear in conducting it?" She says that when you tally the amount of money that taxpayers have put into the mill over the decades, the cost of such a study is surely justified.

On becoming an MLA, she also introduced a Clean Air Act, which the Liberal government did not support. She worries that Nova Scotia has some of the weakest environmental laws in Canada, even North America. She would also like to see more and better air monitoring in Pictou, and she has an issue with the way the emissions testing is done for Northern

Pulp. The company schedules the tests and engages a global company called Stantec to do them. Stantec sends the results to Northern Pulp, which then hands them over to the Nova Scotia Department of Environment. "That's truly unfair," says MacFarlane. "No company should have the authority to conduct their own monitoring. It should be independent and the company should not know when it will take place."

In her view, the push for a cleaner mill should not be confused with a push to close the mill. "Those jobs shouldn't be in jeopardy. If the investments were made by the company to follow rules and regulations and regular maintenance, I honestly believe we wouldn't be where we are today," she says. MacFarlane doesn't think that the government should ever be protecting jobs over health, but admits it is a sensitive issue that has divided friends and families. She is refreshingly – and courageously – candid.

She believes if the mill were cleaned up, the business climate in Pictou would improve. MacFarlane speaks from experience. As the past owner of the Ship Hector Company Store on the waterfront, she recalls how tourists would come up and complain about the smell on the clothing, and she would feel obliged to give them a 10 or 15 percent discount. Not the smell of money, rather the smell of lost money.

Other small business owners in town share the same problems, she says. Some wind up going out of business, or just don't open new ones because they fear the pollution and smell. When, a few years earlier, she was trying to sell a bed and breakfast that she ran in Pictou, she lost prospective buyers from England who told her they didn't want to raise their son in that air. They went instead to the community of Parrsboro on the Bay of Fundy.

"It is a very delicate issue," she says. "I've seen some families divide over this, and they're still not speaking, and it's been very difficult to watch those incidents. It is an emotionally charged issue." She tries to keep all channels open, meeting regularly with the mill and also keeping up a dialogue with the Clean The Mill group. "I work for the people, and I've always made that clear – I don't work for Northern Pulp. But I have constituents who work for Northern Pulp that I represent as well," she says, reaffirming that it's about cleaning it up and not closing it down. MacFarlane has difficulty wrapping her head around the fact that one of the world's richest families owns the mill but doesn't invest the money to clean it up. "There's no doubt a feeling that they're [the various mill owners] dictating to our government and always have."

"I can't say there's been one government that's played a better role than the others. Each has made a step trying to improve but nothing ever came to fruition. It all seemed like lip service, leading up to an election."

She says she wants Nova Scotia's leaders to stand up to the companies that want to come and harvest the trees on our land, that it's up to government to make tougher rules and regulations. But for now, she's in opposition and feels the current Liberal government is being dictated to by large corporations. She's disappointed that the government of Stephen McNeil caved to Northern Pulp in negotiations over its new industrial approval. Most of that didn't happen in the legislature, she says: "Most was behind closed doors, and I don't know who was behind the closed doors."

17

A video, social media, and a new movement to clean the mill (2013-2016)

Let us get away from talk, let us do something, let us get to action.

– Otto Schierbeck[664]

There's a charming, unscripted video posted online in August 2013 that features Matt Gunning (brother to Dave), and the siblings Kathy Gregory and Paul Gregory, who are introducing themselves and the Facebook page they've just created.[665] They're talking about the group page called "Clean Up the Pictou County Pulp Mill."[666] They explain they had been discussing the perennial problems of pollution from the mill, and then one day decided to start a Facebook page to try to garner some attention to the issue and as a forum for documentation and research they were undertaking.

They stress their Facebook page is all about cleaning up and not closing down the mill, thank all their followers for their personal stories, promise to keep the page updated, and pledge to get a "Clean The Mill" website developed soon.[667] This video and the Facebook page mark the beginning of something that would become the largest, most wide-reaching citizens' campaign on the mill's environmental impact since it opened in 1967.

One Saturday morning in early September 2016, Matt Gunning and his wife, Bobbi Morrison, squeeze a couple of hours out of their busy lives to tell me more about the group. Morrison is an associate professor of marketing at St. Francis Xavier University in Antigonish, and Gunning works for a vehicle dealership in Stellarton. With two children involved in many activities and their volunteer work with the Clean The Mill group, spare time is not something they have in abundance. But this morning, over coffee and pastries in their spacious and homey kitchen in a Victorian-style house in Pictou, they take some time to tell me how it all came to be.

Even as a kid growing up in Lyons Brook, Matt Gunning says he knew there was something harmful in the pollution from the mill. Later, when he became an avid kayaker, he would paddle from Pictou out past Lighthouse Beach and the mouth of Boat Harbour, then east several kilometres to the beautiful Melmerby Beach. He would always get a bit wet, and noticed that his gear smelled strange when he took this route past the Boat Harbour outlet.

Gunning had been attending meetings of the Pictou County Watershed Coalition, doing some online research about the mill, and paying more attention to the plumes coming from its stacks and the effluent that was going into the Northumberland Strait. He found himself chatting with others in town about the emissions. Everyone seemed concerned, he says, as the emissions got worse and worse: "You felt you could only mention it behind closed doors, and you had to look over your shoulder before you said anything, and I started realizing that most of the town was doing that." And he adds, "At that point, we still had some hope in our government to regulate it."

It was Paul Gregory who took the decisive move to start a Facebook page and add Gunning's name to his. "I thank him and blame him at the same time," Gunning says, "because he realized we would have talked about it forever, and there was just never going to be a good time to decide to commit our lives to it." The Facebook page, he thinks, "lit the fire" that became a powerful citizens' movement – and for the next couple of years, it took over their lives.

Morrison was still writing her PhD dissertation at the time, so she didn't get fully drawn into the movement until she completed it in September 2013. Till then, she says, "I was one of those really naïve people that thought, yeah, it stinks, yeah, it's atrocious to look at. But they wouldn't be doing it if it wasn't okay, because our government protects us, because the Nova Scotia Department of Environment has rules, and they tell the companies what they can emit. This isn't some Third World country." When her husband started showing her evidence that suggested the government was not protecting the population, she began delving into the mill story herself. "And we started asking questions and started asking the government for more information," she tells me. "The more we learned, the more we realized how unprotected we are."

They began to document their findings and then set up the Clean The Mill website where they posted them. They found that in 2013, Pictou County had the highest incidence of cancer in Nova Scotia, which in turn has the highest incidence of all ten Canadian provinces. Deaths from respiratory disease in the county were also the highest in the province, which again had higher rates than the national average.[668] Cardiovascular disease in Pictou County also exceeded the provincial incidence rate, and the group provided references showing links between cardiovascular mortality and pulp mill chemical exposures among employees.

They didn't stop there. They posted the 2008 findings from the Pictou County Health Authority showing that the rates of stillbirths and infant deaths were both significantly higher in Pictou County than elsewhere in Nova Scotia. They noted there was scientific evidence showing that pulp mill effluent had reproductive effects on fish, reducing levels of sex steroid hormones, size and fertility of gonads, altered secondary sex characteristics, and delayed sexual maturity.[669] And they found that Pictou County had a highly unusual gender ratio of births; for every girl born there were 1.26 boys, while the provincial average was 1:06, very close to the global average. While the Clean The Mill group could not prove a direct link between any of these health issues and the pulp mill, they did locate and cite studies that indicated possible relationships, and very compelling reasons for the government to undertake that epidemiological study that doctors and citizens had been asking for since 1989.

They also scrutinized all the repeated claims the government and the mill made about its economic value to the province. Their analysis of government support between 2009 and 2013 led them to three surprising conclusions. First, "The yearly average of $32 million received in government funding compensates for the mill's losses, thereby functioning as a subsidy to keep the mill in business." Second, they alleged, "With a loss of $24 million/year, Northern Pulp is not contributing corporate tax dollars directly to the province." And lastly, they determined, "Although the Nova Scotia taxpayer is not a direct shareholder of the mill, the subsidies provided by the province suggest that the Nova Scotia taxpayer has a vested interest in the operations and profitability of the facility over and above the health and environmental impact."[670]

They pointed out there had never been a "full cost accounting" of the impact of the mill on the community, which included possible costs of depressed property values, negative effects on other industries such as tourism and the fisheries, and on health, and the true value of those tens of millions of litres of fresh water turned to wastewater every day.

Another area they investigated was the extent to which the mill's effluent and emissions were being monitored. They reported on an undated document from the Department of Environment which stated that toxic sludge from Boat Harbour was being burned as biomass in the mill, and a contradictory statement from the mill saying it was being spread on mill property. A Department of Environment official confirmed in 2017 that both are true, that there was a "small test burn" of "wood fibre from one of the settling ponds" in Boat Harbour in the 1990s, but now the fibre dredged from the settling ponds "is disposed of at the regulated landfill on the Northern Pulp property at Abercrombie Point."[671]

Again, the lack of transparency over the years and the lack of information available on the composition of the mill's effluent led to questions about the way the monitoring was being done and the lack of public access to the results.[672] The activists from the Watershed Coalition and Clean The Mill group uncovered a consultant's report that laid out an Air Management Plan for Northern Pulp, which stated the wet scrubber on the mill's power boiler, key to reducing emissions of particulate matter, had been out of commission since 2006.[673] The report was from 2009, so the province should have known and acted immediately. The Department of Environment did finally issue a directive to the mill to fix this problem, but not until February 2012, as one of the still unmet conditions it had imposed when it extended the company's operating permit for two years in 2011.[674] A freedom of information request by investigative journalist Miles Howe showed this was the very first directive the environment department had given the mill on air or boiler emissions in twenty-three years.[675] Rather than impose a fine on Northern Pulp, the environment department gave the mill until April 2013 – more than a year – to fix the problem, while the NDP government kept giving it loans and grants throughout this period.

Clean The Mill complemented their research work with an online petition and public meetings, and earned increasing media attention, even reaching out to and attracting support from the internationally known environmental activist Erin Brockovich.[676] Their ads in local papers showed the steaming, discoloured, and frothy contents of Boat Harbour, and posed the question: "How much industrial pollution is okay?"

Getting all that information, Morrison tells me, was not easy. The whole group contributed immense amounts of energy and their own time to the research, the very research that she believes elected governments and public civil servants should be doing.

"No matter who's in power, they've given money to the mill," she says. "It boggles my mind." She recalls a day a few years ago when her children, who were attending Pictou Elementary School, came home and told her that the school library was being closed; there wasn't enough money to keep it running. And the very next day the NDP made an announcement down on the waterfront in Pictou that Northern Pulp was going to get more than $20 million, she says. It made her furious that they would be taking books away from children in the province while supporting an industry that was polluting their air and water.

When I ask Morrison and Gunning how much of their time they have devoted to the research and campaigning, Morrison sighs and says it's hard to quantify. "It feels as if it's taken over completely." From 2013 until early 2016, she says some members of the Clean The Mill movement were spending at least twenty hours a week working on it, and the rest of the time thinking about it. One summer, she says, her family headed off for a vacation in Cape Breton, their intention being to take a break from it all. Even then, she recalls their children piping up from the back seat, pleading with their parents: "Could you just not talk about the mill for five minutes, please?" Morrison says she came home from that vacation with a cell phone bill of several hundred dollars because she spent most of it "dealing with the mill stuff."

Matt Gunning spent so much time doing research, or on the phone doing interviews or discussing the mill, that his car dealership in Pictou suffered. He's aware that some in Pictou believe his activism – or "factivism" as he calls it – cost him his business, and that some in the mill might even claim it as a victory. Gunning says a Paper Excellence executive sent him an email "almost gloating" when he closed down his business in Pictou. But Gunning says he moved immediately to a good job in a large dealership in nearby Stellarton, where, he says, he has sold quite a few cars to mill employees. On the whole, they have received largely positive feedback for their efforts. He is intensely aware of the importance of the mill for those whose livelihoods depend on it, adding that from his house he can see the homes of five mill employees.

Gunning believes there have been efforts to make it look like the group wants to close rather than clean up the mill, which he reiterates is simply not true. "It's a difficult conversation to have," he says. "Pictou County is showing all the signs of an abused spouse, you know, forced into silence. So the group's work to launch what he calls the "awkward conversation" has brought out a lot of emotion, sadness, anger, sometimes even hatred. There were those who feared their jobs might be at risk and others who blamed the mill for illnesses, some of them employees themselves. Still, he expected more negative feedback than he's received.

Morrison believes the use of social media has been an invaluable tool that allowed people to share information and voice their concerns. There were, Gunning says, a few fake accounts and trolls earlier on, but the administrators do not censor posts on the Facebook page unless they are racist or outright threatening. "The community deserves an awful lot of credit," says Morrison. "They did the reading and learned an awful lot of things very quickly and when you can do that, then the trolls don't have any power."

Whether it was the use of social media, the quality and quantity of the research findings posted on the website, or just growing public concern and anger over the foul air and water despite all the millions of dollars of public financing to improve the situation, the Clean The Mill group gained a good deal of traction over the next year and eventually, politicians began to recognize the need to respond.

It seemed, initially, as if the new Liberal government of Stephen McNeil was listening. The new premier came in talking tough. In January 2014, at a luncheon at the Halifax Club, he announced that Northern Pulp had approached the Department of Natural Resources for a bailout just before the provincial election, a request that included a guarantee of an extra half million tonnes of green fibre, a forgivable loan of $10 million, and funding for equipment that would have cost about $30 million. McNeil said he had turned it down. "We made it very clear there would be no forgivable loans under our administration, so that was off the table before we started," he told the media. He said his government would stick to his campaign promise not to bail out companies and then call it economic development. "If private sector investors aren't prepared to invest," he said, "we seriously have to ask why are we."[677]

The announcement and the new tone was part of an unprecedented bout of public sparring between the provincial government and Northern Pulp. Shortly before McNeil made his announcement, Don Breen, the mill's manager, had denied the company had made a request for financial support. McNeil countered that this wasn't true, and he was "unhappy" about that report, that it didn't "help the public conversation."[678]

McNeil's comments about Boat Harbour encouraged Matt Gunning and other members of the Clean The Mill group.[679] Gunning was "cautiously optimistic" about McNeil's talk of cleaning up the mill's effluent site. When it came to access to the people's forests, however, McNeil seemed more open to compromise. He had honoured the promise made by the previous NDP government to give Northern Pulp access to an additional 125,000 green metric tons.[680]

And people with concerns that the pulp industry had undue influence on forest policy in the province thought there were worrying signs. There was the hiring in April 2014 of the former woodlands manager at the now-defunct Bowater mill in southern Nova Scotia, as executive director of the renewable resources branch in the Department of Natural Resources.[681] Biologists Bob Bancroft and Donna Crossland were very critical of the appointment. "This is of grave concern to me," Crossland told Michael Gorman of *The Chronicle Herald*. Like Matt Miller at the Ecology Action Centre, Crossland expressed fears about the future of the recently acquired Crown Lands. Bancroft said it was a case of industry wagging the government.[682]

But when it came to cleaning up the mill itself, the Clean The Mill group was stepping up the pressure, and for a time, it looked as if there might be some progress. The Department of Environment's inspection specialist had issued two more directives since the one in 2012 demanding the installation of pollution equipment on the power boiler.[683] One from March 2013 said emissions tests in the fall of 2012 exceeded allowed levels of particulate matter and total reduced sulphur; it gave Northern Pulp until the end of September that year to reduce these emissions.

Later that year, the department again flagged excessive total reduced sulphur, and this time gave the mill until April 2014 to provide it with data on emissions of these compounds and inform the province of what it was doing to remedy the problem. The department's apparent lack of detailed information on what Northern Pulp was doing to curb its emission of some very noxious pollutants and the lack of a penalty were remarkable. It prompted journalist Miles Howe to ask, "Why set limits at all?"[684]

The mill, meanwhile, sent out soothing messages. In June 2014, Northern Pulp announced they were "breaking ground" on the new precipitator for their recovery boiler, a project that would cost $21 million, of which more than half – $12 million – was coming from the provincial government.[685]

The Clean The Mill group responded with a brochure bearing the headline "Just another one of 'those days' in Pictou," superimposed on a photo of the historic downtown, shrouded in what looks like dense fog. The pamphlet was full of damning quotes from visitors to Pictou from various online sites that decried the "disgusting" or "rank" or "foul" stink from the mill.

There was another burst of negative publicity when, in mid-June 2014, there was a major effluent leak from the pipeline at Pictou Landing, which led to a shutdown of the mill and a blockade by the First Nations community and others from the area.[686] This led to more discussion, and another bout of déjà vu, on when and how Boat Harbour would be closed down, and who would pay for the clean-up and an alternate treatment facility. The former was clearly the responsibility of the province that had indemnified the pulp mill for cleaning up the treatment facility back in 1995. But when he was asked if the province would have to pay for a new treatment facility for the mill, Premier McNeil told the media, "Not to my knowledge."[687]

In July 2014, the groundswell of discontent gained more momentum when the local business community joined the chorus of those calling on the government and Northern Pulp to do something about the pollution, and came together as the Clean Pictou Air Group of Businesses. The local media regularly printed letters from disgruntled citizens and tourists, calling on the government and Northern Pulp to close the mill while the problem was fixed. An editorial in *The Advocate* by Steve Goodwin, who had reported on the mill for years, said it was time to "remedy a nearly 50-year-old wrong."[688] Dr. Gerry Farrell wrote a letter saying "enough is enough" and "Surely our health is more important than making money for Northern Pulp's shareholders living far away from the pollution it is presenting to us daily."[689]

The Clean Pictou Air Group of Businesses asked for a meeting with Environment Minister Randy Delorey, Health and Wellness Minister Leo Glavine, and Economic and Rural Development and Tourism Minister, Michel Samson.[690] Anne Emmett, who ran the beautiful Braeside Inn on the Pictou waterfront, told the media the businesses involved in the group merely wanted to run their businesses "unencumbered by air pollution." Members of Clean The Mill met with the business owners, shared information with them, and joined forces to promote their cause of a cleaner mill.

Among those involved in the Clean The Mill group were some prominent business people. President of WearWell Garments Ltd. in Stellarton, Stirling MacLean, wrote personally to the Minister of Environment.[691] In his letter, he points out his company employs 100 people, and he would love to open a factory outlet store in Pictou, but it would be impossible to do so as the smell from the mill would mean the outlet "would be doomed to fail." "Northern Pulp is ruining the livelihoods of thousands of people in Pictou County," he wrote, "not to mention potentially seriously affecting the health of all community members (including many of my own staff), and the Provincial Government supports this practice."

The meeting between the two groups working for a cleaner mill and the three provincial ministers took place on July 16, 2014, at the Braeside Inn. Health Minister Glavine admitted there were some health concerns around the emissions of particulate matter, saying, "It's an issue that the Department of Health must take a look at."[692]

A scant two weeks after the meeting, Environment Minister Delorey dashed hopes that the government was going to take the side of the concerned populace and business owners. Delorey told the CBC that although it was clear the pulp mill was malfunctioning, he had no intention of forcing it to close, and declared, "To date the conclusions that they've made are that there isn't an imminent threat to human health."[693] He didn't identify the "they" who made these conclusions. A spokesperson for the mill said the company was having "logistical" issues bringing in a new precipitator for the recovery boiler, but hoped one would be installed by May 2015.[694] He said if the mill were to shut down in the meantime, it would probably not reopen. Delorey said he was content to live with the mill's timeline to fix the problem.

These statements did not go down well with the public.

Anne Emmett told *The Chronicle Herald* that the mill should be closed down and not reopened until the problem was fixed.[695] Around this time a member of one of Canada's best-known business families had joined the fray, taking aim at the mill and its pollution. Paul Sobey, who had recently retired as CEO of Empire Co. Ltd., told CBC news that the mill's emissions were "criminal."[696] In an interview on CBC's *Mainstreet* program, he said if the mill could not fix its problems, "the government of Nova Scotia is going to have to turn around and protect the health of the people of the province."[697] In a film called *Defenders of the Dawn: Green Rights in the Maritimes*" by filmmaker Silver Donald Cameron, Sobey said pollution from the mill was a "horrific problem for the community."[698]

An email from Northern Pulp to the New Glasgow paper, *The News*, took issue with Sobey, saying that while, "[w]e respect Mr. Sobey's opinions, we have a different view."[699] Then Peter MacKay, MP for Central Nova, Canada's Attorney General and Minister of Justice, added his voice, saying he trusted the decision by Environment Minister Delorey.[700] Three years earlier, MacKay had announced the large federal grant to Northern Pulp for the "green transformation," which Northern Pulp had said would reduce odour emissions "by at least 70 percent."[701] At the time, it was said the investment would benefit "visitors and tourists who visit Pictou County to enjoy all that the region has to offer" and Northern Pulp was to be "doing detailed engineering on the odour emissions project" and "upgrading the mill's boiler to make it cleaner and more efficient which helps improve the mill's operational efficiencies and environmental performance," both of which would be completed by the end of 2011.[702]

Or not.

Three years later, with public outrage over the mill's emissions reaching a crescendo, MacKay released a statement saying while he shared concerns about the health and environmental impacts of the mill, he believed they posed no threat to human health and that this was based on sound research.[703]

On the same day, CBC News published a story saying both the government and Northern Pulp acknowledged the emissions were "well above the legal limits," that the most recent emissions test undertaken the previous November showed levels of particulate matter exceeded limits by 78 percent. And a Nova Scotia Department of Environment engineer admitted it "absolutely could be possible" that the air was now worse than it had been when the tests had been done.[704]

18

Discord, debate, and déjà vu (2014)

One of the real shames that people don't talk about when it comes to Northern Pulp is that there are a lot of skilled workers ... there, that work hard, some of them have put in a lifetime there, and it's really unfair to them the fact that they are led to believe that everything's fine when it's not.

– Terry Mosh Dunbrack,
Clean Up The Pictou County
Pulp Mill Facebook Group[705]

The campaigns to clean the mill didn't go unchallenged. One of those who went to its defence was Don MacKenzie, the president of Local 440 of Unifor, the union that represented 220 mill employees. In an interview on Halifax CBC's *Information Morning*, MacKenzie denied the odour from the emissions was a common topic among workers at the plant.[706] He said he was "getting mixed messages" from the people in the community who were making waves about the mill's pollution. "We're not sure what their goal is," he told host Bob Murphy. "And we find it frustrating sometimes that their opinions, we believe, are based on not all the correct information, or in some cases, maybe they've been misinformed."

Murphy replies, "Well, they want the air cleaned up, that's the main goal here, right? They don't want to see the mill shut down, but they do want this corrected?"

MacKenzie answers, "Well, I believe some of them want the plant shut down, not all of them." He goes on to say the mill has "always followed the laws of the land" and the new owners "try to meet compliances and the regulations."

Then comes a lively back and forth between host and interviewee.[707] Murphy asks, "But they do admit their emissions are beyond standards now?" MacKenzie replies the mill owners have "dumped in excess of $150 million and one of those big projects towards being what we call compliance and following the laws of the land as related to the precipitators which will cost over $20 million ..."

Murphy interjects here. "And a large part of that is paid by taxpayers' money? That $20 million bill?"

MacKenzie wants clarification. "For the precipitators?" Murphy confirms and MacKenzie responds, "I don't believe that's correct. The $150 million that I speak about, that came from the new owner."

Murphy: "Right, but my understanding is that the provincial government is helping to pay for part of the new precipitator?"

MacKenzie: "I'm not sure about that."

The confusion about the figures was hardly surprising. There had been numerous confusing and contradictory reports about just how much the province loaned or gave the mill in April 2013, and what the funding was for. According to one, the province was financing more than half the cost of the new precipitator with a loan of $12 million.[708] A press release from the Department of Economic and Rural Development and Tourism stated that of the $14.7 million repayable loans and $2.5 million forgivable one announced on April 5, 2013, $5 million would go towards "new environmental technology" to "significantly reduce air particulates" and that the new equipment would cost $12 million.[709] And in 2015, another government press release announced it was making the final disbursement to Northern Pulp from the $21.7 million in loans and earned incentives under its jobs fund, of which $12 million was for the precipitator.[710] So MacKenzie can hardly be faulted for being unclear about how much the people of the province would be contributing to the cost of the new precipitator.

After this, Murphy pushes MacKenzie on whether he, as a union rep, is concerned about the health effects of the plume of emissions from the mill, and whether the union does any research when it comes to health concerns.

"Well, you read some of the comments that people say that, you know, it causes cancer," MacKenzie replies. "I'm not a scientist. I'm not a doctor, I don't know ... But I know that in the mill, I've worked there for quite a number of years, and probably since the mill opened in 1967, there's probably been 800 full-time employees worked there ... there's hundreds of them retired in the community, you know, we've had some people but to try and say it's definitely been caused by the mill, I don't see the scientific reports."

The defence of the mill from a union representative was quite a turnaround from earlier days. In 1970, the union that represented the mill workers, the International Brotherhood of Pulp, Sulphite and Paper Mill Workers, had been openly critical of the "devastating ecological effects" of the mill's pollution.[711]

As the summer of 2014 wore on and heated up, so did the debate over the mill's emissions, which was now attracting national media attention. In an interview on CBC's *As It Happens*, David Kerr, vice president of operations for Paper Excellence Canada, maintained the emissions from the stacks were "as best controlled as we can control them" and he stated, "The air is good. There's no plume heading toward Pictou. It's heading towards the north ... there are days when atmospheric conditions cause the plume to fall down onto the harbour."[712]

Progressive Conservative and opposition leader Jamie

Baillie told reporter Steve Goodwin that he was "increasingly alarmed at how local residents are being cornered into making a false choice between good jobs and a healthy environment."[713] And, taking aim at Premier McNeil's earlier claims that he would not be financing private industries in the name of economic development, Baillie said, "Continued inaction by the government is as much of a subsidy for the mill as if they had handed the owners a bucket of taxpayer cash."

Concerned citizens, many identifying with no specific campaign or group, gathered no fewer than three times on the streets of New Glasgow to demand an end to the mill's pollution.[714] Confusion abounded about just what was going on in the mill, why the pollution had become so intense.

Natalie Gordon, born and raised in Pictou County, was working at the time with a local, family-owned FM radio station doing news and hosting a weekly interview show. She tells me, when I visit her in July 2016 in Trenton where she is now living, that she'd never seen the pollution as bad as it was in the summer of 2014. One particular evening is etched in her memory. She had come home from work and fallen asleep on the couch beside an open window in her apartment in Pictou, looking right across at the mill. "I woke up and couldn't see across the room," she says. The air "was completely full like a fog." She moved to her bed, and awoke in the morning, sicker than she'd ever been in her life.

"The only way I can describe it is like I had a chemical burn right down into my lungs ... like it was stripped and burned, and I had trouble breathing and my mind wasn't clear," she said. When she went to work, she could no longer function or even remember passwords she'd used for years, or use the software she used every week for her radio show. Gordon had to take time off, and her doctor advised her to move out of Pictou, which she did. But she was still depending on puffers and having trouble breathing, so in December she left her job and headed to Mexico, where she now spends half the year. Gordon admits that personally she'd like to see the mill closed, but she's also painfully aware of the importance of jobs in the area. She says it's a "crime" that no study has ever been done to determine how much income and how many jobs have been lost in the county because of the mill, and how it might have grown in both residency and tourism, because Pictou was, she says, "a jewel."

The pollution coming from Northern Pulp also took up a great deal of ink in the province's daily paper, *The Chronicle Herald*. On August 23, 2014, it was the subject of the editorial cartoon, two half-page opinion pieces, and two of the paper's prominent columnists also devoted their contributions to the controversy swirling around the mill. Roger Taylor chastised the provincial government for its environmental legislation that was bent to "accommodate industry" and he asked tough questions about the public money that had been lavished on Northern Pulp and why the precipitator had not been installed years earlier.[715]

In August 2014, CBC News reported that the man who had been Northern Pulp's lawyer in charge of environmental compliance for years, Bernie Miller, had in February been named Deputy Minister of Priorities and Planning, having been "hand-picked by Premier McNeil to handle his government's most sensitive files."[716] But Premier McNeil said that after his appointment, Miller was not part of any discussions about the mill: "Things that we've been doing with Northern Pulp have been completely isolated from Bernie."[717] From 2009 until 2014, Bernard F. Miller was registered as an active lobbyist for Northern Pulp with the government of Nova Scotia.[718]

In Pictou itself, staunch supporters came forward to urge the government not to do anything to jeopardize the mill's future. Andy MacGregor, fabrication manager of MacGregors Industrial Group in Pictou County, wanted a "less emotional perspective" on Northern Pulp and argued there was a great deal at stake if the mill were shut down, including "lost jobs and decreased pensions, lost population, increased taxes and a local community unable to sustain itself."[719] He wrote that

Paper Excellence had "injected $150 million" into the mill, without specifying how much of that was public loans and grants. He also said that in a year, the mill put $204 million into the provincial economy.

And so the battle of words and wills raged on, as it had decade after decade. The pollution persisted; the mill continued to ask for time to correct the problem. And the public continued to pressure for immediate action, many of them using the Clean The Mill Facebook page as an outlet for their thoughts, often their frustrations, and sometimes also their anger.

Dave Gunning had joined the Facebook page early on, and then registered the Clean The Mill website. He figured that if anyone were considering instigating legal action against the other campaigners, he would be well placed to deal with it. In 2012, Gunning had taken on the Royal Canadian Mint, which had accused him of copyright infringement because the artwork on the cover of his album *No More Pennies* showed images of the Canadian penny, which the Mint had just stopped producing.

The Mint said he could sell the first 2,000 copies of the album for no charge, but for the next 2,000 copies he would be expected to pay $1,200. Gunning took it all in his stride, and asked his fans to donate pennies at his concerts, which he would bundle up and send to the Mint in Ottawa. After a great deal of negative publicity, the Mint backed down, and Gunning said he would donate all the pennies he'd received to the IWK Children's Hospital in Halifax. An unassuming musician and songwriter he may be, but Gunning was not afraid to confront the powers that be – whether that be the Canadian Mint or Northern Pulp or the provincial government.

The Clean The Air concert he organized in September 2014 on the Pictou waterfront would have as its backdrop the mill and its plume, as they are for us when we sit on his front veranda in June 2016 to talk about the Clean The Mill group, and what it's all meant to him and his family, and the concert.[720]

"I reached out to some buddies of mine," he tells me. "And everybody said yes immediately. We could have done three concerts!" A trucking company transported the stage for free, and the stage was donated by the Stan Rogers Folk Festival that is held each year in Canso, Nova Scotia, while supporters in Halifax provided the sound and lighting free of charge. "I think we probably had 3,000 people through the gate," he says, and local media also used this figure.[721] But, he adds, "The next day, there were troll accounts on the Facebook page saying what a failure it was, claiming that there were only 300 people in the field."

It was at this concert that Dr. Dan Reid had so stridently criticized Dr. John Hamm, and Gunning says there was a little pushback from one local politician because of this. But he says, if his brother Matt's role is to be calm and to collect all the documents, he sees his own role as more of an outspoken activist who tackles people who "won't miss a meal if the mill closes," and who have staunchly supported the mill, whether it's John Hamm or former mill spokesperson and current executive director of the Pictou County Chamber of Commerce Jack Kyte.[722]

Like his brother, Dave Gunning says the experience has been intense. Remembering the summer of 2014 when the emissions were particularly bad, he says, "There would be days I would sit on this porch and I couldn't see the road. And then I would drive by a schoolyard and I'd just get frustrated ...." Here, he stops, his voice cracks and he seems surprised himself at how distressing he finds the memories. He recalls driving past Pictou Academy and seeing kids outside playing baseball and running in the fog of smog, which contained particulate matter from the mill. "I would post this on Facebook," he says, "and another post would come in from a mill worker bragging about how they had just broken all production records that month."

When they started the campaign, Gunning believed they would make a lot of enemies, but he says that hasn't happened.

He's made new friendships, not least Jonathan Beadle, whom he now views as a "brother," and who has done press photos for him.[723] He tells me that sometimes if he's shopping at Sobeys in Pictou, people approach him to say thank you for all the hard work. And on another positive note, he says the activism has inspired his writing; three songs on his internationally acclaimed album *The Lift* have their roots in the Clean The Mill struggle.

But for all Gunning's determined positivity, he's had to withstand a good deal of nastiness aimed his way, especially by a very few followers of the Facebook page who send or post insulting messages – some privately and some public – to him from time to time. His wife and family have not been immune from it all. Sara Delong Gunning admits it's not been easy, the sadness she feels for him when he's on the phone or locked away somewhere handling Clean The Mill work, and missing out on experiences with his family and kids. "But he's doing something he's passionate about," she tells me one lovely summer day in 2016 when we meet to speak, while her husband takes one of their sons to a nearby pond to swim.

She says feedback about their efforts is often positive; the family will be out in public and people will come up and whisper in her ear that they are very proud of what Dave and Matt are doing for the pulp mill, but they don't want anyone to hear them say it because it's such a divisive issue in the community. And sometimes it's a difficult balancing act. A case in point, she tells me, was the Clean The Air concert. "At the end of the concert Dave said something like 'we don't want to see the mill shut down, we don't want to see people lose their jobs, we want it to meet requirements and standards, we want it cleaned up.'"

By walking the fine line, however, he earned criticism from people on both sides of the issue. "It's hard to win," she adds, "because there are so many divisions in the community, with the people who want to pretend there's nothing wrong with it, those that want to see it gone, and people who would like to see it cleaned up."

Like her husband, Delong Gunning falls into the latter group. She is well aware of the problems with the pollution, and recalls all too well watching her sons at a piping-and-drumming camp on the Pictou waterfront one summer, taking deep, deep breaths to play the bagpipes, while she contemplated all that smog going into their "little pink lungs." She has the same concerns, she says, when the plume from the mill blankets the playground at the school where she teaches, and she wonders if the kids would be better off if recess were held inside. But they always strive for balance on the issue, she says.

The work of the Clean The Mill group, combined with that of the Clean Pictou Air Group of Businesses, struck a powerful chord with the public and in the community. For the first time in the nearly forty years since the Northumberland Strait Pollution Committee campaign was at its peak, the local papers filled up with opinion pieces about the mill.[724] Journalist Steve Goodwin at *The Advocate* wrote an editorial saying the Clean The Air concert had "real meaning" and that the people needed "one government to quit stalling and act on this file. Installation of real monitors with the real facts in this day and age is not a lot to ask."[725]

The work of the activists inspired eighty-three-year-old Ella Langille to write a letter to the editor, saying she stood with the group "150 percent" and she urged them to continue: "Don't give up; stand your ground and hold fast."[726] A medical doctor in Pictou, Dr. Catharina Felderhof, who had served the Pictou Landing First Nation for twenty years, wrote a piece saying she had witnessed "the consequences of the bad choices our politicians/leaders have made in allowing Northern Pulp to continue to pollute the air, soil and water first hand, very close up."[727]

The concert created a good deal of media buzz, as did the photo exhibit "Clean Air: A Basic Right" organized by Marianne Fraser and Dr. Gerry Farrell, when it opened at the deCoste

Centre in Pictou in September 2014, before being moved to the Museum of Industry in Stellarton. Once again, letter writers got busy, decrying the absence of MLAs, mayors, councillors, and wardens at the opening of the exhibit, and that only two MLAs and the mayor of New Glasgow bothered to send regrets.[728] Although several prominent people with Northern Pulp were invited, none showed up.[729]

Concerned citizens were still waiting to see what the government was going to do, following Premier McNeil's trip to Shanghai that September, where he met with representatives of Paper Excellence, including deputy CEO Pedro Chang, vice president of operations David Kerr, and chairman Jackson Widjaja.[730] A media report quoted McNeil as saying, "I reiterated the province's position and made it clear that they are expected to fully comply with the environmental laws of Nova Scotia or be shut down."[731]

19

Industrial approval ... and disapproval (2014-2016)

Nova Scotians deserve the same air quality protections afforded in other jurisdictions and if NSE [Nova Scotia Environment] is not prepared to bring this province in line with global emissions limits, they must be prepared to explain that decision to the public.

– Bobbi Morrison[732]

Then it was time to renew Northern Pulp's industrial approval, which would set the conditions for its continued operations. As part of the process, the company was obliged to hold public consultations, with a deadline for public input of November 7, 2014. The Clean Pictou Air Group of Businesses and Clean The Mill sponsored a newspaper ad, urging anyone concerned about "high emission levels, relevant monitoring, regular testing, waste treatment, or the proper enforcement of regulations" to speak their minds. The ad featured quotes from five doctors in the area.[733] It also said that in 2012, Northern Pulp was responsible for 63 percent of all the particulate matter 2.5 in Nova Scotia, more than all other industries combined and more than twice as much as any other pulp mill in the country. And it noted that particulate matter is carcinogenic to humans and that since 2010, Northern Pulp had repeatedly failed stack tests for particulate matter.

Northern Pulp held two open-house sessions, which led to more back-and-forth in the media, with some citizens calling the consultations a "snow job," while others defended the mill. One letter-writer called the protestors' advertisement "fear mongering" and said he was disturbed to see local doctors endorsing the claims in the newspaper ad.[734]

In early November 2014, Dave and Matt Gunning, accompanied by Dr. John Krawczyk, former chief of staff at the Aberdeen Hospital in New Glasgow and a child and adolescent neuropsychiatrist, earned headlines when they delivered the results of an independent environmental report on the soil and water of Boat Harbour to the Pictou office of the Department of Environment.[735] The Clean The Mill group had engaged a chemist who, with the assistance of a resident from the Pictou Landing First Nation, had taken the samples in June 2014 at seven sites around Boat Harbour. [736]

The results showed the presence of heavy metals, and the presence of mercury in three of six samples suggested that at some point there may also have been a mercury spill, which the report recommended be investigated. In an interview he did with CBC's *Information Morning*, Dr. Krawczyk said it was "very alarming" that five heavy metals were present in the samples – mercury, arsenic, cadmium, nickel, and chromium.[737] He described heavy metals in the environment as a "grave concern," particularly when it comes to young people and their developing nervous systems. The amount of brain damage they can cause, he said, depends on whether there is mild or severe contact with the heavy metals, and the damage is permanent.

Environment Minister Delorey said he appreciated that the Clean The Mill group had shared the information with the government and pledged to take it seriously. Later in November, the Departments of Environment and of Health and Wellness, issued a press release saying that levels of mercury and most other chemicals found in the majority of samples were within acceptable levels.[738]

When the results of the mill's October emissions tests were released in 2014, both Northern Pulp and Delorey described them as a step in the right direction.[739] The tests found that this time the emissions of particulate matter from the power boiler were below allowed limits. However, those from the recovery boiler were still above levels stipulated in the company's existing industrial agreement with the province. Northern Pulp's spokesperson, Roger Pike, said that once the electrostatic precipitator was installed by May 2015, emissions would be further reduced.[740]

Matt Gunning was not impressed, pointing out that the emissions from the power boiler should have dropped still further after the installation of a new scrubber in 2012, and the public was being misled. He described the province's environmental standards for Northern Pulp as "notoriously weak." Like Karla MacFarlane, the Progressive Conservative MLA for the area, he also took issue with the process for the testing. "Northern Pulp got to pick the date and time of the stack testing," Gunning told *The Chronicle Herald.* "What we would like to see is Nova Scotia Environment hire a company at a date and time that is unknown to Northern Pulp. We're just worried that things aren't at arms-length enough to consider it a third party."[741]

On December 1, 2014, the province released a sixty-page draft industrial approval for Northern Pulp, which would replace the mill's expiring operating permit. For the first time, the drafting of an industrial approval had involved consultation with both the Pictou Landing First Nation and the community. The draft industrial approval incorporated some of the citizens' concerns about water use and pollution, requiring the mill to gradually reduce its water consumption and effluent production over the coming half-decade, which would mean a 40 percent reduction in both by 2020. As for the emissions, Environment Minister Delorey said a new federal code of conduct would become the new standard for the mill, although the code had yet to be completed. The public had until January 5, 2015, to send their feedback on the draft to the government.[742]

The response from Northern Pulp was non-committal. Manager Bruce Chapman described it as a "draft and a work in progress," and said they would "continue to work with Nova Scotia Environment on this."[743] Matt Gunning, on the other hand, worried about the grey areas and generous time limits for the reductions in emissions, water use, and effluent. He speculated that it had been written to be tough, but it got weakened, watered down with legalese as it passed up the "chain of command" and reached the lawyers. "We're a little discouraged," he told *The News* in New Glasgow.[744]

But the saga of the new industrial approval had only just begun, and as the plot unfolded, it started to bear an uncanny similarity to the story of what had happened to the good intentions behind the new natural resources strategy.

At the end of January 2015, the province released the new industrial approval, which emphasized environmental improvements in three areas – air emissions, water usage, and effluent.[745] A summary of this version stated that once it was implemented, it would be "consistent with what is achieved by other similar mills in North America."[746] There were new caps on emissions of particulate matter, as well as lower annual limits for both particulate matter and sulphur dioxide, with the expectations that when the new precipitator was installed in May, these would be achievable. Testing of emissions from the power and recovery boilers would be done four times a year.

Further, by 2020 the mill would have to reduce its consumption of fresh water by 34.5 percent, with a new daily allowance of 63,000 cubic metres (63 million litres), and monitor the effects of this use on the Middle River lest further reductions were needed. The new maximum for effluent flowing to Boat Harbour would be 67,500 cubic metres (67.5 million litres) per day by 2020, down 25 percent from actual wastewater production. The mill's maximum production of 310,000 tonnes of pulp per year would remain the same, although there were still no daily limits as the Clean The Mill group had requested. Group member Paul Sobey had suggested that although the mill's daily capacity was 400 tonnes of wet pulp, some days it was producing up to 1,000 tonnes.[747]

At a press conference, with what looked like a nod to the hard work of the Pictou Nation First Landing, the Clean The Mill, and Clean Pictou Air Group of Businesses, Environment Minister Delorey said, "We have heard the concerns raised by the people of Pictou County and the new approval demonstrates that the status quo is no longer an option."[748] The new operating conditions had been developed, he said, by referencing "continental standards."[749]

The mill owners disagreed. The deputy CEO of Paper Excellence Canada, Pedro Chang, said the changes would cost the company $90 million, and he derided the new standards as "arbitrary" and "well beyond anything being requested by any province or state anywhere in North America." He said appealing the approval would be the right thing to do for the company and its employees. According to reporter Steve Goodwin, spokespersons for the mill had already warned that if the mill had to close to reduce its emissions, it would not reopen, and if there were a ban on clear cutting, it would no longer be able to operate in the province.[750]

Matt Gunning, however, produced documentation that showed the industrial approval was not requiring Northern Pulp to do anything that similar mills elsewhere were not required to do. Progressive Conservative environment critic and MLA for Pictou West Karla MacFarlane said there should be even larger reductions in how much water the mill used, and asked, not for the first time, for more air monitoring.[751] Her concerns were echoed in a scientific review of environmental studies done on the mill's pollution, which also called for more strategic placement of air monitoring sites and communication of results.[752]

By the end of February, the messages coming from Northern Pulp were loud and clear. General Manager Bruce Chapman said the industrial approval "set the company up for failure."[753] Chapman told *The News* they had met with the Department of Natural Resources on February 24 to express their concerns and to make sure everyone understood how the new approval affected their long-term business. "We are at a serious impasse with Nova Scotia Environment," he said. He denied they were "playing the shutdown card" and repeated the mantra that had been used for so long to appease citizens of Pictou County, the province, and across the country concerned about the environmental costs of the industry: "It doesn't have to be jobs versus the environment, we can have both."

A typo in the first version of the industrial approval resulted in a delay of two months before the province issued an amended version, after which Northern Pulp – and any group that wanted to appeal the approval – had thirty days to submit their requests.[754]

The bell had rung on the next round. The powers that be in the forestry industry rallied around Northern Pulp, as did the union. Shortly after the industrial approval was released, Northern Pulp and a union representative from Unifor met privately with the province's Minister of Natural Resources, Zach Churchill, to try to enlist his support in their demand for concessions on new pollution limits set by the Department of Environment.[755]

Journalist Robert Devet obtained an unsigned copy of a letter that petitioned Premier McNeil, the Minister of the Environment, and the Minister of Natural Resources to stop putting "red tape" in the way of economic growth, citing the "unreasonable Industrial Approval (IA) for Northern Pulp" that would not allow the company to have a long future.[756] The letter was circulated together with a "fact sheet" defending

Northern Pulp and claiming the industrial approval imposed "conditions stricter than North American industry norms," and it would limit the company's "financial stability and the ability to attract capital."[757]

The Clean The Mill group then issued a point-by-point rebuttal to the unsigned "fact sheet" about Northern Pulp's industrial approval.[758] In response to a claim that Paper Excellence had plans to invest in and modernize the mill after it purchased it in 2011, Clean The Mill noted that pulp mills required about $50 million per year of capital investment, whereas in the past forty-four years, the various owners had put only $80 million into upgrades for the mill. The group responded to a statement that the cap on production would hurt the company's finances by pointing out Northern Pulp had increased its production in the summer of 2014, when it knew its pollution control equipment was ailing. Clean The Mill quotes the "facts" and refutes them one by one. As if to add weight to their argument, emissions tests done in March 2015 showed that once again, the mill was pumping out more than the allowed amounts of particulate matter from its power and recovery boilers.[759]

Opposition politician, Progressive Conservative MLA Tim Houston from Pictou West, said the Liberal government had pleased no one with the new industrial approval, and that Minister Delorey had "never even been to the mill" or had "meaningful discussions with stakeholders."[760]

In early April, Clean The Mill and the Pictou Landing First Nation submitted their appeals to the Department of Environment. The Mi'kmaq concerns were focused on the environmental performance of the mill. Clean The Mill requested increased and more transparent monitoring of emissions, and expressed concern that the new approval would not adequately protect human health and wellness. On June 8, the Minister replied to Brian Hebert, the lawyer representing the Pictou Landing Band, and to Clean The Mill. Both of their appeals were denied.[761]

The Northern Pulp appeal, submitted on April 9, 2015, got a different response. The day after he denied the appeals of the First Nations Band and Clean The Mill group, Minister Delorey extended the appeal period for Northern Pulp by thirty days. At this time, the mill was shut down while the new precipitator was installed, a job that involved an additional 600 tradespeople, according to Northern Pulp's communications manager, who said it would go back into production at the end of June.[762]

When Delorey sent Northern Pulp his response in July 2015, it was full of concessions; gone were terms and conditions on a new effluent facility because that would be dealt with in a separate plan to close the Boat Harbour treatment plant by 2020. Also gone were steep cuts in water usage and the mill's obligations to provide reports to the Pictou Landing First Nation.[763] In justifying the concessions, Delorey said there had been in Northern Pulp's appeal "additional information included that's been made available to me that was reviewed as part of the appeal process."[764] That information, he said, came from "consultants hired by the province and Northern Pulp."

But Northern Pulp still hadn't got everything it wanted, and it set out to get it. In August, the company announced it was taking the province, which had lavished it with so many dollars and so many concessions over the years, to court. Northern Pulp's Kathy Cloutier told CBC's Jennifer Henderson that the July response failed to address "multiple issues," so Northern Pulp was keeping "all options" open, including the courts.[765] She said they would prefer to reach an agreement on a new industrial approval through "dialogue" and added, "Conversations underway with government are increasingly constructive." Meanwhile, the company filed documents in the Supreme Court of Nova Scotia that appealed the amended industrial approval.

In late July 2015, Andrew Younger took over from Delorey as Environment Minister. He would remain until November when he was expelled from cabinet and from the Liberal caucus for a personal legal issue, after which Younger became an Independent MLA before leaving politics in the run-up to the 2017 provincial election.

At one point during his tenure as minister, Andrew Younger recalls being shown a PowerPoint presentation that compared Northern Pulp's water use and other statistics with those of other pulp mills. During an interview in the summer of 2016, Younger tells me the presentation suggested that Northern Pulp was the worst performing mill in North America. He said it fuelled his concerns about the mill's water use, which he believes cannot be sustained and that also limits any new industries in the area that require water. After he was ousted as minister and from the Liberal caucus, he wanted to review the facts he saw in the presentation and filed a Freedom of Information request for the PowerPoint. He forwarded to me what he received back: the first four title pages were there but the ten remaining pages had been removed, or as a handwritten note on page five said, "severed."[766]

In the autumn of 2015, with the court challenge still lurking in the wings, Northern Pulp launched its own public relations campaign, filling the media airwaves with advertisements about what it was doing for the province and its forests. It also commissioned its own study of the "economic impacts" of the mill and its press release on the findings contained quotes from its own executives and the executive director of the Forest Products Association of Nova Scotia.[767] Northern Pulp, it claimed, created "over 2,040 full-time equivalent jobs ... with workers earning $101 million in income." It employed 339 at the mill itself, produced and exported 280,000 tonnes of pulp each year, was one of the largest shippers with the Halifax Port Authority, and purchased over 90 percent of the wood chips produced in Nova Scotia, "receiving on average 120 trucks of fibre" each day.

The mill seemed to be riding high on the wave of positive publicity it had generated for itself with its PR blitz. The mill manager, Bruce Chapman, announced at a business breakfast hosted by the Pictou County Chamber of Commerce that the biggest issue all along had been "communication" that would help Northern Pulp re-engage with the community.[768]

Shortly thereafter the results from the September 2015 emissions tests were made public. The new precipitator, which the company now claimed cost $35 million, had indeed reduced emissions of particulate matter from the recovery boiler to below permitted levels. But the power boiler was still pumping out too much particulate matter, causing the Department of Environment to issue a directive that Northern Pulp undertake an independent review of the entire boiler system by the end of November.[769] This was the second such directive in just a year; in June 2015 the mill had been ordered to provide a written report on what it planned to do about the power boiler.[770]

This was not the first time the mill's power boiler had been an issue; its power boiler scrubber had been "offline" since 2006 and had been the subject of a 2012 government directive to fix it.[771] In June 2013, Northern Pulp's website announced, "We are pleased to report that we completed the task on time and the upgraded scrubbing system is in operation and working well."[772] Then in August 2014, the vice president for operations for Paper Excellence Canada, David Kerr, told CBC *Mainstreet* host Stephanie Domet there were "good cleaning and scrubbing systems on the power boiler." He said the boiler that was causing "the exceedances and the plume" that summer was the recovery boiler."[773]

"And what concerns are outstanding about emissions from the power boiler?" Domet asked him then.

"No concerns whatsoever," he replied. "We're in total compliance with the power boiler." Less than a year later, the province issued the first of two directives about excessive emissions from the power boiler.

In late summer and into the fall of 2015, the Department of Environment hired an environmental engineering firm,

CBCL Limited, to assess the feasibility of the terms it wanted to impose on Northern Pulp in the new industrial approval. The report found that Northern Pulp could indeed meet the terms, that reducing water consumption by 30 percent was "technically feasible" and this would make it conform to North American averages for similar mills, and so was a 23 percent reduction in wastewater.[774]

Northern Pulp disagreed with the report. In its appeal to the Supreme Court, it was asking that all those reductions be scrapped, and it be allowed to increase its annual pulp production. A peer-reviewed article that compared emissions limits from five other pulp mills in Canada also undermined Northern Pulp's claims that the new industrial approval went "beyond industry standards in Canada" and it showed that in some cases, even the new emission limits were "less stringent than other jurisdictions."[775]

Still, it was just a matter of weeks before the province would capitulate. In early February 2016, Margaret Miller, the new Environment Minister – the third in less than a year – wrote to Northern Pulp's technical manager with a final decision on the appeal.[776] Despite the Department of Environment's earlier good intentions to impose tougher standards, McNeil's tough talk, and Delorey's claims about the status quo no longer being an option, it looked as if it was after all.

The new industrial approval gave Northern Pulp nearly everything it had asked for. Gone were the lowered limits on water use and wastewater production; the mill would be allowed to use 92,310 cubic metres (92.3 million litres, 20.3 million Imperial gallons) every single day. Also gone was the sustainability study of the effect of the water draw on the Middle River Watershed, and the cap on pulp production of 310,000 tonnes per year.[777] Instead, the mill would be asked to propose its own water reduction projects, provide an annual report on sulphur in wastewater, and it could increase annual production to 330,000 tonnes.

In return for these concessions, Northern Pulp withdrew

its appeal to the Supreme Court of Nova Scotia. The reaction of the many activists who had devoted years of their lives to the struggle to get the government to force the mill to reduce its environmental footprint was poignant, sometimes even pain-filled.

"The government has failed to even gently pressure this mill to meet standards being met by every other pulp mill in the country," Dave Gunning told CBC News. "The mill wanted an increase in production and they got it. They wanted to use more water and they got it. They wanted to put in more efflu-ent and they got basically everything they were looking for."[778] Jocelyne Rankin of the Ecology Action Centre also expressed concern that the water consumption could be averaged over the whole year at 80,000 cubic metres per day by January 30, 2018, which would allow excessive amounts taken out in times when the Middle River was low and threatening fish, a growing concern because of climate change and increasingly erratic rainfall patterns.[779]

The industrial approval stipulated that Northern Pulp had to have an environmental management plan. When asked why this plan was not available on their website, respondents from the Department of Environment said it must be applied for in accordance with the Freedom of Information and Pro-tection of Privacy Act.[780]

Ron Kelly of the Pictou County Watershed Coalition penned a letter to *The Advocate* noting a refrain about how, historically, the mill had run the show, the bureaucrats aided and abetted them, and the politicians stood by and watched.[781] He had hoped the Liberal government would change this "un-healthy dynamic" and he expressed his disappointment that with the new industrial approval, it seemed to be "making a hasty retreat."

Renowned poet and author Sheree Fitch joined many others to write letters to the Liberal government protesting the watered down industrial approval. To no avail. The mill, once again, had won. The response Fitch received from the

Minister of Environment stated, "The mill must meet all of the compliance limits as outlined in the amended industrial approval, and we will continue to monitor for compliance. I have taken the time necessary to consider the factors put forward in my decision. This industrial approval will reduce immediate risk to the environment and encourage the mill to look for ways to further reduce emissions and water usage."[782] This was a form letter, identical to ones sent to other citizens who had taken the time to write and express their concern to their elected government.

In April 2016, Dr. John Hamm, chair of the Board of Northern Resources Nova Scotia Corporation, parent to Northern Pulp Nova Scotia Corporation, announced the addition of two new board members.[783] One was Terri Fraser, formerly the Technical Manager at Northern Pulp, who had been so much a part of the industrial approval negotiations. The other was James MacConnell, who had run the campaign for Sean Fraser, the candidate who had won the seat for the Liberals in the 2015 federal election and was now the MP for Central Nova. As one of the dedicated followers of the Clean Up The Pictou Pulp Mill Facebook page put it, "With John Hamm as the Chairman of the Board and now Jim MacConnell sitting with him, Northern Pulp has an influential Conservative and an influential Liberal on the Northern Pulp Board of Directors."[784]

As for the Community Liaison Committee that was also a condition of the new industrial approval, its membership was selected by Northern Pulp. The summary notes from biannual meetings made available online are one-pagers merely listing what was discussed but without details of the actual discussions or outcomes, and as of this writing, the most recent meeting documented was in June 2016.[785]

For Dave Gunning, the lack of transparency and openness of the Liaison Committee defeats the whole purpose of having one. Frustrated by this and continued problems with the emissions through the spring and early summer of 2016, when on some days the air was so foul he and his wife had to bring the children in from outdoors, turn off the ventilation system, and close all the windows, in June that year Dave Gunning wrote to Premier McNeil. He again pointed out Northern Pulp decided when the emissions tests would be, that there were not enough air monitoring stations, and that people were feeling they had exhausted their options and had stopped complaining because they "were very much alone in this with no support or assistance from our own government."

A month later he received a reply, not from the premier but from Environment Minister Margaret Miller, saying, "Production at the mill was normal on June 24, 2016 and there were no reported upsets." The letter continued: "Nova Scotia Environment continues to monitor the mill for compliance and take appropriate action when required to address any incidents of non-compliance with their industrial operating approval."[786]

Gunning replied, this time attaching a photo of the dark plume coming from the mill and smeared across the horizon, and questioned whether this might relate to the power boiler. He also informed Minister Miller, who had claimed there had been "no recent exceedances for the power boiler," that Northern Pulp had admitted to the media that it failed the power boiler test in June 2016 for the second time in five tests.[787] "So you lied to me," he wrote, "and possibly someone lied to you." And, he added, the "owners of Northern Pulp/Paper Excellence/Asia Pulp and Paper have a direct line of communication with Stephen McNeil and can reach him any time they need him. But he has not even once responded to any of my letters sent to him over the past 3-4 years."[788]

When the mill failed its stack tests because the level of particulate matter from its power boiler exceeded permitted levels in June 2016, the government fined the mill $697.50. "Pathetic," was Dave Gunning's response. "I wonder if Northern Pulp will rally their 'stakeholders' to lobby the government for a forgivable loan to cover this enormous fine," he said to Francis Campbell, then writing for the *Local Xpress.* "Or will Northern Pulp board members have to give up their golf memberships?"[789]

It's early 2017 when I go back to see Dave Gunning for an update on the Clean The Mill group. It's a frigid but sunny winter day, and from his front yard it looks like the mill has produced its very own dark cloud as if to hide itself from view. The brownish plume drifts towards the north, suspended over the length of Pictou Landing like a giant phantom shark.

Gunning is home in Lyons Brook only briefly, just back from one gig before heading off to the next one in Kansas the following week. I am taken aback at how tired he looks. He says the whole Clean The Mill group is exhausted; they continue to pay attention to what is happening but they just don't know what else to do. They've installed a permanent camera in town that helps them monitor the emissions, visually. But this is hardly a substitute for more rigorous, transparent, and comprehensive testing of what is coming out of the stacks at all times of day and night.

Still, ever the positive thinker, Gunning says they are proud of what they have accomplished, convinced it was all the publicity the concerned citizens drew to the mill's emissions and effluent that led to so much money being spent on a new precipitator. And this, in turn, created extra employment in the area. He also believes that because of the adverse publicity they generated, Northern Pulp has made real efforts to ingratiate itself with the community. He thinks employees are being treated better than they once were, and that the mill is trying to woo the community with donations and support for local sports and activities.

But he also wonders if the group hadn't pushed so hard on the issue and inundated the media with advertisements, the mill might not have pushed back so hard, and government might have just pulled the plug and not propped it up with concessions on the industrial approval and access to Crown land. He's relieved the government passed a law that will close

Boat Harbour by January 2020, and indeed was invited to speak about the bill at the Law Amendments Committee in the Legislature before it was passed.[790] But he – like many others – wonders about the alternative once Boat Harbour is closed.

20

Boat Harbour – full circle? (2005-2017)

I think we need to move away from this area altogether and maybe come back in 500 years. But right now, whatever they do with it [Boat Harbour], it's not going to solve the problem. It's just too far gone."

– Sarah Francis[791]

When Rodney MacDonald took over as premier in 2006, he inherited the four-decades-old problem of Boat Harbour and the mill's waste. Eight premiers had come and gone, as had repeated promises by the province to close or clean up the facility. More than 200 studies had been done on Boat Harbour.[792] But a review of that research showed even when the mill had failed to comply with pollution limits, regulatory enforcement had been lacking. There were "very few reports" with information to address community concerns about pollution, and the lack of data limited the "ability to evaluate potential local ecological and human health exposures."[793]

In late 2008, three provincial cabinet ministers – Minister of Transportation and Infrastructure Renewal Murray Scott, Minister of Natural Resources David Morse, and Minister of Aboriginal Affairs Michael Baker – met twice with Pictou Landing First Nation representatives, including Chief Anne Francis-Muise, to discuss Boat Harbour.[794] The Band made it clear it wanted the entire treatment facility removed.[795]

Following those meetings, Minister Scott wrote an extraordinarily candid letter to Chief Francis-Muise, reiterating the words of Minister Baker: "To say that the Band has been long suffering would be a masterful understatement of the obvious." And he continued, "It is our unwavering intention to end that suffering as quickly as possible. It should have been done long ago." He said the first step would be to find another location to discharge the mill's effluent that did not involve Boat Harbour, and then to clean the harbour and return it to a tidal state.[796]

This, he said, would "take time." Then came this intriguing paragraph: "In grateful response to the band's cooperative spirit we wish to make a contribution to the community recognizing the negative impact of delay in closing the facility from [what had been] the intended completion date of December 31, 2008, to the final completion of this major task." This would involve striking a committee consisting of the Band chief and a provincial minister.

"Let me make our government's position perfectly clear," Minister Scott wrote in closing. "We believe your community has suffered from the negative effects of the Boat Harbour Treatment Facility for far too long. We are fully committed to ending that suffering as quickly as it is practical to do so."

At the end of December, Northern Pulp proposed a new "accommodation agreement" to the Band, which recognized the ongoing negotiations between the province and the First Nation for returning Boat Harbour to a tidal estuary. It would give the mill until January 31, 2009, to continue operating the existing treatment facility. For this, Northern Pulp would pay the Band $110,000 on or before that date, and another $95,000 that was payable under the first amending agreement of 2006.[797] The Band's lawyer, Brian Hebert, sent the $110,000 back, saying that no new agreement had been reached on extending the agreement.[798] Then in June 2009, Rodney MacDonald's government was shown the door by the Nova Scotian electorate, ushering in the NDP government of Darrell Dexter.

Just before that, in April 2009, the landmark investigation by the University of King's College journalism students put Boat Harbour into the public conscience the way it hadn't been for many years, if ever. Despite all the agreements and memoranda of understanding that had been signed and the promises made to close the facility and clean up Boat Harbour, the effluent still flowed, the air still reeked. A technical committee that had been set up in 1993 after the out-of-court settlement with the federal government, which comprised the Chief, the Band Council and some council members and their legal counsel, representatives of the mill, and federal and provincial governments, was still meeting every month.[799] But it looked as if it had made no headway; everything was again up in the air. In the words of the journalism students in their damning articles on Boat Harbour, this left "the province with no plan."[800]

The Dexter government didn't seem inclined to respect the promises made by former minister Murray Scott to the Band. In March 2010, the NDP Minister of Transportation and Infrastructure Renewal, Bill Estabrooks, told Beverley Ware of *The Chronicle Herald* that the letter by his predecessor pledging action on Boat Harbour didn't apply to the new government. "It's not the focus of where I'm going," he told her.[801] Chief Aileen Francis said this betrayal of promises made by the province was "insulting," marking "fifteen years of unfulfilled expectations." In April 2010, the Band asked the province to terminate the mill's license to use Boat Harbour by the end of June. The date came and went.

The residents of Pictou Landing First Nation demanded a meeting with NDP Premier Darrell Dexter. Instead, they were granted an hour-long session with the Transportation Minister Bill Estabrooks. Once again – for the umpteenth time in forty-five years – they demanded the treatment facility be closed down.[802]

The Band's "patience," which Scott had praised in his letter to Chief Francis Muise in 2008, had apparently run out, yet again. Their legal counsel, Brian Hebert, advised them to put an end to the seventeen years of monthly technical meetings and to exercise their legal rights. In July 2010, the Band gave notice of an intended lawsuit against the province, which would involve an injunction to shut down the treatment facility.[803] The Band Council would be prepared to negotiate a solution with the province, but it said such negotiations would happen alongside and not instead of legal action. In September 2010, the Band filed the lawsuit against the province, Northern Pulp, and all its former owners.[804]

When the government offered them $3 million to put the lawsuit on hold for three years, the members of the Band voted to reject what journalist Miles Howe dubbed an attempt at paying "hush money."[805] The new chief of the Pictou Landing Band, Andrea Paul, took up the Boat Harbour issue with the federal Minister of Indian and Northern Affairs at a meeting of First Nations in Ottawa, asking for the government to finally do something about the mess.

Meanwhile, the Pictou Landing First Nation was struggling to find ways to pay for the ongoing lawsuit. Speaking to *The Chronicle Herald*, Chief Paul said the Band could not afford to use precious funding for social programming for the lawsuit, which lawyer Brian Hebert said would cost millions of dollars because of the amount of research it required.[806] But they were not going to be deterred. The Band Council decided to try to get a court order from the Supreme Court of Nova Scotia that would force the province to fund their lawsuit, which would be a historical first because this would mean the province was funding a lawsuit against itself. Hebert said there were legal precedents for such a case from British Columbia and Alberta. In 2014, however, the Nova Scotia Supreme Court rejected the request.[807]

In April that year, things reached a breaking point – yet again – when Environment Minister Randy Delorey approved the extension of Northern Pulp's old industrial approval until the end of the year, which meant the mill could continue to pipe effluent into Boat Harbour in spite of all the promises and pledges made to have it closed.[808] Delorey defended the extension, saying it gave him more time to consult with the First Nation. Chief Andrea Paul didn't see it that way, and threatened to use "any means necessary to protect our land and our people," accusing the government of "ignoring the law."[809]

Then in the early evening of June 9, 2014, Jonathan Beadle and his son were walking along the park-like manicured fields towards the pipeline outlet at the Boat Harbour facility, as he often did in his quest for photos and video footage.[810] He noticed there was none of the smelly wastewater coming up from the underground pipeline that fed the effluent to the Boat Harbour facility. Both he and his son sensed something was wrong. Turns out it they were right.

Northern Pulp reported that it discovered a pipeline break at 7:40 the next morning, where the line came ashore on the Pictou Landing side of East River, about 110 metres from the Pictou Harbour shoreline.[811] The mill immediately halted operations, but by then, the faulty pipeline had spewed an estimated 47 million litres of untreated effluent into a wetland area, from where it flowed into East River and Pictou Harbour.[812]

An eyewitness account by a member of the Band described a scene that was both "heartbreaking and terrifying," as the effluent flowed over Indian Cross Point and into East River, which was discoloured.[813] The pipeline had been "unlawfully buried" there without the consent of the First Nation, and it was routed across lands where the Mi'kmaq sacred burial grounds were located, lands that the province had no legal right to expropriate.

Chief Andrea Paul contacted the government and Northern Pulp and asked how they proposed to clean up after the spill, but the province reportedly declined to pass on this information.[814]

Court documents later showed the pipeline, nearly a metre in diameter, was in an "advanced stage of deterioration" where it had ruptured, and a section about 1.5 metres long had been "completely delaminated," with "visible cracks, leaks, and extensive corrosion," and an oval-shaped hole of thirty-five centimetres where the leak occurred.[815] Further, according to the court decision, while the mill did have an inspection plan for its pipeline, there had been no internal inspection done on the land-based line since Northern Pulp had taken over responsibility for the "operation and maintenance of the effluent pipeline and treatment facility in 2008 – this despite there having been several leaks that had required repair or replacement of sections of the pipeline in previous years."[816]

This latest pipeline break sparked outrage in the Pictou Landing First Nation.[817] Within hours the Band Council mounted a peaceful blockade on the road leading to the site of the toxic spill, and said they would not stand down and allow the mill to resume operations until the province and Northern Pulp committed to closing Boat Harbour and restoring the lagoon.[818]

Speaking to *The Chronicle Herald*, Chief Andrea Paul said, "In 1991, '95, '97 and 2008 we were promised they would clean up Boat Harbour ... so today in 2014 it has come to this ... if we back down now, we'll be in the same situation we were in before."[819]

The blockade spurred the provincial government into action. The government organized a meeting with Chief Paul and the Band Council. It was reportedly a difficult meeting that ended only when Environment Minister Delorey signed an agreement in principle that by June 2015, the government would have agreed to a timeline for stopping the flow of wastewater into Boat Harbour and its remediation.[820] If the province failed to deliver, it would pay the Band $1 million. Based on these conditions, the Band agreed to end the blockade.

An evaluation of samples collected by Northern Pulp at the site found they were "acutely lethal to fish," while analyses of Environment Canada samples revealed elevated pH levels, high enough to have "sub-lethal toxic effects on fish."[821] A report done for the Mi'kmaq Conservation Group concluded that the concentrations of mercury at three sample sites were above safe standards.[822]

In August 2014, an environmental report on the effect of the pipeline break showed the presence of five different dioxins and furans in the area where the effluent had spilled, and one kind of dioxin was found as far away as Melmerby Beach, where dead fish had been reported.[823] Melmerby, about twenty kilometres east of Abercrombie Point, is one of the most popular swimming spots on the Northumberland Strait and the site of a provincial park. An Environment Department engineer told *The News* that under federal regulations, once wastewater has been treated there should be no detectable dioxins and furans.[824] She added the results would lead to further investigations. The leak also revealed that Northern Pulp was exceeding the provincially approved levels of biochemical oxygen demand and total suspended solids in its effluent.[825]

An inspection specialist for the Department of Environment in Pictou said the "consequences" had not yet been determined because the initial focus was on repair and monitoring after the spill.[826]

On January 20, 2016, Northern Pulp pled guilty to "unlawfully depositing or permitting the deposit of a deleterious substance, namely pulp and paper effluent, in water frequented by fish" in contravention of the Canadian Fisheries Act, and prosecution proceeded in the case of R. v. Northern Pulp Nova Scotia Corporation.[827] The Pictou Landing First Nation contributed a 160-page Victim Impact Statement that recounted the sorry history of Boat Harbour.[828] The language and the content of the statement are both stark and moving. At one point it states, "The wastewater facility has been like a heavy weight dragging down the community – physically, emotionally, spiritually, culturally, socially and economically – for decades. The community had lost hope and trust after decades of broken promises by the Province and the owners of the mill."[829] The community members managed to find a silver lining in the spill, noting that it meant the mill was shut down for two weeks, during which time they "felt relief" because the air pollution and stench disappeared.[830]

Presiding Judge Del W. Atwood decided the ruptured pipeline was "an accident waiting to happen," meaning Northern Pulp was "midway on the scale of culpability." The court fined the company $225,000, a third of which would go to the Mi'Kmaw Conservation Group, another $75,000 to the Pictou County Rivers Association, and the final third to the Pictou Landing First Nation for the protection or restoration of fish habitat. In his decision, Judge Atwood noted that "the truth of the damaging impact that the pulp mill at Abercrombie Point and its toxic effluent-treatment site at Boat Harbour has had on the well-being of the Pictou Landing First Nation – and continues to have – is so conspicuous and notorious as to be beyond dispute."[831]

Four years earlier, the Pictou Landing Native Women's Group had embarked on a six-year community-based participatory study that sought to answer the question, "Is Boat Harbour making us sick?"[832] Its final report presented glaring proof that there were gaping regulatory lapses when it came to Boat Harbour. It noted that legislation in Nova Scotia has never required human health risk assessments, and that federal regulations for pulp and paper effluent had permitted the mill to operate twenty years without quality control of its wastewater.[833] It also found Boat Harbour was toxic to both fish and amphibians, none of which survived past seven days in undiluted water from the facility. It noted almost half of the households on the Reserve depend entirely on social assistance, concluding, "If, indeed, the pulp mill was brought to Nova Scotia to benefit the residents of the region, these benefits have clearly not materialized in the community that may be paying the highest price."[834]

In April 2015, the momentous news broke that the Liberal government was fulfilling its pledge to take firm action on Boat Harbour, that it had drafted legislation that would lead to the cessation of the use of the lagoon for receiving mill effluent by the end of January 2020.[835] Before finalizing Bill 89, the Boat Harbour Act, the Liberal party contacted the Clean The Mill group for input, and Dave Gunning travelled to Halifax to speak at the Law Amendments Committee.

In his passionate address, Gunning thanked the Pictou Landing First Nation, and particularly Chief Andrea Paul and the Band Council, for their hard work, and also the government "for facing an extremely complex and difficult situation head-on for the first time" in nearly fifty years since the mill opened. He also pointed out the clean-up of Boat Harbour and the construction of a new industrial treatment facility with infrastructure improvements at the mill could create a lot of jobs. "This whole movement to clean up Boat Harbour is being seen as a very positive step and will not only entice former residents to retire back home from out West," he told the House, "but will also help attract new residents to the area along with new business opportunities."[836]

But, he said, echoing the words of Chief Andrea Paul, "We remain cautiously optimistic," and he reminded the legislators there was a long history of "non-compliance and lack of enforcement by the Department of Environment." This lack of accountability by mill operators and governments, he said, was what had "gotten us into this mess." And, he noted, it was not really fair to blame previous generations for the mess, because so much was not known about health and environmental impacts. But in 2015, he said, "we know better and therefore we have to do better."

This was not the view of Jack Kyte, the executive director of the Pictou County Chamber of Commerce. Speaking with Jennifer Henderson on CBC Halifax *Information Morning* in April 2015, he said that, "Contrary to popular belief, the wastewater treatment system at Boat Harbour, which has its issues, treats wastewater extremely well."[837] Kyte pointed out there were "lots of questions" about who was going to pay for a new treatment system, and whether the mill was "in a position to spend many millions of dollars on something like this when there's no real return on investment."

The déjà vu was remarkable; twenty-four years earlier Kyte, then public affairs manager for Scott, had told journalist Reg Fendick of the erstwhile *Daily News* almost exactly the same thing, when a consultant's study had shown the mill, owned then by Scott, needed a new $74-million effluent treatment plant to replace the Boat Harbour facility. At the time Kyte said, "Seventy-four million dollars plus several million dollars to operate a new system would be a major undertaking for our company at this time," and "It would be most difficult for us to come up with those sorts of dollars ourselves."[838]

In the 2015 interview on CBC, he said a new treatment facility would have to meet federal standards that had changed over the years. "You're not going to be designing it to do much better than the standard because of the cost of it," he told Henderson. "So ironically, in the end you could end up with wastewater that may not be treated as well as it is today." And he repeated his view about the existing treatment facility at Boat Harbour: "Possibly, but ironically, the current system, despite its problems, treats wastewater extremely well."[839]

But the government was determined to close Boat Harbour, and the Act passed Third Reading in May 2015, which obliged the province to close and restore Boat Harbour by 2020. The next step was to figure out how that was going to be done, and what kind of new treatment facility was going to be put in place, and who was going to pay for it. Ken Swain, project leader for the clean-up with the Department of Transportation and Infrastructure Renewal, told reporter Michael Gorman, then reporting for the *Local Xpress*, that there were "information gaps" that needed to be filled.[840] He noted that "a couple of hundred studies" had been done on what was in Boat Harbour, but much was still not understood about its hydrology and hydrogeology, and even the extent of the contamination and its depth on the harbour floor.

In October 2016, Nova Scotia Lands, a provincial Crown corporation responsible for remediating and redeveloping Crown-owned properties, held an information session in the firehall in Pictou Landing to introduce the remediation plans for Boat Harbour. The presenters, led by Ken Swain, described a pilot project that would involve building a barrier in one corner of the harbour to create a cove. This could be drained and then dredged to determine what material had collected on the harbour bottom over fifty years, and what would need to be done with it. If successful, this could then be applied to the whole harbour. They said the government had set aside $88 million for the remediation, but this would likely have to increase.

About one hundred people showed up for the session, including many familiar faces from groups that had struggled over the years to have the mill cleaned up – Jonathan Beadle, Robert Christie, Dave Gunning, Matt Gunning, Alexander MacKenzie, Fergie MacKay, Stirling MacLean, Marsha Sobey, among others – in addition to Progressive Conservative MLAs Tim Houston and Karla MacFarlane from Pictou County.

Many present seemed satisfied by the progress on the remediation plans. But there were others concerned that the presenters could not answer questions about a new treatment facility.

A few weeks later, Northern Pulp chose the Montreal engineering firm KSH to study options for a new treatment facility, which would be located within Northern Pulp's existing mill site.[841] It would look at changes that would be made at the mill, the best treatment process, and also the route that a new pipeline would take. Although it was reported that Northern Pulp had "agreed to cost share the study with the province," their contribution and the total cost of the study were not made public. The government contributed $300,000. In a report to Northern Pulp, which the company then submitted to the Law Amendment Committee on the Boat Harbour Act in April 2015, KSH Consulting had stated that there was a "50-50 chance" of completing the project to close Boat Harbour and complete a new wastewater treatment facility by the deadline of January 2020, proposed in the new law.[842]

In June 2017, Ken Swain, the project leader for the cleanup, said a consulting firm, GHD, had been chosen to develop a plan for the remediation, and the province had added $44.5 million to its estimated budget for the work, which now stood at $133 million. He said the actual remediation work would start in 2020 and take from three to five years.[843] There was still no official statement on what would happen to the mill's effluent after that date, although Northern Pulp's general manager, Bruce Chapman, said it would probably be built on Northern Pulp property close to the mill.[844] It was estimated that a new treatment plant would cost $100 million, and because the government of John Hamm had signed a lease in 2002 that allowed the mill to use Boat Harbour until 2030, it wasn't clear who would be paying for the new treatment facility, the people of Nova Scotia or Northern Pulp.

On September 1, 2017, CBC's Paul Withers reported that Northern Pulp had qualified for a faster environmental assessment for a new treatment facility proposed for mill property, and that consultants were looking at possible release points for the treated effluent, both in Northumberland Strait and in Pictou Harbour. How much it would cost and who would pay for it were not revealed.[845]

Brian Hebert, the lawyer for the Band, is watching and waiting. In an interview in March 2017, he tells me the province has a duty to consult with the First Nation on any decision they make about Boat Harbour and an alternate treatment system. "We've already put them on notice that the potential outfall [for the waste], depending on where it's located, could have an adverse impact on the community. So we're looking closely at that."

The lawsuit that was filed in 2010 is still live before the courts; neither the province nor the previous owners of the mill have filed any defence, according to Hebert. And for the time being, he says, the Pictou Landing First Nation is fine with that, and waiting to see what happens, whether the treatment facility is actually closed, Boat Harbour cleaned up and an acceptable alternative found. "It ain't over till it's over," he adds.

Chief Andrea Paul says she prays that her grandchildren will see Boat Harbour as it once was. "It has to be better than it is now," she said in the film *A'Se'k*. "You can't get any worse."[846]

The people of Pictou Landing First Nation are already looking ahead to the day when their beloved "A'Se'K" will be healed. In November 2016, women from the community gathered under a full moon to start the process of cleansing the waters around Boat Harbour. The water ceremony, organized by Tonya Francis, was performed by women while men guarded a sacred fire.[847] Francis told journalist Debbi Harvie of *The Advocate* that the hope is the ancestors will lead the way in healing the waters, so that it will be clean, the way it once was before the pulp mill came.

"To see that things are actually happening, that has been a positive. It's time to clean this mess up," Chief Andrea Paul told journalist Francis Campbell. "It's long, long, long overdue."[848]

Epilogue

The paper in the book you are holding in your hands right now is made from the shavings of spruce, and birches that were expressly felled (that is to say, killed) for this purpose.

— Peter Wohlleben[849]

As I write this, it's just over a year since the smell of the pulp mill came calling in my neck of the woods in northern Nova Scotia, prompting me to start asking questions that led to that pivotal telephone conversation with Dave Gunning and, eventually, this book. In many ways it has been a positive journey of learning and meeting many people whose deep passion for healthy communities and forests, for clean air and water, has driven them to devote immense amounts of their time and their expertise to the cause of cleaning up the mill and improving the way the pulp industry operates in Nova Scotia. Their dedication, courage, and commitment have been inspiring, informing this book and providing good reasons for optimism.

Without all the hard work that concerned citizens have done in the past fifty years to pressure government and industry to make the mill and the pulp industry more accountable and responsible, it's difficult to imagine where we might be. It's possible there would still be absolutely no treatment of the waste coming out of the mill, that the air in Pictou would be far less breathable than it is, and that there would be even more clear cutting and aerial spraying of chemicals than there has been on the woodlands of Nova Scotia.

Today there seems to be an awakening, not just in Nova Scotia but around the world, to the value of trees in landscapes and of healthy ecosystems and forests, which do so much more than provide timber, biomass, and pulp. It is encouraging to see young people taking up where previous generations left off, trying to draw attention to all that is wrong with the kind of intensive industrial forestry that has been practised in the region for the past century or two and to find better ways of managing and indeed benefitting from forests.

One of those is Dale Prest, son of Wade Prest, a well-known defender of Nova Scotia's diverse forests and woodlot owners,[850] and one of the driving forces behind the Otter Pond Demonstration Forest near Mooseland,[851] which is where his uncle, the late Murray Prest, stood up to Scott Paper in the 1960s and refused to clear cut the Crown land he was leasing from the company. Today, Dale Prest is following in their foot-steps, defending Acadian forests and working as Ecosystems Services Specialist with Community Forests International, which aims to combat climate change by helping rural communities to work with nature.[852]

Prest's work on a demonstration woodlot in New Brunswick shows that by carefully managing the Acadian forest, it is possible not just to keep greenhouse gases out of the atmosphere but also to pull carbon out of it for storage in trees and soil.[853] The Acadian forest is particularly well suited to carbon storage, he says, and it can be managed to produce high value and quality trees, which can do a lot to strengthen rural economies and help small woodlot owners thrive. A diverse Acadian forest can store three times as much carbon as can monoculture softwood plantations so favoured by the pulp industry, and Prest points out there is a very big problem with the clear cutting regime that goes with this kind of forestry.

When a forest is clear cut and large machines run back and forth over it, the soil is exposed to the elements and it rapidly loses carbon that is stored there. He says there is twice as much carbon stored in the first metre of soil under a forest as there is in all the trees above ground. Clear cutting speeds up the release of that soil carbon – which may have been stored there for a thousand years – into the atmosphere, contributing to climate change. Eventually, after enough clear cutting, the soil will be so poor that trees will hardly be able to grow back, something Prest is already observing in the Maritimes.

"If you think about trees, they're really just solar-powered carbon vacuums," he tells me. "If you invented a machine that does what a tree does, you would be a miracle maker. They just need a little bit of sun and water to operate, and you can leave them outside all winter ... and when they get old and start to wear out, they replace themselves." And then he plants this image and idea in my mind: "They're actually an incredible, elegantly designed partial solution to the climate change problem we have."

It is interactions like these, with the next generation that is working so hard to correct some of the wrongs of the past half-century – people like Dale Prest, Matt Miller, the Gunning family, Jonathan Beadle, and many more – that inspired me so much over the past year of research and interviews for this book.

On the other hand, it has been disheartening to discover the lack of government and industry transparency and accountability in my home province. A request for interviews with mill management was declined; neither management nor the board would participate in this "project." Letters to my premier went unanswered, as did a letter to my former premier turned chair of the board of Northern Pulp, which swallows up public money, makes demands for and gets control over publicly owned lands and trees. In Nova Scotia, citizens do not seem to have the right to know the details of the loans and grants their government makes with their money to large foreign companies, and even a freedom of information request resulted in no details on those loans and grants.

Paul Pross, the former coordinator of the Healthy Forest Coalition, has had a long career as a professor of public administration at Dalhousie University, with a special interest in public interest groups. So he knows all too well what they are up against when they take on a cause for the public good. "We hear a lot today about 'the lobbies' and their ability to influence, even control, democratic governments," he writes. "Too often, the public, represented by groups like ours [Healthy Forest Coalition], is beaten back simply by the capacity of business lobbies to outlast us. Business can overwhelm us with TV ads, spin doctors, carefully chosen 'good works' and cynical exercises in public consultation because businesses are organized to persist." And, he adds, "Business leaders come and go, there is always someone to replace those who leave. The costs of lobbying can be written off as 'business expenses', which means that we taxpayers help to pay to be fooled."[854]

Too often our governments appear to be complicit in trying to keep citizens in the dark. Investigative journalist Linda Pannozzo has tried in vain to get the Department of Natural Resources to cough up data on the actual state of our forests, and, as she details in a remarkable series of articles, been thwarted in her quest to get those data through freedom of information requests that reveal the lack of access to information in Nova Scotia.[855] Much to her surprise, when she did find the data she was looking for, which she had been told by the Department of Natural Resources didn't exist, it was because it had been provided to a pipeline company based in Texas.

It has been immensely depressing to see how governments led by all three major political parties have caved to the demands of the mill's owners and been captured by the pulp industry to make policies to suit them and their profits at the expense of the welfare and best interests of the people who elected them and pay their salaries.

It reminds me all too much of the same kind of collusion and lack of transparency that I observed over decades of living in, reporting on, and writing about politics and business in very young democracies and non-democracies in the developing world. It also reminds me of so much that is wrong with what is so often called "economic development" and the prevailing economic dogma, unfettered capitalism and consumerism that drive extractive industries that destroy the world around us and all those things on which we depend for life – water, air, soil, biodiverse flora and fauna and forests. This kind of dead-end and blinkered economic ideology is leading to environmental catastrophe and fuelling climate change.

The pulp mill in Pictou is merely a microcosm, one miniscule example, of the kind of destructive economic activity that is so often conflated with economic "development" and progress around the world. In the eloquent words of author and journalist Linda Pannozzo, "If we were to count all the costs – the soil loss, habitat loss, and species loss – associated with the clear cutting, and add this to the environmental and health costs of making pulp, including the severing of millennia-old ties between the Mi'kmaq and the surrounding lands, what would we have then? Only an economic system pumped with delusion could ever count such a venture profitable."[856]

To paraphrase Dr. Seuss in his fable *The Lorax*, UNLESS we struggle very hard to reverse the trend of governance by and for those with money and power – with all the negative environmental, health, political, and economic effects that brings – then things will not get better; they won't. For fifty years, however, the mill has produced not just pulp – it has inspired caring citizens to press for change. This book would not have been written were it not for all those who cared and who have sacrificed so much in their efforts to improve the quality of life for their community and for generations to come.

Acknowledgements

I owe a great deal to a great many people who either inspired or contributed to this book, directly or indirectly, and in some cases, all of the above. Some generously offered their time to meet with, speak to, or share documents or information with me, including Bob Bancroft, Jonathan Beadle, Gary Burrill, Lorne Burrows, Robert Christie, June Daley, Dale Downey, Terry Mosh Dunbrack, Heather Fairbairn, Dr. Gerry Farrell, Sheree Fitch, Natalie Gordon, Mary Gorman, Dave Gunning, Matt Gunning, Sara Delong Gunning, Percy Hayne, Brian Hebert, Beth Henderson, Catherine Hughes, Paul Keats, Ron Kelly, Stephen Kimber, Bernadette MacDonald, Karla MacFarlane, Ferguson (Fergie) MacKay, Alexander MacKenzie, Donald MacKenzie, Stirling MacLean, Edgar McLellan, Matt Miller, Tom Miller, Bobbi Morrison, Ishbel Munro, Charlie Parker, Dr. Daniel N. Paul, Raymond Plourde, Dale Prest, Paul Pross, Janet Proudfoot, Dr. Dan Reid, Jordan Sprague, Barbara Sproull Seplaki, David Sutherland, Marc Theriault, Jane Sproull Thomson, Harry Thurston, Trudy Watts, Gregor Wilson, Andrew Younger, and all those who requested their names not be used. I am grateful too that Elizabeth May agreed to revisit her own experiences and write a foreword for this book.

I would also like to thank the many others who have been involved in trying to clean up the mill and improve forestry in this province over the years, whom I was either unable to reach or just couldn't fit into the book.

Many more people have worked tirelessly to encourage successive provincial and federal governments to better regu-

late and monitor the pulp and paper industry to protect human health and the environment, and we are all in their debt;
this includes the Pictou Landing First Nation, the late David
Orton and Judy Davis, members of the Northumberland Strait
Pollution Committee, Citizens Against Pollution, the Scott Boycott Committee and other groups that fought herbicide use
on the provincial forests, including the Clean The Mill group,
Clean Up the Pictou County Mill Facebook page (both founders and followers), Eastern Shore Forest Watch, the Ecology
Action Centre, Healthy Forest Coalition, Pictou County Watershed Coalition, among many others.

Special thanks to Dr. Gerry Farrell for so generously
contributing the photograph on the cover of this book, to
Marianne Fraser for her photos and work to organize a photo
exhibit to illustrate how the mill affects the community, and to
Dave Gunning and Smokey Dymny for the permission to use
the lyrics of songs they wrote about pulp mills.

I am also grateful to all those who helped me find historical records, including Debbie Clark, Reference & Heritage
Clerk at the New Glasgow Library, the patient crew at the Nova
Scotia Archives, and the reference librarians at the Halifax Regional Library. I am also indebted to those who devoted so
much energy to collecting and saving documents and newspaper clippings that were invaluable for this book, including
Ferguson MacKay, the late Henry Ferguson, and the late W.A.
Robertson of Trenton, whose meticulously kept scrapbooks
were loaned to the New Glasgow Library by Bill Robertson of
Scarborough, Ontario.

Immense gratitude is also due the groundbreaking work
to document the toxic legacy of Boat Harbour by the University
of King's College investigative workshop in 2009 and dozens
of dedicated journalists over the years who documented
the story of the mill. And for their seminal work on forestry
in Nova Scotia and bringing the situation to the attention of
people in the province, many thanks are owed to the team
that put together the reports on forest indicators to document

the health of our forests for Genuine Progress Index (GPI) for Atlantic Canada – Linda Pannozzo, Minga O'Brien, and Ronald Colman.

Gratitude is also due the Pictou Landing Native Women's Group and the entire team that did the research for and wrote *Our Ancestors Are In Our Land, Water, and Air: A Two-Eyed Seeing Approach to Researching Environmental Health Concerns with Pictou Landing First Nation – Final Report.*

My thanks also to those who read the manuscript at various stages, among them David Baxter, Elizabeth Baxter, Linda Pannozzo, Wade Prest, and Jamie Simpson. And my gratitude always to Lesley Choyce and Pottersfield Press, and a special deep bow to Peggy Amirault and Julia Swan for their tireless editing work. And last but not least, to my husband for his enduring patience and understanding.

Endnotes

Introduction (pages 13-19, notes 1 to 6)

1 Wright, Ronald. 2004. *A short history of progress*. Toronto, Ontario: House of Anansi Press, p 5

2 Mendes, Errol. Canada's reputation is tainted by bribery and abuse. Only boards can rescue it. March 13, 2013. *The Globe and Mail*. https://www. theglobeandmail.com/opinion/canadas-reputation-is-tainted-by-bribery-and-abuse-only-boards-can-rescue-it/article9299575/ [Accessed June 1, 2017]

3 Clean Up The Pictou County Pulp Mill Facebook Group: https://www. facebook.com/groups/545965902107532/ [Accessed June 2, 2016]

4 Northern Pulp website, local economic impact. http://northernpulp.ca/ our-company/local-economic-impact/ [Accessed June 2, 2016]

5 http://cleanthemill.com/ [Accessed June 2, 2016]

6 Some background on the creation of the Facebook page and the Group is provided in a video available at: https://www.youtube.com/ watch?v=cvQmzfjxqfc [Accessed September 25, 2016]

Chapter 1 (pages 20-26, notes 7 to 14)

7 Lyrics from "The Smell of Money," a song by Smokey Dymny © 1999, used with permission. Tune: "Blackleg Miner"

8 *Lonely Planet*, Introduction to Pictou, Nova Scotia. http://www. lonelyplanet.com/canada/nova-scotia/pictou/introduction [Accessed October 24, 2016]

9 Johnson, Clarence. Pulp plant operation to involve 1,000 persons. July 14, 1967. *The Chronicle-Herald*, p 11

10 New plant to produce 172,000 tons bleached pulp annually. November 14, 1967. *The Mail-Star*, p S-3

11 A doctor gives us some free advice (Editorial). October 7, 1970. *The Evening News*

12 Stephenson, Marilla. With Northern Pulp, protecting jobs comes first. August 23, 2014. *The Chronicle Herald*

13 Cloutier, Kathy. Cloutier's corner: If you don't tell your own story, someone else will. *Northern Pulse*, December 2015. p 3. http://northernpulp.ca/assets/Uploads/Northern-Pulse-E-Newsletter-4th-Quarter-2015.pdf [Accessed June 26, 2017]

14 A written request (January 11, 2017) was made to Northern Pulp Board Chair Dr. John Hamm, and requests were made by telephone, email, and letter in January 2017 to Northern Pulp communications director Kathy Cloutier for interviews for this book. In an email (January 23, 2017), Cloutier replied saying there had been discussions within the parent company Paper Excellence, and Northern Pulp's board and executive team, and a decision had been made not to participate in this project.

Chapter 2 (pages 27-34, notes 15 to 41)

15 MacDonald, Ron. Pulp mill for Pictou County: Announcement of details slated within 24 hours. December 23, 1964. *The Chronicle-Herald*

16 Stevens, Geoffrey. 1973. *Stanfield*. Toronto, Ontario: McClelland and Stewart, p 29

17 Watkins, Lyndon. Mill is boon to the economy. December 24, 1964. *The Chronicle-Herald*

18 Canada began using the metric system in 1970, so before that volumes and weights are non-metric. Thus, in this book, "tons" refers to 2,000 pounds and "tonnes" refers to 1,000 kilograms.

19 Poitras, Jacques. 2014. *Irving vs. Irving: Canada's feuding billionaires and the stories they won't tell*. Toronto, Ontario: The Penguin Group, p 16

20 Bruce, Harry. 1985. *Frank Sobey: the man and the empire*. Toronto, Ontario: MacMillan of Canada, pp 261-262

21 Ibid

22 Ralph S. Johnson papers. n.d. Brief outline of history of Hollingsworth & Whitney Ltd. and Scott Paper Co. in Nova Scotia. p 79, Public Archives of Nova Scotia (PANS) TP140 B329

23 Bates, John S. 1983. *By the way 1883-1983*. Hantsport, NS: Lancelot Press. PANS FS175 A881 S741 1-0088327

24 Creighton, Wilfrid. 1988. *Forestkeeping: A history of the Department of Lands and Forests in Nova Scotia 1962-1969.* Halifax, NS: Province of Nova Scotia, The Department of Lands and Forests, pp 101-102

25 Bruce, Harry. 1985. *Frank Sobey: the man and the empire.* Toronto, Ontario: MacMillan of Canada, pp 261-262

26 Ibid

27 Expected to play major role in Pictou County's economy. November 14, 1967. *The Mail-Star*, p S-4

28 The Scott brothers started with a pushcart and a loan. November 14, 1967. *The Mail-Star,* p S-6

29 Pulp, paper industry: New plants, new products, bright future. *Nova Scotia Newsletter,* September 1966, Vol 5(9), p 3. Halifax, NS: Nova Scotia Information Service

30 Dennis, Eric. Scott Paper Co. acquires pulp mill at Sheet Harbour. September 9, 1964. *The Chronicle-Herald*

31 Dennis, Eric. Scott Paper Co. acquires pulp mill at Sheet Harbour. September 9, 1964. *The Chronicle-Herald*; MacDonald, Ron. Speculation on new pulp and paper mill. November 7, 1964. *The Chronicle-Herald*

32 Feds' Satellite Forest Monitoring Map illustrates intensity of forest harvesting in Nova Scotia. *Nova Scotia Forest Notes.* Healthy Forest Coalition. (www.healthyforestcoalition.ca) February 11, 2017. http://nsforestnotes.ca/2017/02/11/feds-satellite-forest-monitoring-map-illustrates-intensity-of-forest-harvesting-in-nova-scotia/#more-5065 [Accessed February 11, 2017]

33 Bissix, Glyn and Sandberg, L. Anders. 1992. The political economy of Nova Scotia's Forest Improvement Act 1962-1986. *In:* Sandberg, L. Anders (ed). *Trouble in the woods: forest policy and social conflict in Nova Scotia and New Brunswick.* Fredericton, NB: Acadiensis Press for the Gorsebrook Research Institute for Atlantic Canada Studies

34 Sandberg, L. Anders and Clancy, Peter. 2000. *Against the grain: foresters and politics in Nova Scotia.* Vancouver, BC: UBC Press

35 Bissix, Glyn and Sandberg, L. Anders. 1992. The political economy of Nova Scotia's Forest Improvement Act 1962-1986. *In:* Sandberg, L. Anders (ed). *Trouble in the woods: forest policy and social conflict in Nova Scotia and New Brunswick.* Fredericton, NB: Acadiensis Press for the Gorsebrook Research Institute for Atlantic Canada Studies, p 173

36 Ibid

37 Smith once known as "Hatchet Man." September 15, 1967. *The Evening News*

38 Sandberg, L. Anders and Clancy, Peter. 2000. *Against the grain: foresters and politics in Nova Scotia.* Vancouver, BC: UBC Press, p 119

39 Ibid

40 Expected to play major role in Pictou County's economy. November 14, 1967. *The Mail-Star,* p S-4.

41 Freeman, William A. Scott is planning a new pulp mill. December 24, 1964. *The New York Times*. http://www.nytimes.com/1964/12/24/scott-is-planning-a-new-pulp-mill.html [Accessed September 12, 2016]

Chapter 3 (pages 35-43, notes 42 to 57)

42 Miller, Walter, cited in: Pulp, paper industry: New plants, new products, bright future. September 1966. *Nova Scotia Newsletter* Vol 5(9) Halifax, NS: Nova Scotia Information Service

43 Scott Maritimes Limited Agreement (1965) Act. http://nslegislature.ca/legc/statutes/scottmar.htm [Accessed August 27, 2016]

44 Thurston, Harry. Prest's last stand: keeping Kafka and the bureaucrats out of the Acadian woods. *Harrowsmith,* Aug/Sept 1983, pp 23-30

45 Sunder, Rae. Scott can see woods for trees. February 9, 1970. *The Chronicle-Herald*

46 Johnson, Clarence. Pulp plant operation to involve 1,000 persons. July 14, 1967. *The Chronicle-Herald*, p 11

47 Sandberg, L. Anders and Clancy, Peter. 2000. *Against the grain: foresters and politics in Nova Scotia*. Vancouver, BC: UBC Press, p. 89

48 Seakem Oceanography Limited. 1990. Preliminary environmental profile – Pictou Harbour. A report to Environment Canada Conservation and Protection

49 Agreement between Her Majesty the Queen and Scott Maritime Pulp Limited. September 30, 1970

50 Report for the Executive Council. November 30, 1965. Signed by Minister under the Water Act, R.L. Stanfield on April 6, 1966

51 Ibid

52 Agreement between Her Majesty the Queen and Scott Maritime Pulp Limited. September 30, 1970

53 Ibid

54 Thurston, Harry. Prest's last stand: keeping Kafka and the bureaucrats out of the Acadian woods. *Harrowsmith,* Aug/Sept 1983, pp 23-30

55 Bruce, Harry. 1985. *Frank Sobey: the man and the empire.* Toronto, Ontario: MacMillan of Canada, p 262

56 Agreement between the Province of Nova Scotia and Scott Maritimes Pulp Limited. September 30, 1970

57 University of King's College Investigative Workshop. Pulp mill's warm welcome to Pictou County sealed fate of Boat Harbour. April 23, 2009. (In 2009, students of the investigative workshop at the University of King's College School of Journalism undertook a six-week study of Boat Harbour and its toxic legacy. Their landmark reports and source materials were posted online, although the platform and URL are no longer functional. The reports can still be viewed using the Internet archive "wayback machine" using the URL: http://boatharbour.kingsjournalism.com/)

Chapter 4 (pages 44-55, notes 58 to 94)

58 Pictou Landing Native Women's Group (c/o Sheila Francis, Past President), Castleden, H., Lewis, D., Jamieson, R., Gibson, M., Rainham, D., Russell, R., Martin, D., and Hart, C. (2016). "Our Ancestors Are in Our Land, Water, and Air": A Two-Eyed Seeing Approach to Researching Environmental Health Concerns with Pictou Landing First Nation – Final Report, p 1

59 Pictou Landing First Nations history. http://www.plfn.ca/cultural-history/history/ [Accessed September 20, 2016]

60 Francis, Sheila. Statement made during presentation at Halifax Regional Library by women of Pictou Landing First Nation: "Our Ancestors Are in Our Land, Water, and Air": A Two-Eyed Seeing Approach to Researching Environmental Health Concerns with Pictou Landing First Nation. November 30, 2016

61 MacKay, Ferguson. 2014. *A history of Pictou Landing.* Stellarton, NS: Self-published.

62 National park at Pictou Landing. February 23, 1923. *The Pictou Advocate,* p 1

63 University of King's College Investigative Workshop. Pulp mill's warm welcome to Pictou County sealed fate of Boat Harbour. April 23, 2009

64 Interview with John Seaman Bates by Claude Vickery in "The Deal," an episode of CBC television program, *Land and Sea,* 1988

65 Sandberg, L. Anders and Clancy, Peter. 2000. *Against the grain: foresters and politics in Nova Scotia.* Vancouver, BC: UBC Press, p 88

66 University of King's College Investigative Workshop. Pulp mill welcome to Pictou sealed fate of Boat Harbour. April 23, 2009

67 Bates, Dr. John S. Damage and disgrace. *Atlantic Advocate.* 1964. Vol 55(4): 17- 24

68 Ibid

69 Harder, Steve. Boat Harbour: its dark waters reflect price of industrial gain. October 1, 1988. *The Chronicle-Herald*

70 One of the most impressive plants anywhere. November 24, 1967. *The Chronicle-Herald*

71 Bates, John S. 1983. *By the way 1883-1983.* Hantsport, NS: Lancelot Press, p 80. PANS, TP 140 B329

72 Ibid p 80

73 Letter to The Honourable John R. Nicholson from the Nova Scotia Water Authority. July 19, 1965. PANS, "File concerning pollution at Boat Harbour," MGI Vol. 1437 No. 17A

74 Memorandum to F.B. McKinnon, Regional Supervisor, Indian Agencies, Amherst, NS from W.A. MacDonald, Regional Development Officer, Re: Meeting at Pictou Landing Reserve re Use of Boat Harbour, Aug. 25th. September 9, 1965. PANS, "File concerning pollution at Boat Harbour," MGI Vol. 1437 No. 17A

75 Letter from John R. Nicholson to W.S.K. Jones, Nova Scotia Minister of Trade and Industry. September 20, 1965. PANS, "File concerning pollution at Boat Harbour," MGI Vol. 1437 No. 17A

76 Michael Denny speaking in "The Deal," an episode of CBC television program *Land and Sea,* 1988

77 Paul, Daniel N. 2006. *We were not the savages: collision between European and native American civilizations,* 3rd edition. Blackpoint, NS and Winnipeg, Manitoba: Fernwood Publishing

78 Memorandum from W.P. McIntyre, Regional Director Indian Agencies, Nova Scotia, Re: Proposed use of Boat Harbour, Pictou County, for waste water treatment. October 14, 1965. PANS, "File concerning pollution at Boat Harbour," MGI Vol. 1437 No. 17A

79 Paul, Daniel N. 2006. *We were not the savages: collision between European and native American civilizations,* 3rd edition. Blackpoint, NS and Winnipeg, Manitoba: Fernwood Publishing

80 "It's all gone now." Episode of CBC program *Country Calendar,* presented by Peter Brock. April 17, 1970

81 Boat Harbour project still in study stage. October 18, 1965. *The Evening News*

82 A.F. Wigglesworth assures residents raw waste will not empty into bay. October 21, 1965. *The Pictou Advocate*

83 MacDonald, Dr. J.B. Letter to Rust and Associates Consulting Engineers. March 22, 1970

84 Report for the Executive Council, signed by R.L. Stanfield, Minister under the Water Act. April 6, 1966

85 Agreement with the Governor General in Council. Governor House, Ottawa. September 2, 1966

86 Memorandum from Regional Director W.P. McIntyre re: B.C.R. from Pictou Landing Consenting to use of Boat Harbour as waste water disposal area. October 22, 1965. PANS, "File concerning pollution at Boat Harbour," MGI Vol. 1437 No. 17A

87 Agreement with the Governor General in Council. Governor House, Ottawa. September 2, 1966

88 Paul, Daniel N. 2006. *We were not the savages: collision between European and native American civilizations,* 3rd edition. Blackpoint, NS and Winnipeg, Manitoba: Fernwood Publishing

89 "It's all gone now." Episode of CBC program *Country Calendar,* presented by Peter Brock. April 17, 1970

90 Water Authority general manager resigns post. April 1966. *The Evening News*

91 Rowe new chairman of N.S. Water Authority. July 26, 1966. *The Mail-Star*

92 *The Canadian Encyclopedia*: http://www.thecanadianencyclopedia.ca/en/article/john-seaman-bates/ [Accessed September 21, 2016]

93 *Queen's County Times*: Order of Canada recipients: Armand F. Wigglesworth, C.M., B.E.M., C.D. http://www.queenscountytimes.ca/OC/page2.html [Accessed September 22, 2016]

94 Paul, Daniel N. 2006. *We were not the savages: collision between European and native American civilizations,* 3rd edition. Blackpoint, NS and Winnipeg, Manitoba: Fernwood Publishing, p 242

Chapter 5 (pages 56-68, notes 95 to 120)

95 Pannozzo, Linda. 2016. *About Canada: The environment.* Halifax, NS and Winnipeg, Manitoba: Fernwood Publishing, p 142

96 Paul, Daniel N. 2006. *We were not the savages: collision between European and native American civilizations,* 3rd edition. Blackpoint, NS and Winnipeg, Manitoba: Fernwood Publishing, p 242

97 What does McEwan say about Boat Harbour? Letter to the editor by "Interested reader." February 27, 1969. *The Pictou Advocate*

98 Land already expropriated $11.50 acre offers refused. n.d. *The Pictou Advocate*

99 Effluent line to be completed to Boat Harbor area by October this year. March 1966. *The Evening News*

100 Krauel, David P. December 1969. Tidal flushing of Pictou Harbour – Pictou Road. Fishers Research Board of Canada, Technical Report No. 146. Dartmouth, NS: Marine Ecology Laboratory, Bedford Institute, p i

101 Effluent line to be completed to Boat Harbour area by October of this year. March 1966. *The Evening News*

102 Tenders called for dams on Boat Harbor for Scott Paper mill. October 11, 1966. *The Evening News*

103 Decision of the County Court of District Number Five, by Judge Lusby September 2, 1969 In the Matter of Chapter 91 of the Revised Statutes of Nova Scotia 1954, entitled the Expropriation Act, and In The Matter of the Expropriation of certain lands situated at Boat Harbour, in the registration district two of the County of Pictou, and In The Matter of the Claim for Compensation of Henry G. Ferguson as a land owner.

104 Residents feel frustrated regarding waste disposal. n.d. *The Pictou Advocate*

105 Water Authority chairman surprised at hue and cry. n.d. *The Pictou Advocate*

106 Stephen T. Pyke officiates at ceremony. November 14, 1967. *The Evening News*

107 Filling Stanfield's shoes "no bed of roses." February 26, 1969. *The Evening News*

108 Michael Denny speaking in "The Deal," an episode of CBC television program *Land and Sea*, 1988

109 Effluent line to be completed to Boat Harbour area by October of this year. March 1966. *The Evening News*

110 Pollution of air and water could offset tourist industry (Editorial). December 19, 1968. *The Pictou Advocate*

111 Lobster fishery: little concern over Scott Mill disposal. February 8, 1968. *The Evening News*

112 Clr. Henry Ferguson bitter about Boat Harbor pollution. October 3, 1968. *The Pictou Advocate*

113 MacDonald, Henry. Correspondence, letter to the editor. August 7, 1968. *The Evening News*

114 Boat Harbor situation: Says local MLAs should be working harder on matter. October 19, 1968. *The Evening News*

115 Hon. Donald MacLeod: Minister would rather swim at Boat Harbor than in polluted East River waters. November 25, 1968. *The Evening News*

116 Ibid

117 Says pollution 1000% percent more than allowed in Quebec. December 19, 1968. *The Pictou Advocate*

118 Feels Boat Harbor process equal to any system. Presents chart showing system in other mills. June 3, 1969. *The Evening News*

119 Sunder, Rae. Cabinet committee to lead fight against pollution in N.S. March 13, 1969. *The Chronicle-Herald*

120 Regan welcomes appointment of pollution committee; blasts government for situation in County. March 14, 1969. *The Chronicle-Herald*

Chapter 6 (pages 69-83, notes 121 to 173)

121 Presented by Lionel G. Morash of Trenton. Beautiful scenic spot dead and foul-smelling. March 26, 1970. *The Evening News*

122 Councillor Henry Ferguson kept a scrapbook of newspaper clippings that documented the pollution and controversy caused by the mill, which was a valuable source of reference material for this book.

123 MacKay, Fergie. 2014. *A history of Pictou Landing.* Self-published.

124 J.A. Delaney & Associates. Interim Report No. 1: Sea pollution from Boat Harbor, N.S. July 31, 1969

125 To say Boat Harbor isn't working is a fallacy, declares Delaney but ... November 18, 1969. *The Evening News*

126 Delaney report proposes solution for Boat Harbor: plan presented on behalf of citizens to Premier Smith. November 18, 1969. *The Mail-Star*

127 Pictou County tackles pollution problems. n.d. *The Chronicle-Herald*

128 Ogden, J. Gordon. Biologist admits he's hysterical about Boat Harbor – and explains why (Letter to the editor). November 27, 1969. *The Pictou Advocate*

129 Scott's general manager writes explanatory letter to employees. n.d. *The Evening News*

130 Problem can be solved – engineer. n.d. *The Chronicle-Herald*

131 MacDonald, J.B. "Not unreasonable cost". n.d. *The Chronicle-Herald*

132 Other matters discussed at PC meeting: says Boat Harbor is not a breeding or living place for lobsters. December 6, 1969. *The Evening News*

133 Fishermen take exception to statements by Veniot. December 8, 1969. *The Pictou Advocate*

134 Pictou County controversy: Government "permissive" about pollution. March 17, 1970. *The Chronicle-Herald*

135 MacDonald, Dr. J.B. Letter to Rust Associates and Consulting Engineers. March 22, 1970

136 Tests refute charges, says Scott manager. March 17, 1970. *The Chronicle-Herald*

137 Consultants will meet citizens – Rowe. March 17, 1970. *The Chronicle-Herald*

138 Scott effluent blasted: Pictonians protest. March 26, 1970. *The Chronicle-Herald*

139 30 presentations made at pollution hearing. March 26, 1970. *The Evening News*

140 Union expresses concern over pollution from mill. March 20, 1970. *The Evening News*

141 Water resources chairman clashes with Margeson, McLellan & Delaney. March 26, 1970. *The Evening News*

142 Letters to the editor: Resolution on pollution. May 25, 1970. *The Pictou Advocate*

143 Teachers concerned about Boat Harbor. May 21, 1970. *The Pictou Advocate*

144 Troyer, Warner. 1977. *No safe place.* Toronto, Ontario and Vancouver, BC: Clarke, Irwin & Company Limited

145 Ibid

146 Jack Pink of Canso Chemicals says: We didn't come here to poison people. April 28, 1970. *The Evening News*

147 Plant is given green light. August 11, 1970. *The Evening News*

148 Expansion underway at Canso Chemicals. October 16, 1970. *The Chronicle-Herald*

149 Foshay, Rae. Rust report findings may be "too general." June 6, 1970. *The Chronicle-Herald*

150 Foshay, Rae. Rust report remains clouded in secrecy; MacLeod silent. June 17, 1970. *The Chronicle-Herald*

151 Local Pollution Committee discusses secrecy of report. June 19, 1970. *The Evening News*

152 Charges government deliberately suppressing importance of report. July 23, 1970. *The Pictou Advocate*

153 Meerburg, Peter. Rust report crushing blow to Pictou hopes. July 30, 1970. *The Chronicle-Herald*

154 Rust report challenged. July 31, 1970. *The Chronicle-Herald*

155 Lukewarm attitude of MacLeod and Rowe no surprise, says NDP's Cormier. August 3, 1970. *The Evening News*

156 Party leader Regan says: Government has responsibility to area. August 8, 1970. *The Evening News*

157 Hinds, Barbara. Rust report challenged. July 31, 1970. *The Chronicle-Herald*

158 Delaney says Rust report compiled to block cleanup of Boat Harbor. August 10, 1970. *The Evening News*

159 Scott Maritimes already taking action to improve its screening equipment. July 31, 1970. *The Evening News*

160 Scott image "tarnished." August 1, 1970. *The Chronicle-Herald*

161 Booming support. August 13, 1970. *The Pictou Advocate*

162 Gass, Reverend D.H. Letter to Nova Scotia Premier G.I. Smith. August 16, 1970

163 Rowe, E.L.L. Letter to Reverend D.H. Gass Re: County of Pictou – Boat Harbour waste treatment facilities – address to Rotary Club. August 31, 1970

164 Foshay, Rae. Boat Harbor pollution: Legal action gets approval. August 28, 1970. *The Chronicle-Herald*

165 Foshay, Rae. Legal action plans to curb pollution held in abeyance. September 5, 1970. *The Chronicle-Herald*

166 Scott reveals $1.5 million on-site environmental control plan: mill's program to deal with odor, solid wastes and stack emissions. September 17, 1970. *The Evening News*

167 Scott reveals $1.5 million on-site environmental control plan: Donald R. announces program for Boat Harbor – Scott Mill. September 17, 1970. *The Evening News*

168 Scott program praised, but government plans condemned. September 18, 1970. *The Chronicle-Herald*

169 Fillmore, Nick. Boat Harbor scheme shaky. September 24, 1970. *The 4th Estate*

170 Pictou East MLA, local Pollution Committee visit mill in Maine. October 28, 1970. *The Evening News*

171 Pictou West MLA "smokes out" Fergie MacKay government appointment. February 18, 1972. *The Evening News*

172 Ferguson MacKay replies to charges by Harvey Veniot. February 21, 1972. *The Evening News*

173 *Nova Scotia Water.* Halifax, NS: The Nova Scotia Water Resources Commission. 1972. PANS MG100 Vol. 202 #21-21a

Chapter 7 (pages 84-104, notes 174 to 246)

174 Pictou Landing Band Office. R. v. Northern Pulp Nova Scotia Corporation: Victim impact statement. February 17, 2016. p 2. http://canadianaboriginallaw.com/wordpress1/wp-content/uploads/2016/02/PLFN-Victim-Impact-Statement-2016-02-221.pdf [Accessed February 28, 2017]

175 Foshay, Rae. Pictou area successfully combatting water pollution at Boat Harbour. January 2, 1974. *The Chronicle Herald*

176 Currie, Brian. $650,000 lawsuit launched by province. June 23, 1976. *The 4th Estate*

177 Ibid

178 Canadian Press. Plant told to cut mysterious mercury losses. June 20, 1977. *The Montreal Gazette*

179 Ibid

180 For a detailed account of this mercury poisoning, its devastating effects on the First Nation communities and their environment, and the "scandalous" response of both federal and provincial governments when it was happening in the 1960s, see the 1977 book by Warner Troyer, *No safe place,* published by Clarke, Irwin & Company Limited.

181 Poisson, James and Bruser, David. Mercury-tainted soil found upstream from Grassy Narrows First Nation. January 12, 2017. *Toronto Star.* https://www.thestar.com/news/investigations/2017/01/12/mercury-tainted-soil-found-upstream-from-grassy-narrows-first-nation.html [Accessed March 16, 2017]

182 Poisson, James and Bruser, David. Ontario "completely committed" to mercury cleanup at Grassy Narrows. February 13, 2017. *Toronto Star.* https://www.thestar.com/news/canada/2017/02/13/ontario-completely-committed-to-mercury-cleanup-at-grassy-narrows.html [Accessed March 16, 2017]

183 Warden calls for subsidization to keep Canso Chemicals going. December 11, 1978. *The Evening News*

184 Federal government will help Canso – MacKay. December 11, 1978. *The Evening News*

185 For a detailed account of the citizen action to prevent the aerial spraying of forests in Cape Breton and the pressure from the pulp industry on governments to approve the spraying, see: May, Elizabeth. 1982.

Budworm battles – The fight to stop the aerial insecticide spraying of the forests of Eastern Canada. Glen Margaret, NS: Four East Publications Ltd.

186 Federal government will help Canso – MacKay. December 11, 1978. *The Evening News*

187 Assurances of work until at least 1984. Early Christmas gift for Canso Chemicals. December 20, 1978. *The Evening News*

188 Scott modernization shows confidence in future. September 1, 1982. *The Chronicle-Herald*

189 Taylor, Wilkie. Scott strike will not end until attitude changes, says union. February 24, 1983. *The Chronicle-Herald*

190 Vibert, Jim. Premier gives no assurances: 10,000 demand end of strike at Scott paper. April 15, 1983. *The Mail-Star*

191 Taylor, Wilkie. Scott cancels plans for $51 million modernization. May 25, 1983. *The Chronicle-Herald*

192 Taylor, Wilkie. Scott Maritimes workers vote to end strike. May 31, 1983. *The Chronicle-Herald*

193 Harder, Steve. April 20, 1985. *The Nova Scotian.* (In a telephone conversation on July 5, 2016, Jack Kyte declined to be interviewed for this book.)

194 Harder, Steve. April 20, 1985.*The Nova Scotian*

195 Swift, Jamie. Pulp friction: the growing controversy over kraft-mill pollution. *Harrowsmith,* January/February 1990, pp 35-43

196 CBC *fifth estate*, 1988. Canadian Broadcasting Corporation. Available at: https://www.youtube.com/watch?v=3Tto9FP7m_U [Accessed July 21, 2016]

197 Jobb, Dean. 1994. *Calculated risk: Greed, politics, and the Westray tragedy.* Halifax, NS: Nimbus Publishing Limited, p 186

198 Ibid

199 Majka, Christopher G. Fast facts: Power to the people? June 14, 2012. Canadian Centre for Policy Alternatives. https://www.policyalternatives.ca/publications/commentary/fast-facts-power-people [Accessed June 1, 2017]

200 Harder, Steve. Boat Harbour: its dark waters reflect price of industrial gain. October 1, 1988. *The Chronicle-Herald*

201 Swift, Jamie. Pulp friction: the growing controversy over kraft-mill pollution. *Harrowsmith,* January/February 1990, p 39

202 Christie, Robert E.K. December 1988. Technical proposal #1. The establishment of a systematic biomonitoring regimen at the Boat Harbour Industrial Wastes Treatment Facility: an integrated ecotoxicological report. Citizens Against Pollution Technical Research Committee

203 Interview with Robert Christie, August 25, 2016

204 Citizens Against Pollution (CAP) leaflet for members. n.d.

205 Fraser, Peter and Christie, Robert. The $mell of money. *Between the Issues:* Oct.-Dec. 1989, pp 13-15

206 Ibid

207 CAP News 1991.

208 Olsen, Michael. Boat Harbour effluent caused beach closure: govt' official. September 16, 1989. *The Evening News*

209 Boat Harbour effluent treatment facility: mercury discovered in sediment samples. October 17, 1989. *The Evening News*

210 Environment Department checking Boat Harbor. October 13, 1990. *The Evening News*

211 Feds drop case on Boat Harbour. April 10, 1991. *The Daily News*

212 Ibid

213 Morrison, Campbell. Feds won't reveal rules for Boat Harbour. April 10, 1991. *The Daily News*

214 Harder, Steve. Boat Harbour: Environment Department looks for new operator, September 9, 1989. *The Chronicle Herald*; and Interview with CBC's Jennifer Henderson for *Information Morning* (Halifax). April 20, 2015. http://www.cbc.ca/player/play/2664862121 [Accessed January 4, 2017]

215 Feds drop case on Boat Harbour. April 10, 1991. *The Daily News*

216 Byrne, Gerry. To the people of Pictou County. September 25, 1989. *Scott Environmental Management Plan*

217 Ibid

218 Olsen, Michael. Boat Harbour effluent caused beach closure: govt' official. September 16, 1989. *The Evening News*

219 Industry Minister Don Cameron says: time for Scott to build a new treatment facility. October 17, 1990. *The Evening News*

220 Swift, Jamie. Pulp friction: the growing controversy over kraft-mill pollution. *Harrowsmith:* January/February 1990, pp 35-43

221 Ibid

222 Ibid

223 Ibid p 41

224 CAP Newsflash. Simons study on treating Scott's waste released. November 1991.

225 Ibid

226 Butler, Ishbel. Air-born dioxins: Scott's new environmental experiment will mean breathing dioxins and furans. *CAP News,* Nov-Dec 1991

227 Correspondence from Ishbel Butler (Munro), Citizens Against Pollution, to Jane Sproull Thomson, Moodie Cove Residents Co-op

228 Ibid

229 Underhill, Brian. Tobin says he'll stop Boat Harbour project to protect fish habitat. March 26, 1994. *The Chronicle-Herald*

230 Harder, Steve. Boat Harbour plan sparks debate. 1994. *The Chronicle Herald*

231 Byrnes, Gerry. Letter to Scott employees. Reprinted in: CAP newsletter, April/May 1994

232 Sweet, Barb. CAP feels legal review of agreement with Scott will spell the end of Boat Harbour. April 1, 1991. *The Evening News*

233 Renouf, Mark. Province told it can break B. Harbour waste pact. April 25, 1991. *The Daily News*

234 Scharper, Stephen Bede. Grassy Narrows mercury disaster a form of environmental racism. June 29, 2016. *Toronto Star*. https://www.thestar.com/opinion/commentary/2016/06/29/grassy-narrows-mercury-disaster-a-form-of-environmental-racism.html [Accessed March 5, 2017]

235 Christie, Robert. Letter from Robert Christie to CAP members. *Citizens against pollution news* November/December 1991

236 What's new: Northern Pulp reaffirms environmental stewardship commitment. May 27, 2010. http://northernpulp.ca/news/article/2010-May-Stewardship [Accessed January 28, 2015]

237 Ibid

238 Northern Pulp signs environmental stewardship agreement. May 31, 2010. *The News* (New Glasgow). http://www.ngnews.ca/news/local/2010/5/31/northern-pulp-signs-environment-stewards-1204456.html [Accessed March 16, 2017]

239 Scott Maritimes. Environmental Management Plan. 1992

240 Safer, Andrew. Forestry company phases out chlorine bleach: Scott Maritimes puts millions into environmental upgrade. *Atlantic Business Report,* September 1992

241 Scott Maritimes. Environmental Management Plan. 1993

242 Ibid

243 Taylor, Wilkie. Modification will allow mill to produce cleaner pulp. January 15, 1992. *The Chronicle-Herald,* p B12

244 Scott Maritimes. Environmental Management Plan. 1993

245 Blackmer, Andrew J. Letter to Dan Currie, General Manager, Canso Chemicals, to accompany presentation of six copies of "Canso Chemicals site decommissioning final report." January 26, 2000

246 Ibid pp 35, 37

Chapter 8 (pages 105-118, notes 247 to 287)

247 Quoted by Ted Poole in essay "Conversations with North American Indians." *In:* Osborne Ralph (ed.). 1972. *Who is the Chairman of This Meeting?: A Collection of Essays.* Toronto: Neewin Publishing, p. 43.

248 Cited by the University of King's College Investigative Workshop. Laid to waste – Boat Harbour clean-up plans gone stale. April 23, 2009

249 Indians plan action on Boat Harbor: seek to declare agreement illegal. September 22, 1970. *The Chronicle-Herald*

250 Soss, Mollie. Noel Doucette tells Indian meeting: can't see anyone in their right mind go near Boat Harbor and not complain. September 22, 1970. *The Evening News*

251 Next time we will bring bulldozers, Indians charge at Boat Harbour ditch. September 23, 1970. *The Evening News*

252 Foshay, Rae. Indians block effluent ditch. September 23, 1970. *The Chronicle-Herald*

253 O'Reilly, James, letter to Jean Chrétien, cc to Raymond Francis and Noel Doucette. October 7, 1970. PANS "Pollution at Boat Harbour," MGI Vol. 1437 No. 17A

254 Chrétien, Jean. Letter from Minister of Indian Affairs and Northern Development to James O'Reilly. November 4, 1970. PANS "Pollution at Boat Harbour," MGI Vol. 1437 No. 17A

255 Hon. Glen Bagnell releases statement at press conference on Boat Harbor. February 19, 1972. *The Evening News*

256 Big "Mixmasters" threshing Boat Harbor system effluent. September 18, 1973. *The Evening News*

257 Sweet, Barb. At Boat Harbor: Natives set up successful blockade. April 17, 1991. *The Evening News*

258 The University of King's College Investigative Workshop. Laid to waste – Boat Harbour clean-up plans gone stale. April 23, 2009

259 Paul, Daniel N. 2006. *We were not the savages: collision between European and native American civilizations,* 3rd edition. Blackpoint, NS and Winnipeg, Manitoba: Fernwood Publishing, p 242

260 University of King's College Investigative Workshop. Boat Harbour: on toxic pond. April 23, 2009

261 Harder, Steve. Boat Harbour: its dark waters reflect price of industrial gain. October 1, 1988. *The Chronicle-Herald*

262 University of King's College Investigative Workshop. Laid to waste – Boat Harbour clean-up plans gone stale. April 23, 2009

263 Statement of Defence, T-1075-86, in the Federal Court of Canada Trial Division, Between Roderick Frances, Kenneth Frances, Robert Frances, and John Prosper, Plaintiffs, and Her Majesty the Queen, Defendant. August 12, 1986

264 Ibid

265 Paul, Daniel N. 2006. *We were not the savages: collision between European and native American civilizations,* 3rd edition. Blackpoint, NS and Winnipeg, Manitoba: Fernwood Publishing, pp 242, 248, and interview with Daniel Paul, December 20, 2016

266 Harder, Steve. Final Boat Harbour payments by April: Micmacs will have received $35 million from Ottawa. December 1994. *The Evening News*

267 Pictou Landing Band Council. Open letter to all members of the Pictou Landing Indian Band entitled to vote in the referendum on this matter. May 6, 2002

268 The Canadian Press. Boat Harbour settlement divides Pictou Micmacs. June 23, 1993. *The Chronicle-Herald*

269 Jones, Randy. Paying for pollution: Micmac reserve split on Boat Harbour deal. June 26, 1993. *The Chronicle-Herald,* pp B1-2

270 Pictou Landing Band Council. Open letter to all members of the Pictou Landing Indian Band entitled to vote in the referendum on this matter. May 6, 2002

271 Collins, Glen. Kimberly-Clark to buy Scott Paper, challenging P&G. July 18, 1995. *The New York Times.* http://www.nytimes.com/1995/07/18/business/kimberly-clark-to-buy-scott-paper-challenging-p-g.html [Accessed December 12, 2016]

272 Byrnes, Gerry. Letter to Scott employees. Reprinted in: CAP newsletter, April/May 1994

273 Memorandum of Understanding between Her Majesty the Queen in Right of the Province of Nova Scotia and Scott Maritimes Limited. December 1, 1995

274 Ibid

275 Harder, Steve. Feds OK Boat Harbour extension: Ownership of effluent system must be settled by 1996. January 5, 1994. *The Chronicle-Herald*

276 Nova Scotia Department of Supply and Services. Boat Harbour transfer (Press Release). January 12, 1996. http://novascotia.ca/cmns/msrv/viewRel.asp?relID=/cmns/msrv/nr-1996/nr96-01/96011203.htm [Accessed December 12, 2016]

277 Indemnity Agreement between Her Majesty the Queen in Right of the Province of Nova Scotia and Scott Maritimes Limited. December 31, 1995.

278 Lease Agreement between Her Majesty the Queen in Right of the Province of Nova Scotia and Scott Maritimes Limited. December 31, 1995.

279 Harder, Steve. Notorious lagoon to be shut down: Boat Harbour system will close in 10 years, N.S. says. January 13, 1996. *The Chronicle-Herald*

280 Ibid

281 University of King's College Journalism Students. A decade (and more) of plans. April 23, 2009

282 MacEachern, Lana. Boat Harbour cleanup hits algae snag. September 29, 2005. *The Evening News*

283 Pictou Landing Band Council. Open letter to all members of the Pictou Landing Indian Band entitled to vote in the referendum on this matter. May 6, 2002

284 Government of Nova Scotia, Department of Transportation and Public Works. Boat Harbour Progress (press release). October 4, 2002.

285 Ibid

286 Ibid

287 University of King's College Journalism Students. Boat Harbour by the numbers. April 23, 2009

Chapter 9 (pages 119-125, notes 288 to 298)

288 Troyer, Warner. 1977. *No safe place*. Toronto, Ontario and Vancouver, BC: Clarke, Irwin & Company Limited, pp 35-36

289 University of King's College Journalism Students. It's not fair – Some landowners say they should be compensated too. April 23, 2009

290 Pictou County this week: Boat Harbour protester supports lawsuit. April 2, 2002. *The Evening News*

291 Correspondence from Jane Sproull Thomson to Chris Moir, Nova Scotia Department of Transportation and Public Works. November 1, 2006. Correspondence between Jane Sproull Thomson and Peter MacKay (MP)

292 Ibid

293 Draft Minutes: Boat Harbour Committee Meeting. November 29, 2006

294 Goodwin, Steve. MacKenzie protesting pulp mill's emissions. July 30, 2014. *The Pictou Advocate*

295 Effluent fallout: more breaks than thought. December 5, 2008. *The News* (New Glasgow)

296 Paul, Daniel N. 2006. *We were not the savages: collision between European and native American civilizations,* 3rd edition. Blackpoint, NS and Winnipeg, Manitoba: Fernwood Publishing, p 246

297 Ballot box bandit causes problems in Pictou. November 28, 2000. CBC News. http://www.cbc.ca/news/canada/ballot-box-bandit-causes-problems-in-pictou-1.209156 [Accessed January 5, 2017]

298 The Canadian Press. 'Ballot Box Bandit' gets suspended sentence. May 12, 2006. *The Globe and Mail*. http://www.theglobeandmail.com/news/national/ballot-box-bandit-gets-suspended-sentence/article23004230/ [Accessed October 15, 2016]

Chapter 10 (pages 126-138, notes 299 to 355)

299 Johnson, Ralph S. 1986. *Forests of Nova Scotia: a history.* Halifax, NS: Province of Nova Scotia, Department of Lands and Forests and Four East Publications, p xv

300 Webster, Paul L.H. 1991. *Pining for trees: the history of dissent against forest destruction in Nova Scotia 1749-1991.* Submitted in partial fulfillment of the requirements for the degree of Master of Arts, Dalhousie University

301 Simpson, Jamie. 2015. *Restoring the Acadian forest: a guide to forest stewardship for woodlot owners in the Maritimes.* Halifax, NS: Nimbus Publishing

302 Simpson, Jamie. 2014. *Journeys through eastern old-growth forests: a narrative guide.* Halifax, NS: Nimbus Publishing, p ix

303 Frazer, Jennifer. No tree is an island and no place is this truer than a forest. May 9, 2015. *Scientific American*. https://blogs.scientificamerican.com/artful-amoeba/dying-trees-can-send-food-to-neighbors-of-different-species/ [Accessed January 26, 2017] and Wohlleben, Peter. 2016. *The Hidden Life of Trees: What They Feel, How They Communicate – Discoveries from a Secret World*. Vancouver, BC: Greystone Books

304 Thurston, Harry. Prest's last stand: keeping Kafka and the bureaucrats out of the Acadian woods. *Harrowsmith,* Aug/Sept 1983, pp 23-30

305 Genuine Progress Index for Atlantic Canada. Abstract: The Nova Scotia GPI Forest Accounts Volume 1: Indicators of ecological, economic & social values of forests in Nova Scotia. 2001. http://www.gpiatlantic.org/publications/abstracts/forest-ab1.htm [Accessed November 20, 2016]

306 Patterson, George. 1877. A history of the County of Pictou, Nova Scotia, 1824-1897. PANS. https://archive.org/details/historyofcountyo00pattuoft [Accessed November 21, 2016]

307 For a comprehensive fictional account of how rapidly forests were destroyed in eastern Canada and the US after the arrival of European colonists, see: Proulx, Annie. *Barkskins*. New York, NY: Dead Line Ltd.

308 Ralph Johnson papers. n.d. Treatments to natural forests. Public Archives of Nova Scotia (PANS) MGI Vol. 2861 #16

309 Webster, Paul L.H. 1991. *Pining for trees: the history of dissent against forest destruction in Nova Scotia 1749-1991.* Submitted in partial fulfillment of the requirements for the degree of Master of Arts, Dalhousie University

310 McMahon, Julia. The new forest in Nova Scotia. *In:* Burrill, Gary and McKay, Ian (eds). 1987. *People, resources, and power: critical perspectives on underdevelopment and primary industries in the Atlantic region.* Fredericton, NB: Acadiensis Press for the Gorsebrook Research Institute of Atlantic Canada Studies, p 99

311 Hawboldt, L.S. Woodlands: The forest resource of Nova Scotia. *Canadian Pulp and Paper Industry.* August 1965. PANS V/F V. 77 #12

312 Ibid

313 Ibid

314 Sandberg, L. Anders and Clancy, Peter. 2000. *Against the grain: foresters and politics in Nova Scotia.* Vancouver, BC: UBC Press, p 52

315 Sandberg, L. Anders. Forest policy in Nova Scotia: the big Lease, Cape Breton Island, 1899-1960. *In:* Sandberg, L. Anders (ed). 1992. *Trouble in the woods: forest policy and social conflict in Nova Scotia and New Brunswick.* Fredericton, NB: Acadiensis Press for the Gorsebrook Research Institute for Atlantic Canada Studies, pp 66-89

316 Hawboldt, L.S. Woodlands: The forest resource of Nova Scotia. *Canadian Pulp and Paper Industry.* August 1965. PANS V/F V. 77 #12

317 Webster, Paul L.H. 1991. *Pining for trees: the history of dissent against forest destruction in Nova Scotia 1749-1991.* Submitted in partial fulfillment of the requirements for the degree of Master of Arts, Dalhousie University, p 186

318 Bissix, Glyn and Sandberg, L. Anders. The political economy of Nova Scotia's Forest Improvement Act, 1962-1986. *In:* Sandberg, L. Anders (ed). 1992. *Trouble in the woods: forest policy and social conflict in Nova Scotia and New Brunswick.* Gorsebrook Research Institute for Atlantic Canada Studies. Fredericton, NB: Acadiensis Press

319 Creighton, G.W.I. Do Nova Scotians really want industry? October 15, 1971. *The Chronicle-Herald*

320 Sources for this are cited by Webster, Paul L.H. 1991. *Pining for trees: the history of dissent against forest destruction in Nova Scotia 1749-1991.* Submitted in partial fulfillment of the requirements for the degree of Master of Arts, Dalhousie University, pp 65-69

321 Tattrie, Jon. Meet the real Edward Cornwallis. March 11, 2012. *The Chronicle Herald.* http://thechronicleherald.ca/thenovascotian/72328-meet-real-edward-cornwallis [Accessed January 16, 2017]

322 Webster, Paul L.H. 1991. *Pining for trees: the history of dissent against forest destruction in Nova Scotia 1749-1991.* Submitted in partial fulfillment of the requirements for the degree of Master of Arts, Dalhousie University, p 66

323 Hoegg Ryan, Judith. 1995. *The birthplace of New Scotland: an illustrated history of Pictou County, Canada's cradle of industry.* Halifax, NS: Formac Publishing Company Limited, p 28

324 Cited by Webster, Paul. 1991. *Pining for trees: the history of dissent against forest destruction in Nova Scotia 1749-1991.* Submitted in partial fulfillment of the requirements for the degree of Master of Arts, Dalhousie University, p 177

325 Sandberg, L. Anders and Clancy, Peter. 2000. *Against the grain: foresters and politics in Nova Scotia.* Vancouver, BC: UBC Press

326 Ibid pp 101-102

327 Ibid p 102

328 Ibid p 115

329 MacDonald, Ron. Speculation on new pulp and paper mill. November 7, 1964. *The Chronicle-Herald*

330 Bissix, Glyn and Sandberg, L. Anders. The political economy of Nova Scotia's Forest Improvement Act, 1962-1986. *In:* Sandberg, L. Anders (ed). 1992. *Trouble in the woods: forest policy and social conflict in Nova Scotia and New Brunswick.* Fredericton, NB: Acadiensis Press for the Gorsebrook Research Institute for Atlantic Canada Studies

331 Ralph Johnson papers. n.d. Brief outline of history of Hollingsworth & Whitney Ltd. and Scott Paper Co. in Nova Scotia. PANS, MGI Vol. 2861 #16

332 Johnson, Clarence. Pulp plant operation to involve 1,000 persons. July 14, 1967. *The Chronicle-Herald,* p 11.

333 Ralph Johnson papers. n.d. Treatments to natural forests. PANS, MGI Vol. 2861 #16

334 Orton, David. Pulpwood forestry in Nova Scotia. *Green Web Bulletin* #10. April 1983

335 McMahon, Julia. 1987. The new forest in Nova Scotia. *In:* Burrill, Gary and McKay, Ian (eds). 1987. *People, resources, and power: critical perspectives on underdevelopment and primary industries in the Atlantic region.* Fredericton, NB: Acadiensis Press for the Gorsebrook Research Institute of Atlantic Canada Studies

336 Smith, G.I. Speech at annual meeting of N.S. Forest Productions Association. *N.S. Forest Products Association Newsletter* Vol. 2(2). 1968. PANS SD1 N93 N55

337 Ibid

338 Sandberg, L. Anders and Clancy, Peter. 2000. *Against the grain: foresters and politics in Nova Scotia.* Vancouver, BC: UBC Press, p 180

339 Ibid p 53

340 Webster, Paul L.H. 1991. *Pining for trees: the history of dissent against forest destruction in Nova Scotia 1749-1991.* Submitted in partial fulfillment of the requirements for the degree of Master of Arts, Dalhousie University, p 189

341 Ibid

342 Thurston, Harry. Prest's last stand: keeping Kafka and the bureaucrats out of the Acadian woods. *Harrowsmith,* Aug/Sept 1983, pp 23-30

343 Ibid p 27

344 Ibid

345 Webster, Paul L.H. 1991. *Pining for trees: the history of dissent against forest destruction in Nova Scotia 1749-1991.* Submitted in partial fulfillment of the requirements for the degree of Master of Arts, Dalhousie University

346 Ibid p 194

347 Thurston, Harry. Prest's last stand: keeping Kafka and the bureaucrats out of the Acadian woods. *Harrowsmith,* Aug/Sept 1983, p 27

348 Foulds, Jim and Manley, Stephen. 1990. "Toothpicks" and the forests of tomorrow. *New Maritimes,* July/August 1990, pp 12-13. PANS O/S 11 D 8402 N532

349 Johnson, Ralph S. 1986. *Forests of Nova Scotia: A history.* Halifax, NS: Province of Nova Scotia, Department of Lands and Forests and Four East Publications, p 355

350 Johnson, Ralph S. 1986. *Forests of Nova Scotia: A history.* Halifax, NS: Province of Nova Scotia, Department of Lands and Forests and Four East Publications, p 356

351 Cited by Webster, Paul L.H. 1991. *Pining for trees: the history of dissent against forest destruction in Nova Scotia 1749-1991.* Submitted in partial fulfillment of the requirements for the degree of Master of Arts, Dalhousie University, p 198, from correspondence between R.S. Johnson to T.C. de Fayer. February 7, 1985. PANS MGI Vol. 2863 #40

352 Ibid

353 Wilson, Sara, Colman, Ronald, O'Brien, Minga, and Pannozzo, Linda. Ecological, economic and social valuation of forest resources related to resource management, harvest practices, and multiple resource usage. Halifax, Nova Scotia: The Nova Scotia GPI Forest Accounts Volume 1: Indicators of Ecological, Economic & Social Values of Forests in Nova Scotia. 2001. http://www.gpiatlantic.org/publications/abstracts/forest-ab1.htm [Accessed January 22, 2017]

354 Johnson, Ralph S. 1986. *Forests of Nova Scotia: A history.* Halifax, NS: Province of Nova Scotia, Department of Lands and Forests and Four East Publications, p xvi

355 Parker, Mike. 1992, 2012. *Woodchips and beans: life in the early lumber woods of Nova Scotia.* Halifax, NS: Nimbus, p 151

Chapter 11 (pages 139-155, notes 356 to 390)

356 Surette, Ralph. Split DNR and put its agenda through the chipper. March 9, 2015. *The Chronicle Herald.* http://thechronicleherald.ca/opinion/1273166-surette-split-dnr-and-put-its-agenda-through-the-chipper [Accessed March 9, 2017]

357 McMahon, Julia. 1987. The new forest in Nova Scotia. *In:* Burrill, Gary and McKay, Ian (eds). 1987. *People, resources, and power: critical perspectives on underdevelopment and primary industries in the Atlantic region.* Fredericton, NB: Acadiensis Press for the Gorsebrook Research Institute of Atlantic Canada Studies

358 Ibid p 99

359 Parenteau, Bill. Pulp, paper and poverty. Then and now: past to present in the New Brunswick woods. *New Maritimes,* March/April 1989, pp 22-26

360 Ibid

361 McMahon, Julia. The new forest in Nova Scotia. *In:* Burrill, Gary and McKay, Ian (eds). 1987. *People, resources, and power: critical perspectives on underdevelopment and primary industries in the Atlantic region.* Fredericton, NB: Acadiensis Press for the Gorsebrook Research Institute of Atlantic Canada Studies

362 Hoegg Ryan, Judith. 1995. *The birthplace of New Scotland: an illustrated history of Pictou County, Canada's cradle of industry.* Halifax, NS: Formac Publishing Company Limited, p 114

363 McMahon, Julia. 1987. The new forest in Nova Scotia. *In:* Burrill, Gary and McKay, Ian (eds). 1987. *People, resources, and power: critical perspectives on underdevelopment and primary industries in the Atlantic region.* Fredericton, NB: Acadiensis Press for the Gorsebrook Research Institute of Atlantic Canada Studies, p 100

364 Orton, David. Pulpwood forestry in Nova Scotia. Presentation by the Socialist Environmental Protection and Occupational Health Group to a Public Hearing held by the Royal Commission on Forestry, Halifax, April 19, 1983. *Green Web Bulletin* #10

365 The trees around us. Forest Practices Improvement Board. 1980. p 10, cited by Orton, David. Pulpwood forestry in Nova Scotia: presentation to a Public Hearing held by the Royal Commission on Forestry, Halifax. April 19, 1983. Saltsprings, NS: Green Web Publications

366 Ralph S. Johnson papers. Brief outline of history of Hollingsworth & Whitney Ltd. and Scott Paper Co. in Nova Scotia. n.d. PANS MGI Vol. 2861 #16

367 Cited by Clancy, Peter. The politics of pulpwood marketing in Nova Scotia, 1960-1985. *In:* Sandberg, L. Anders (ed.). 1992. *Trouble in the woods: forest policy and social conflict in Nova Scotia and New Brunswick.* Fredericton, NB: Acadiensis Press for the Gorsebrook Research Institute for Atlantic Canada Studies, p 142

368 Ibid

369 Sandberg, L. Anders and Clancy, Peter. 2000. *Against the grain: foresters and politics in Nova Scotia.* Vancouver, BC: UBC Press

370 Ibid

371 Nova Scotia Woodlot Owners and Operators Association, Our Mission. http://www.nswooa.ca/ [Accessed January 17, 2017]

372 Sandberg, L. Anders and Clancy, Peter. 2000. *Against the grain: foresters and politics in Nova Scotia.* Vancouver, BC: UBC Press, p 214

373 Ibid pp 208-209

374 Dennis, Eric. Scott Paper Co. acquires pulp mill at Sheet Harbour. September 9, 1964. *The Chronicle-Herald*

375 Cited by Clancy, Peter. The politics of pulpwood marketing in Nova Scotia, 1960-1985. *In:* Sandberg, L. Anders (ed). *Trouble in the woods: forest policy and social conflict in Nova Scotia and New Brunswick.* Fredericton, NB: Acadiensis Press for the Gorsebrook Research Institute for Atlantic Canada Studies, p 156

376 Ibid

377 Schneider, Aaron. Underdeveloping Nova Scotia's forests and the role of corporate counterintelligence. *In:* Schneider, Aaron (ed). 1989. *Deforestation and "development" in Canada and the tropics.* Sydney, Cape Breton: Centre for International Studies, University College of Cape Breton, pp 181-183

378 Clancy, Peter. The politics of pulpwood marketing in Nova Scotia, 1960-1985. *In:* Sandberg, L. Anders (ed.). 1992. *Trouble in the woods: forest policy and social conflict in Nova Scotia and New Brunswick.* Fredericton, NB: Acadiensis Press for the Gorsebrook Research Institute for Atlantic Canada Studies, p 142

379 Orton, David. Forest spraying: A gathering storm. *Canadian Dimension.* October 1990, pp 29-30

380 Nova Scotia's forests under assault. The Coalition for Alternatives to Pesticides and the Green Web. September 7, 1992. Saltsprings, Nova Scotia: Green Web

381 Ibid

382 Orton, David. Pulpwood forestry in Nova Scotia. Presentation by the Socialist Environmental Protection and Occupational Health Group to a Public Hearing held by the Royal Commission on Forestry, Halifax, April 19, 1983. *Green Web Bulletin* #10, p 2

383 Orton, David. Pulp and paper primer: Nova Scotia. *Green Web Bulletin* #26. April 1991

384 Ibid

385 Webster, Paul L.H. 1991. *Pining for trees: the history of dissent against forest destruction in Nova Scotia 1749-1991.* Submitted in partial fulfillment of the requirements for the degree of Master of Arts, Dalhousie University, p 198

386 McMahon, Julia. The new forest in Nova Scotia. *In:* Burrill, Gary and McKay, Ian (eds). 1987. *People, resources, and power: critical perspectives on underdevelopment and primary industries in the Atlantic region.* Fredericton, NB: Acadiensis Press for the Gorsebrook Research Institute of Atlantic Canada Studies, p. 105

387 Friends of the Redtail Society. Website: http://friendsofredtail.ca/our-mandate/

388 Orton, David. Pulpwood forestry in Nova Scotia. Presentation by the Socialist Environmental Protection and Occupational Health Group to a Public Hearing held by the Royal Commission on Forestry, Halifax, April 19, 1983. *Green Web Bulletin* #10

389 http://www.bankofcanada.ca/rates/related/inflation-calculator/ [Accessed January 24, 2017]

390 Ecology Action Centre https://ecologyaction.ca/

Chapter 12 (pages 156-171, notes 391 to 442)

391 Ralph S. Johnson papers. Scott Paper Company's Forest Management Program in Nova Scotia, n.d. PANS MGI Vol. 2861 #16

392 Ibid

393 Swift, Jamie. 1983. *Cut and run: the assault on Canada's forests.* Toronto, Ontario: Between The Lines.

394 Ibid p 178

395 Sandberg, L. Anders and Clancy, Peter. 2000. *Against the grain: foresters and politics in Nova Scotia.* Vancouver, BC: UBC Press, p 116

396 For a detailed account of this campaign, see: May, Elizabeth. 1982. *Budworm battles: The fight to stop the aerial insecticide spraying of the forests of Eastern Canada.* Glen Margaret, NS: Four East Publications Ltd.

397 Ibid p 15

398 Ibid p 61

399 Ibid pp 93-94

400 Donavan, Mike. Budworm spraying: Battle of the year. *Atlantic Issues*, Vol 1(1): February-April 1977. http://bit.ly/2qbVC6U [Accessed May 30, 2017]

401 May, Elizabeth. 1982. *Budworm battles: The fight to stop the aerial insecticide spraying of the forests of Eastern Canada.* Glen Margaret, NS: Four East Publications Ltd., p 78

402 Ralph S. Johnson papers. Scott Paper Company's Forest Management Program in Nova Scotia. n.d. PANS MGI Vol. 2861 #16

403 Wildsmith, Bruce H. Of herbicides and humankind: Palmer's common law lessons. *Osgoode Hall Law Journal* 1986, Vol. 24(1): 161-186 http://digitalcommons.osgoode.yorku.ca/ohlj/vol24/iss1/6 [Accessed January 18, 2017]

404 Peabody, George. *Herbicides.* 1983. Halifax, Nova Scotia: Ecology Action Centre.

405 n.d. Agent Orange: background on Monsanto's involvement. http://www.monsanto.com/newsviews/pages/agent-orange-background-monsanto-involvement.aspx [Accessed January 25, 2017]

406 The Canadian government allowed the US military to spray Agent Orange and other carcinogenic herbicides on the military training grounds around CFB Gagetown in New Brunswick from 1956 until 1984, unbeknownst to the Canadian forces working and stationed there. For many years the government denied the full extent of the spraying. [Agent Orange Association of Canada, Inc. Website: http://www.agentorangecanada.com/ Accessed May 28, 2017]. Then in 2007, the Canadian government set aside $100 million to compensate those harmed by the herbicides, but in 2014 victims were still struggling to get compensation for the serious health problems, including high rates of cancer, caused by the herbicide spraying. [CFB Gagetown Agent Orange victims urged to seek compensation. December 16, 2014. CBC News. http://www.cbc.ca/news/canada/new-brunswick/cfb-gagetown-agent-orange-victims-urged-to-seek-compensation-1.2874785] [Accessed May 28, 2017].

407 Quoted from *St. Croix Courier,* St. Stephen, NB, July 23, 1980, *In*: Swift, Jamie. 1983. *Cut and run: the assault on Canada's forests.* Toronto, Ontario: Between The Lines, p 200.

408 Swift, Jamie. 1983. *Cut and run: the assault on Canada's forests.* Toronto, Ontario: Between The Lines, p 201

409 Livingston, Neal (Director). Herbicide trials. National Film Board of Canada. 1984. http://onf-nfb.gc.ca/en/our-collection/?idfilm=14603 [Accessed January 25, 2017]

410 Peabody, George. *Herbicides.* 1983. Halifax, Nova Scotia: Ecology Action Centre.

411 Elizabeth May, biography. http://www.loe.org/images/content/081003/Elizabeth_bio_long.pdf [Accessed March 19, 2017]

412 Guyton, Kathryn Z, Loomis, Dana, Grosse, Yann, El Ghissassi, Fatiha, Benbrahim-Tallaa, Lamia, Guha, Neela, Scoccianti, Chiara, Mattack, Heidi, Straif, Kurt, on behalf of the International Agency for Research on Cancer Monograph Working Group, IARC, Lyon, France. March 20, 2015. Carcinogenicity of tetrachlorvinphos, parathion, malathion, diazinon, and glyphosate. *The Lancet.* http://www.thelancet.com/journals/lanonc/article/PIIS1470-2045%2815%2970134-8/abstract [Accessed January 25, 2017]

413 Mesnage, Robin, Renney, George, Séralini, Ward, Malcole, Antoniou, Michael N. Multiomics reveal non-alcoholic fatty liver disease in rats following chronic exposure to an ultra-low dose of Roundup herbicide. Nature: *Scientific Reports* 7, 2017. Article number: 39328. http://www.nature.com/articles/srep39328 [Accessed January 25, 2017]

414 Hakim, Danny. Monsanto weed killer Roundup faces new doubts on safety in unsealed documents. March 14, 2017. *The New York Times.* https://www.nytimes.com/2017/03/14/business/monsanto-roundup-safety-lawsuit.html?hp&action=click&pgtype=Homepage&clickSource=story-heading&module=second-column-region&region=top-news&WT.nav=top-news&_r=1 [Accessed March 19, 2017]

415 California to list glyphosate as cancer-causing. June 27, 2017. CBC News. http://www.cbc.ca/news/health/california-lists-glyphosate-as-cancer-causing-1.4179685 [Accessed June 30, 2017]

416 Restino, Charles. Herbicide chemicals in the forest. January 1993. *In: The national and global crisis in Canada's forests.* New Denver, BC: Canada's Future Forest Alliance

417 Scott's herbicide program 1986. *Trees and people*, a publication prepared by the Public Affairs Department of Scott, Canadian Timber-lands Division, and Scott Maritimes Ltd. August 1986. Issue 11, p 4

418 Goodfellow, W.G. Message from the Timberlands Manager: A new forest policy. *Trees and people.* A quarterly publication of Scott Paper International, Canadian Timberland Division. April 1986. Issue 10, p 1

419 Herbicide season 1987. *Trees and people.* A publication prepared by the Public Affairs Department of Scott, Canadian Timberlands, and Scott Maritimes Limited. December 1987. No. 13, p 5

420 Boycott Scott Paper pamphlet. The Scott Boycott Committee. n.d.

421 Kyte, J.D. Letter to Zachary Lyons, President, Centre for Economic Democracy, PO Box 64, Olympia, Washington, U.S.A. from Scott Maritimes Manager of Public Affairs. July 19, 1991

422 Ibid

423 Pulp and paper primer: Nova Scotia. April 1991. Saltsprings, NS: *Green Web Bulletin* #26

424 Rural residents oppose spray: Press Release. n.d. Contacts: Debbie MacBurnie, Brenda MacBurnie, Dan Purdy, Judy Davis

425 Bornais, Stephen. Spraying foes throw rocks as three arrested. September 10, 1988. *The Daily News,* p 3

426 Judy Davis's testimony delivered at Tatamagouche Provincial Court. September 21, 1988, provided by June Daley

427 Sandberg, L. Anders and Clancy, Peter. 2000. *Against the grain: foresters and politics in Nova Scotia.* Vancouver, BC: UBC Press, p 187

428 Ibid p 188

429 McCoag, Tom. Scott guilty of harming trout spawning area. March 3, 1989. *The Chronicle Herald*

430 Ibid

431 Fendick, Reg. Scott stumpage rates to soar. September 28, 1988. *The Daily News*

432 Byrne, Gerry. To the people of Pictou County. September 25, 1989. *Scott Environmental Management Plan*

433 1993. Environmental Management Plan. Scott Maritimes Limited

434 Goodwin, Steve. Aerial spraying raises concerns. August 17, 2005. *The Pictou Advocate*

435 Ibid

436 Ibid

437 Ban aerial spraying of herbicide, group urges. July 26, 2007. CBC News. http://www.cbc.ca/news/canada/nova-scotia/ban-aerial-spraying-of-herbicide-group-urges-1.637091 [Accessed January 30, 2017]

438 Howe, Miles. Exclusive: The Cumberland Files – Part Two: Stonewalled deer biologist turns towards governmental education: Internal documents. October 14, 2015. *Halifax Media Co-op.* http://halifax.mediacoop.ca/story/exclusive-cumberland-files-part-two/34015 [Accessed January 30, 2017]

439 http://stopthespray.com/ [Accessed January 30, 2017]

440 Devet, Robert. Glyphosate spraying on Nova Scotia forests continues. August 18, 2016. *Nova Scotia Advocate.* https://nsadvocate.org/2016/08/18/glyphosate-in-nova-scotia-an-update/ [Accessed January 30, 2017]

441 Vegetation Management Notification, Northern Pulp Nova Scotia Corporation. July 29, 2016. *The Chronicle Herald*, p B3

442 McGregor, Phlis. Public concerns about herbicide use in Nova Scotia rising, though usage steady: Opposing views on the health risks associated with glyphosate. September 14, 2016. CBC News. http://www.cbc.ca/news/canada/nova-scotia/herbicide-spraying-forests-glyphosate-northern-pulp-1.3760549 [Accessed January 30, 2017]

Chapter 13 (pages 172-183, notes 443 to 512)

443 Troyer, Warner. 1977. *No safe place*. Toronto, Ontario and Vancouver, BC: Clarke, Irwin & Company Limited, p 202

444 Kimberly-Clark to evaluate spin-off of paper and Canadian pulp operations (press release). Kimberly-Clark. February 2, 2004. http://investor.kimberly-clark.com/releasedetail.cfm?releaseid=129476 [Accessed January 8, 2017]

445 Ibid

446 Neenah Paper – Timberland Purchase and Sale Agreement. May 5, 2006. Available at: http://www.techagreements.com/agreement-preview.aspx?title=Neenah%20Paper%20-%20Timberland%20Purchase%20And%20Sale%20Agreement&num=576743 [Accessed January 8, 2017]

447 Webster, Katharine. Timber firm guards privacy of investors. April 18, 2005. *Bangor Daily News*. Available at: https://web.archive.org/web/20141109172147/http://archive.bangordailynews.com/2005/04/18/timber-firm-guards-privacy-of-investors; Wagner Forest Management, Ltd. Smith, Gambrell, Russell, LLC. Trust the Leaders (12): summer 2005. http://www.sgrlaw.com/wagner/ [Accessed January 9, 2017]

448 Yankee Farm Credit, biography of Tom Colgan. March 30, 2012. https://www.yankeeaca.com/en/About-Us/News-and-Events/Tom-Colgan [Accessed January 8, 2017]; Ertel, Laura. Nicholas School alums- take three paths to leadership in the forestland/conservation investment sector. Duke Nicholas School of the Environment. May 27, 2015. https://nicholas.duke. edu/about/news/nicholas-school-alums-take-three-paths-leadership-forestlandconservation-investment [Accessed January 9, 2017]

449 Wagner Forest Management, Ltd. Smith, Gambrell, Russell, LLC. Trust the Leaders (12): summer 2005. http://www.sgrlaw.com/wagner/ [Accessed January 9, 2017]

450 St. Pierre, Jym. Doing big deals in Maine. 1999. http://www. forestecologynetwork.org/tmwfall99_07.html [Accessed January 9, 2017]

451 Ibid

452 St. Pierre, Jym. End of an era: The 'American paper century' in Maine is history. 2005. *Times Record*. Available at: http://www.restore.org/Forests/ end_of_era.html [Accessed January 9, 2017]

453 Webster, Katharine. Timber firm guards privacy of investors. April 18, 2005. *Bangor Daily News*. Available at: https://web.archive.org/ web/20141109172147/http://archive.bangordailynews.com/2005/04/18/ timber-firm-guards-privacy-of-investors; Wagner Forest Management, Ltd. Smith, Gambrell, Russell, LLC. Trust the Leaders (12): summer 2005. http:// www.sgrlaw.com/wagner/ [Accessed January 9, 2017]

454 Sale of woodlands. Washington, D.C.: United States Securities and Exchange Commission, Form 10-Q. March 2008. Available at: http://www. wikinvest.com/stock/Neenah_Paper_(NP)/Filing/10-Q/2008/F6137248 [Accessed January 9, 2017]

455 Wagner Forest Management Limited website, Home. http://www. wagnerforest.com/ [Accessed January 8, 2017]

456 Rainforest Alliance and FSC. Forest management certification assessment report for Wagner Forest Management, Ltd. in Lyme, NH, USA. 2008. http://www.wagnerforest.com/pdf/ wagnerforestmanagementpubsum08.pdf [Accessed January 9, 2017]

457 A call made to Wagner Forest NS on January 9, 2017 to obtain an update on land holdings and certification status was not returned.

458 Neenah Paper divests Pictou pulp mill. May 15, 2008. *Toronto Star*. https://www.thestar.com/business/2008/05/15/neenah_paper_divests_ pictou_pulp_mill.html [Accessed January 8, 2017]

459 Neenah sale of Pictou mill and woodlands. Excerpts taken from filed NP 10-K. March 12, 2009. http://www.wikinvest.com/stock/Neenah_Paper_ (NP)/Sale%20Pictou%20Mill%20Woodlands [Accessed January 9, 2017]

460 Northern Pulp completes purchase of N.S. kraft pulp mill. June 25, 2008. *The News* (New Glasgow)

461 Ibid

462 MacFadyen, Ken. Adam Blumenthal: In the rough. July 2011. Mergers & Acquisitions

463 Ibid

464 Moore, Heidi. Michael Bloomberg defends Steve Rattner: "A great public servant." April 24, 2009. Wall Street Journal. http://blogs.wsj.com/ deals/2009/04/24/mayor-mike-steve-rattner-why-do-you-ask/ [Accessed July 16, 2016]; Edeleman, Susan and Adams Otis, Ginger. The great nest egg robberies: Who's afraid of the big, bad blue wolf? April 26, 2009. *The New York Post*

465 A registered letter sent on January 11, 2017, to Dr. John Hamm requesting an interview for this book received no reply.

466 After he stepped down as premier, Dr. Hamm received a series of awards. In 2009, he was made an officer of the Order of Canada for his contributions to the province as premier, physician, and community leader. In 2015, the University of King's College honoured him with a Doctor of Civil Law for his service to the university, the community, and the province, and the same year he was named an Honorary Fellow of the Royal College of Physicians and Surgeons of Canada.

467 Vardy, Jennifer. Pulp mill payday: province loans $15 million to Northern Pulp. March 27, 2009. *The News* (New Glasgow). http://www. ngnews.ca/business/2009/12/29/pulp-mill-payday-311585.html [Accessed January 10, 2017]

468 Ibid

469 Blue Wolf Capital's and Atlas Holdings' Northern Pulp Nova Scotia acquires 475,000 acres of timberland (Blue Wolf Capital Partners LLC News and press releases). March 1, 2010

470 Regan, Sarah. Neenah paper plant finds new owners. May 16, 2008. *The News* (New Glasgow). http://www.ngnews.ca/ Employment/2008-05-16/article-322187/Neenah-Paper-plant-finds-new-owners/1 [Accessed January 9, 2017]

471 Fugazy, Danielle. Blue Wolf expands ownership in Nova Scotia. *Buyouts Magazine*, Fall 2010. http://www.bluewolfcapital.com/press-releases/2010/blue-wolf-expands-ownership-nova-scotia.pdf [Accessed January 9, 2017]

472 Hinchliffe, Aethne. Making a bio-mess of Nova Scotia's forests. December 25, 2009. *The Dominion*. http://www.dominionpaper.ca/articles/3082 [Accessed January 9, 2017]

473 Fugazy, Danielle. Blue Wolf expands ownership in Nova Scotia. *Buyouts Magazine*, Fall 2010. http://www.bluewolfcapital.com/press-releases/2010/blue-wolf-expands-ownership-nova-scotia.pdf [Accessed January 9, 2017]

474 Atlas announces two acquisitions: Bridgewell Resources and a major woodland purchase (Atlas Holdings press release). March 2, 2010. http://www.atlasholdingsllc.com/news/?id=17 [Accessed January 9, 2017]

475 New role for former premier. September 9, 2010. *The News* (New Glasgow). http://www.ngnews.ca/News/Local/2010-08-09/article-1664112/New-role-for-former-premier-/1 [Accessed January 9, 2017]

476 Fugazy, Danielle. Blue Wolf expands ownership in Nova Scotia. *Buyouts Magazine*, Fall 2010. http://www.bluewolfcapital.com/press-releases/2010/blue-wolf-expands-ownership-nova-scotia.pdf [Accessed January 9, 2017]

477 Ibid

478 Pannozzo, Linda. Boat Harbour: Paradise lost for local Mi'kmaq. March 10, 2010. *The Chronicle Herald*

479 MacIntyre, Mary Ellen. No fix yet for Boat Harbour: Pictou Landing native band threatens legal action against province, pulp mill over failure to clean up polluted lagoon. July 3, 2009. *The Chronicle Herald*

480 February 2009. A Boat Harbour update from Chief and Council, Chief and Council Message. *A'Se'K' News* (3): 1

481 Pöyry (Vancouver) Inc. Northern Pulp Nova Scotia Corporation, Air Emission Management Plan. September 25, 2009

482 Fugazy, Danielle. Blue Wolf expands ownership in Nova Scotia. *Buyouts Magazine*, Fall 2010. http://www.bluewolfcapital.com/press-releases/2010/blue-wolf-expands-ownership-nova-scotia.pdf [Accessed January 9, 2017]

483 Hinchliffe, Aethne. Making a bio-mess of Nova Scotia's forests. December 25, 2009. *The Dominion*. http://www.dominionpaper.ca/ articles/3082 [Accessed January 9, 2017]

484 Simpson, Jamie. 2014. *Journeys through eastern old-growth forests: a narrative guide*. Halifax, NS: Nimbus Publishing, p 70

485 Ibid pp 72, 74

486 Ibid p 76

487 Paglia, Todd. If you can't beat them, try to silence them with lawyers: really, SFI? *Huffington Post*. June 22, 2013. http://www.huffingtonpost. com/todd-paglia/if-you-cant-beat-them-try_b_3103529.html [Accessed May 28, 2017]

488 Hinchliffe, Aethne. Making a bio-mess of Nova Scotia's forests. December 25, 2009. *The Dominion*. http://www.dominionpaper.ca/ articles/3082 [Accessed January 9, 2017]

489 Ibid

490 Fugazy, Danielle. Blue Wolf expands ownership in Nova Scotia. *Buyouts Magazine*, Fall 2010. http://www.bluewolfcapital.com/press-releases/2010/blue-wolf-expands-ownership-nova-scotia.pdf [Accessed January 9, 2017]

491 A phone call to Darrell Dexter at Global Public Affairs on February 26, 2017, in which a request was made for an interview, was not returned.

492 Keen, Kip. Atlantic forestry: Exit Neenah. Blog page of Kip Keen. April 2010. http://www.kipkeen.ca/2014/02/exit-neenah.html [Accessed January 11, 2017]

493 More details on this and other loans and grants to Northern Pulp were requested from Nova Scotia Business Inc. (NSBI), which advised that a Freedom of Information request would have to be made to obtain this information. A Freedom of Information request on the status of this and other recent loans and repayments was submitted to Nova Scotia Business Inc. on March 29, 2017. The results of the FOI issued on June 8, 2017, did not include details on terms or interest rates for this or any other loans, all of which were redacted. A request for a review was submitted to the Access to Information and Privacy Commissioner on June 13, 2017. An officer from the FOI Office reported back on June 16, 2017, that this process can take anywhere from 90 days to two years.

494 Neenah land purchase. Nova Scotia Department of Natural Resources (government press release). 2010. http://novascotia.ca/natr/land/neenah-2010/ [Accessed January 11, 2017]

495 Atlas announces two acquisitions: Bridgewell Resources and a major woodland purchase (Atlas Holdings press release). March 2, 2010. http://www.atlasholdingsllc.com/news/?id=17 [Accessed January 9, 2017]

496 Vardy, Jennifer. Pulp mill payday: province loans $15 million to Northern Pulp. March 27, 2009. *The News* (New Glasgow)

497 Neenah land purchase. Nova Scotia Department of Natural Resources (government press release). 2010. http://novascotia.ca/natr/land/neenah-2010/ [Accessed January 11, 2017]

498 Ibid

499 Ibid

500 Atlas First Quarter 2010 Review (Atlas Holdings press releases). April 26, 2010. http://www.atlasholdingsllc.com/news/?id=16 [Accessed January 11, 2017]

501 New role for former premier. August 9, 2010. *The News* (New Glasgow)

502 Neenah land purchase. Nova Scotia Department of Natural Resources (government press release). 2010. http://novascotia.ca/natr/land/neenah-2010/ [Accessed January 11, 2017]

503 Delaney, Gordon. $75 million loan to NP slammed. March 5, 2010. *The Chronicle Herald*

504 Ibid

505 Sunder, Rae. Scott can see woods for trees. February 9, 1970. *The Chronicle-Herald*

506 Province of Nova Scotia and Northern Pulp, "Investing in Nova Scotia's Future" map showing the land Northern Pulp acquired and the land Nova Scotia then immediately bought from Northern Pulp. https://novascotia.ca/natr/land/neenah-2010/pdf/NP_landpurchase.pdf [Accessed June 27, 2017]

507 Baxter, Joan. How a government loan helped wreck Wentworth Valley vistas. June 21, 2017. *Local Xpress*. https://www.localxpress.ca/opinions/opinion-how-a-government-loan-helped-wreck-wentworth-valley-vistas-649062 [Accessed June 27, 2017]

508 Minister responds to clear cutting concerns. June 26, 2017. CBC Halifax *Information Morning*. http://www.cbc.ca/news/canada/nova-scotia/ programs/informationmorningns/minister-responds-to-clear cutting-concerns-1.4178242 [Accessed June 27, 2017]

509 Anderson, Stephen. Northern Pulp projects receive boost. January 24, 2011. *Pulp and Paper News*. http://beta.pulppapernews. com/20161229/2565/northern-pulp-projects-receive-boost [Accessed January 30, 2017]

510 Northern Pulp website, Frequently Asked Questions. http:// northernpulp.ca/our-company/frequently-asked-questions/ [Accessed July 30, 2016]

511 Ibid

512 These are: Northern Resources Nova Scotia Corporation (ID 3249154); Northern Pulp Nova Scotia Corporation (ID 3227808); Northern Pulp NS GP ULC (ID 3227817); Northern Pulp Nova Scotia (ID 3228675); Northern Pulp (ID 3228674); Northern Timber Nova Scotia Corporation (ID 3242556); 3243722 Nova Scotia Limited (ID 3243722); Northern Timber Nova Scotia LP (ID 3243946). https://rjsc.gov.ns.ca/rjsc/ [Accessed January 10, 2017]

Chapter 14 (pages 184-199, notes 513 to 588)

513 http://www.paperexcellence.com/ [Accessed March 16, 2017]

514 Greenpeace. Asia Pulp and Paper in Canada. June 2, 2011. http://www. greenpeace.org/canada/en/campaigns/More/Resources/Background-documents/Asia-Pulp-and-Paper-in-Canada/ [Accessed February 4, 2017]

515 Pulp and Paper Mills owned by Paper Excellence, Paper Excellence, "Mills", Website for Paper Excellence, www.paperexcellence.com viewed January 2012, cited by: van Gelder, Jan Willem and Spaargaren, Petra. Dutch private companies related to APP: Update research paper prepared for Greenpeace Netherlands. May 2012. Available at: www.profundo.nl/ files/download/Greenpeace1205a.pdf [Accessed February 2, 2017]

516 Paper Excellence website, "Mills." http://www.paperexcellence.com/ mills/ [Accessed February 2, 2017]

517 Paper Excellence will be here for a century, says executive. June 16, 2015. *Pulp & Paper Canada*. https://www.workingforest.com/paper-excellence-will-be-here-for-a-century-says-executive/ [Accessed June 28, 2017]

518 Ibid

519 van Gelder, Jan Willem and Spaargaren, Petra. Dutch private companies related to APP – update research paper prepared for Greenpeace Netherlands. May 2012. Available at: www.profundo.nl/files/download/Greenpeace1205a.pdf [Accessed January 11, 2017]

520 Ibid

521 Ibid

522 Ibid p i

523 Ibid

524 Ibid p 6, citing Dun & Bradstreet, "Northern Pulp Nova Scotia Corporation", Dun & Bradstreet, April 21, 2011; Reed Elsevier Inc LexisNexis®Corporate Affliliations, "Howe Sound Pulp & Paper LP", Reed Elsevier Inc LexisNexis®Corporate Affliliations, November 23, 2011

525 Paper Excellence will be here for a century, says executive. June 16, 2015. *Pulp & Paper Canada*. https://www.workingforest.com/paper-excellence-will-be-here-for-a-century-says-executive/ [Accessed June 28, 2017]

526 Final bids in for NewPage mill. Paper Excellence, Stern Partners want to keep paper plant going. December 16, 2011. CBC News. http://www.cbc.ca/news/canada/nova-scotia/final-bids-in-for-newpage-mill-1.1044528 [Accessed January 4, 2017]

527 Hamilton, Gordon. Asian paper giant sees growth opportunity in Canada. June 6, 2011. *Vancouver Sun*. http://globalnews.ca/news/122490/asian-paper-giant-sees-growth-opportunity-in-canada/ [Accessed February 4, 2017]

528 Goodwin, Steve. Northern Pulp emissions installations on schedule. August 17, 2011. *The Advocate*

529 Borsuk, Richard and Webb, Sara. The rise and plummet of APP's Widjaja Family. March 5, 2001. *The Wall Street Journal*. https://www.wsj.com/articles/SB983734299575537180 [Accessed February 4, 2017]

530 Yong, David and Langner, Christopher. Worst Asian default forgiven as Indonesia billionaire sells debt. April 27, 2015. *Bloomberg*. https://www.bloomberg.com/news/articles/2015-04-27/worst-asian-default-forgiven-as-indonesia-billionaire-sells-debt [Accessed February 4, 2017]

531 Preparing to pulp the pulp merchants? Cambodia government announces legal action against predatory paper giant (press release). December 31, 2004. *Global Witness*. https://www.globalwitness.org/en/archive/preparing-pulp-pulp-merchants-cambodian-hgovernment-announces-legal-action-against-predatory/ [Accessed February 4, 2017]

532 Bettinger, Keith Andrew. A forest falls in Cambodia. January 6, 2005. *Asia Times online*. http://www.atimes.com/atimes/Southeast_Asia/ GA06Ae01.html [Accessed February 4, 2017]

533 Asia Pulp & Paper. Forest Stewardship Council (FSC) https://ic.fsc.org/ en/stakeholders/dispute-resolution/current-cases/asia-pulp-and-paper-app [Accessed January 4, 2017]

534 Peterson, Molly. Mattel breaks up with Asia Pulp and Paper after Greenpeace's Barbie-based campaign [UPDATE]. October 5, 2011. 89.3 KPCC. http://www.scpr.org/news/2011/10/05/29262/mattel-breaks-asia-pulp-and-paper-after-greenpeace/ [Accessed February 4, 2017]

535 Harvey, Fiona. Multinationals vow to boycott APP after outcry over illegal logging. April 2, 2012. *The Guardian*. https://www.theguardian.com/ environment/2012/apr/02/boycott-app-illegal-logging [Accessed February 4, 2017]

536 In response to this boycott, in 2013, Asia Pulp & Paper announced it would end "the clearing of natural forest across its entire supply chain in Indonesia." This "no deforestation" pledge was followed six months later by an announcement that APP would be building a new mega-pulp mill in the country, its third, with $2.5 billion in financing from Chinese state-owned banks. The new PT OKI Pulp and Paper Mill would double APP's demand for wood in Indonesia, and it would produce between 2 and 3.2 million tonnes of pulp each year, making it one of the world's largest mills. In 2016, a report undertaken by 12 NGOs of how this would affect AP&P's pledge to stop deforestation, Will Asia Pulp and Paper default on its "zero deforestation" commitment, [available at: https://www.wetlands. org/publications/will-asia-pulp-paper-default-on-its-zero-deforestation-commitment/ Accessed June 12, 2017] casts doubt on whether APP's plantations could meet the voracious needs of the giant mill. It also noted these plantations are often on drained peatland and vulnerable to fires, which raged through the company's concessions in 2015, causing disastrous haze throughout Southeast Asia. The report also notes the use of peatland for plantations results in "high levels of annual carbon emissions," and calls on the company to show how it will be able to feed its mill, phase out plantations on drained peatland, and put a moratorium on any new land acquisitions until the rights of indigenous people are respected.

537 Howe, Miles. Pulp dreams: Pictou mill is Asia Pulp and Paper's latest acquisition. July 6, 2011. *The Dominion*

538 Asia Pulp and Paper in Canada, Greenpeace Canada. June 2, 2011. http://www.greenpeace.org/canada/en/campaigns/More/Resources/ Background-documents/Asia-Pulp-and-Paper-in-Canada/ [Accessed February 4, 2017]

539 Goodwin, Steve. Mill purchase good for county: Hamm. April 14, 2011. *The Pictou Advocate*

540 MacInnis, Adam. Scotsburn sawmill reopening under new owner. October 3, 2012. *The News* (New Glasgow). http://www.ngnews.ca/business/2012/10/3/scotsburn-sawmill-reopening-under-new-ow-3092099.html [Accessed February 6, 2017]; Power, Bill. Ligni Bel lumber mill expected to open this month. October 1, 2012. *The Chronicle Herald*. http://thechronicleherald.ca/business/142340-ligni-bel-lumber-mill-restart-expected-this-month [Accessed June 27, 2017]

541 Nova Scotia Registry of Joint Stock Companies. https://rjsc.gov.ns.ca/rjsc/search/viewProfile.do [Accessed February 8, 2017]

542 WestFor Management Inc. website, "member profiles." http://www.westfor.org/who-we-are/member-profiles [Accessed February 8, 2017]

543 Sproull Thomson, Jane. No more tax dollars up in smoke with pulp mill. April 20, 2011. *The Advocate*

544 Gunning, Matt. Taxpayers should have financial interest in paper mill. May 11, 2011. *The Advocate*

545 Goodwin, Steve. Christie: Costly clean up looming at several sites. May 18, 2011. *The Advocate*

546 Goodwin, Steve. Northern Pulp emissions installations on schedule. August 17, 2011. *The Advocate*

547 Secret deal with Northern Pulp "seriously undermines" Western Crown lands consultation (media release). February 4, 2017. Ecology Action Centre

548 Ibid

549 Province buys Bowater lands. December 10, 2012. CBC News. http://www.cbc.ca/news/canada/nova-scotia/province-buys-bowater-lands-1.1186704 [Accessed February 5, 2017]

550 Mersey rescue: Credible plan. December 2, 2011. *The Chronicle Herald*. http://thechronicleherald.ca/editorials/39049-mersey-rescue-credible-plan [Accessed February 5, 2017]

551 Province buys Bowater lands. December 10, 2012. CBC News. http://www.cbc.ca/news/canada/nova-scotia/province-buys-bowater-lands-1.1186704 [Accessed February 5, 2017]

552 Epstein, Howard. 2015. *Rise again: Nova Scotia's NDP on the rocks*. Halifax, NS: Empty Mirrors Press, p 143

553 Ibid

554 Province buys Bowater lands. December 10, 2012. CBC News. http://www.cbc.ca/news/canada/nova-scotia/province-buys-bowater-lands-1.1186704 [Accessed February 5, 2017]

555 McKenna, Barrie. For government subsidies, what price is too high to save a job? September 30, 2012. *The Globe and Mail.* https://www.theglobeandmail.com/report-on-business/economy/for-government-subsidies-what-price-is-too-high-to-save-a-job/article4577935/ [Accessed May 30, 2017]

556 Epstein, Howard. 2015. *Rise again: Nova Scotia's NDP on the rocks.* Halifax, NS: Empty Mirrors Press, p 143

557 Zaccacga, Remo. Northern Pulp deal rapped. February 24, 2014. *The Chronicle Herald*

558 Pannozzo, Linda. Forest tragedy: how the forest industry and compliant bureaucrats hijacked the public will. September 13, 2016. *Halifax Examiner.* https://www.halifaxexaminer.ca/province-house/forest-tragedy/#%E2%80%9CPure%20Economics%E2%80%9D [Accessed June 27, 2017]

559 Letter from Diane P. MacDonald (DNR) on behalf of Duff Montgomerie to all DNR staff. April 25, 2014

560 Zaccacga, Remo. Northern Pulp deal rapped. February 24, 2014. *The Chronicle Herald*

561 Pannozzo, Linda. Forest tragedy: how the forest industry and compliant bureaucrats hijacked the public will. September 13, 2016. *Halifax Examiner.* https://www.halifaxexaminer.ca/province-house/forest-tragedy/#%E2%80%9CPure%20Economics%E2%80%9D [Accessed June 27, 2017]

562 Ibid

563 Guderly, Helga. Opinion: N.S. Crown land forests: Who is managing them? February 14, 2017. *The Chronicle Herald.* http://thechronicleherald.ca/opinion/1441376-opinion-n.s.-crown-land-forests-who-is-managing-them [Accessed May 29, 2017]

564 Gorman, Michael. Opponents say Crown lease would chop down forest health. March 13, 2017. CBC News. http://www.cbc.ca/news/canada/nova-scotia/western-crown-land-forest-management-natural-resources-westfor-1.4022875 [Accessed March 20, 2017]

565 Who is managing our Crown land? Healthy Forest Coalition blog. January 31, 2017. http://www.healthyforestcoalition.ca/hfc-blog/archives/01-2017 [Accessed February 6, 2017]

566 Ibid

567 Medway District forest certification changed. Nova Scotia Department of Natural Resources. February 29, 2016. http://novascotia.ca/news/release/?id=20160229002 [Accessed February 6, 2017]

568 Pollon, Christopher. The war over eco-certified wood. June 3, 2009. *The Tyee.* https://thetyee.ca/News/2009/06/03/EcoWood/ [Accessed February 6, 2017]

569 Devet, Robert. DNR drops acclaimed forestry certification program in Western Nova Scotia. March 31, 2016. *Nova Scotia Advocate.* https://nsadvocate.org/2016/03/01/dnr-drops-acclaimed-forestry-certification-program-in-western-nova-scotia/ [Accessed February 6, 2017]

570 Pannozzo, Linda. Forest tragedy: how the forest industry and compliant bureaucrats hijacked the public will. September 13, 2016. *Halifax Examiner.* https://www.halifaxexaminer.ca/province-house/forest-tragedy/#%E2%80%9CPure%20Economics%E2%80%9D [Accessed June 27, 2017]

571 Ibid

572 Interview with Bob Bancroft, June 17, 2016

573 Pannozzo, Linda. Forest tragedy: how the forest industry and compliant bureaucrats hijacked the public will. September 13, 2016. *Halifax Examiner.* https://www.halifaxexaminer.ca/province-house/forest-tragedy/#%E2%80%9CPure%20Economics%E2%80%9D [Accessed June 27, 2017]

574 Interview with Bob Bancroft, June 17, 2016

575 The Government of Nova Scotia, JobsHere. The path we share: A Natural Resources Strategy for Nova Scotia 2011 – 2020. http://novascotia.ca/natr/strategy/pdf/Strategy_Strategy.pdf [Accessed March 20, 2017]

576 Economic impact analysis of timber management and supply changes on Nova Scotia's Forestry Industry, prepared for Government of Nova Scotia Department of Natural Resources. May 2011. Woodbridge Associates. https://novascotia.ca/natr/strategy/pdf/Woodbridge-May-2011.pdf [Accessed May 29, 2017]

577 Pannozzo, Linda. Forest tragedy: how the forest industry and compliant bureaucrats hijacked the public will. September 13, 2016. *Halifax Examiner*. https://www.halifaxexaminer.ca/province-house/forest-tragedy/#%E2%80%9CPure%20Economics%E2%80%9D [Accessed June 27, 2017]

578 Withers, Paul. Nova Scotia forest management cleaned up, province says. August 17, 2016. CBC News. http://www.cbc.ca/news/canada/nova-scotia/forestry-management-report-card-medway-1.3723879

579 Interview with Burrill, Gary. March 2, 2017

580 Plourde, Raymond. Personal communication. June 23, 2017

581 May, Geoffrey. Letter to Stephen McNeil. Posted on April 5, 2017, at: http://www.friends-of-nature.ca/does-forestry-in-nova-scotia-have-a-future/ [Accessed April 5, 2017]

582 Bancroft, Bob. Give our forests back to the people. March 4, 2016. *The Chronicle Herald*. http://thechronicleherald.ca/opinion/1346864-give-our-forests-back-to-the-people [Accessed February 6, 2017]

583 http://nsforestnotes.ca/wp-content/uploads/2017/04/BudgetAddress.jpg [Accessed May 29, 2017]

584 Independent review of forestry announced in Nova Scotia budget address. *Nova Scotia Forest Notes*. May 1, 2017. http://nsforestnotes.ca/2017/04/27/independent-review-of-forestry-announced-in-nova-scotia-budget-address/ [Accessed May 29, 2017]

585 Election 2017 priority issue: clear cutting. Ecology Action Centre. https://ecologyaction.ca/issue-area/election-2017-priority-issue-clear cutting [Accessed May 29, 2017]

586 No long term leases of Nova Scotia Crown Land for now but current cutting continues even near Protected Areas. *Nova Scotia Forest Notes*. May 24, 2017. http://nsforestnotes.ca/2017/05/24/no-long-term-leases-of-nova-scotia-crown-land-for-now-but-current-cutting-continues-even-near-protected-areas/ [Accessed May 29, 2017]

587 Nova Scotia Forest Notes, June 20, 2017. http://nsforestnotes.ca/2017/06/20/nova-scotia-state-of-the-forest-2016-report-released/ [Accessed June 26, 2017]

588 State of the Forest 2016. Nova Scotia Department of Natural Resources. April 2017. p 3 https://novascotia.ca/natr/forestry/reports/State_of_the_Forest_2016.pdf [Accessed June 29, 2017]

Chapter 15 (pages 200-214, notes 589 to 631)

589 Perry, Anne. 1998. *A twisted root*. New York, NY: Ballantine Books, p 245

590 St-Jean, S.D., Stephens, R.E., Courtenay, S.C., and Reinisch, C.L. 2005. Detecting family proteins in haemocytic leukemia cells of Mytilus edulis from Pictou Harbour, Nova Scotia, Canada. *Canadian Journal of Fisheries and Aquatic Sciences* 2005, 62(9): 2055-2066. http://www. nrcresearchpress.com/doi/abs/10.1139/f05-119#.WG6ZGpJNo-8 [Accessed January 5, 2017]

591 Yorke, Laura. May finds advocate for health review. August 1, 2009. *The News* (New Glasgow)

592 Morin, Brandi. Alberta doctor that found higher rates of cancer in First Nation Community fired by Health Board. May 11, 2015. *APTN National News*. http://aptnnews.ca/2015/05/11/alberta-doctor-found-higher-rates-cancer-first-nation-communities-fired-health-board/ [Accessed May 29, 2017]

593 Goodwin, Steve. Seeking cleanup of pollution sources. August 5, 2009. *The Advocate*

594 MacIntrye, Mary Ellen. Polluted sites rapped: Group appalled at Boat Harbour effluent lagoon. August 1, 2009. *The Chronicle Herald*

595 Yorke, Laura. May finds advocate for health review. August 1, 2009. *The News* (New Glasgow)

596 Kelly, Ron, spokesperson for the Pictou Country Watershed Coalition. Letter to Sterling Belliveau, Nova Scotia Minister of the Environment. September 1, 2009

597 Pictou County's Watershed Coalition gets support from other organizations. December 17, 2009. *The Advocate*

598 Another leak causes the closure of Northern Pulp. June 3, 2009. *The Chronicle Herald*

599 More breaks than thought. December 5, 2008. *The News* (New Glasgow)

600 Kelly, Ron, spokesperson for the Pictou Country Watershed Coalition. Letter to Sterling Belliveau, Nova Scotia Minister of the Environment. November 30, 2009

601 Ibid

602 Ibid

603 MacDonald, Maureen. Letter to Ron Kelly, spokesperson, Pictou County Watershed Coalition. January 20, 2010

604 Kelly, Ron. Watershed Coalition losing patience over lack of health study. March 12, 2011. *The News* (New Glasgow)

605 Kelly, Ron, for the Pictou County Watershed Coalition. Letter to Maureen MacDonald, Nova Scotia Minister of Health. April 14, 2011

606 Pictou County Watershed Coalition. Dexter government ignores health concerns. Press release. November 28, 2011

607 County doctors back provincial body in deploring pollution. June 11, 1970. *The Evening News*

608 Documentary by Doug Huskilson. "Scott Paper Mill's (NS) emissions reach PEI." CBC *Maritime Magazine*. July 8, 1989. PANS Ar 8211, # Mfs-634, Accession 1990-11

609 Ibid

610 Reid, Dr. Daniel S. Pictonians, pulp mill and pulmonary diseases. *The Nova Scotia Medical Journal*, December 1989: pp 146-148

611 Solet, David, Zoloth, Stephen R., Sullivan Clare, Jewett John, and Michaels, David M. Patterns of mortality in pulp and paper workers. *Journal of Occupational Medicine*, July 1989: 31(7), 627-630

612 https://www.youtube.com/watch?v=w_KYl5PszHg [Accessed January 31, 2017]

613 Hamm slammed for involvement in Northern Pulp. September 10, 2014. CBC News. http://www.cbc.ca/news/canada/nova-scotia/dr-john-hamm-slammed-for-involvement-with-northern-pulp-1.2762171 [Accessed January 30, 2017]

614 Ibid

615 Ibid

616 Ibid

617 Campbell, Francis. Exhibit pictures impact of Pictou County mill. August 20, 2014. *The Chronicle Herald*. http://thechronicleherald.ca/novascotia/1230803-exhibit-pictures-impact-of-pictou-county-mill [Accessed February 1, 2017]

618 Bundale, Brett. Erin Brockovich slams Pictou pulp mill. September 3, 2014. *The Chronicle Herald.* http://thechronicleherald.ca/ novascotia/1233905-erin-brockovich-slams-pictou-county-pulp-mill-pollution [Accessed February 1, 2017]

619 Not his real name. "Duncan" requested anonymity.

620 Keats, Paul (Inspection, Compliance and Enforcement Division, Nova Scotia Department of Environment, District Manager, Antigonish, Acting Regional Director Northern Region), March 23, 2017. Emailed response to questions. According to the manager of Nova Scotia's Environment's Inspection, Compliance and Enforcement Division in eastern Nova Scotia, the mill does continuously measure total reduced sulphur (and of several sulfur compounds) emissions from its recovery boiler and lime kiln. (Email of March 23, 2017)

621 Keats, Paul (Inspection, Compliance and Enforcement Division, Nova Scotia Department of Environment, District Manager, Antigonish, Acting Regional Director Northern Region), (Email of March 23, 2017.) Reply to emailed question about why such 24-hour-a-day emissions readings were not done for the pulp mill: "Continuous emission monitors are generally required based on the type and level of air contaminant being emitted by the Approval Holder, the source of the emission, and the capability/ reliability of the technology for the application. Continuous emission monitors measure sulphur dioxide at Units #1-3, and nitrogen oxides at Units #1-6 at Tufts Cove Generating Station. Continuous emission monitors measure total reduced sulphur at the recovery boiler and the lime kiln at Northern Pulp."

622 Environment and Climate Change Canada: Historical substance reports: Northern Pulp Nova Scotia Corporation. http://ec.gc.ca/inrp-npri/donnees-data/index.cfm?do=facility_history&lang=En&opt_npri_id=0000000815&opt_report_year=2015 and List of National Pollutant Release Inventory (NPRI) substances for 2016 and 2017. https://www.ec.gc.ca/inrp-npri/default.asp?lang=En&n=9617CEC8-1 [Accessed March 7, 2017]

623 An emailed response on April 5, 2017, from an Environmental Program Officer with the National Pollutant Release Inventory to a question on how these threshold levels were established and what criteria are used to establish them reads: "It is important to note that these thresholds are not used to determine acceptable levels of pollutants released to the environment, but only to determine if facilities are required to report to the NPRI."

624 Hoffman, E., Bernier, M., Blotnicky, B., Golden, P.G., Janes, J., Kader, A, Kovacs-da Vosta, R., Pettipas, S., Vermeulen, S., and Walker, T.R. Assessment of public perception and environmental compliance at a pulp and paper facility: A Canadian case study. *Environmental Monitoring and Assessment*, 2015, Dec. 187: 766 (https://link.springer.com/article/10.1007/s10661-015-4985-5)

625 The air we breathe: Nova Scotia's air quality report, 2000-2007. Nova Scotia Environment. 2009. https://novascotia.ca/nse/air/docs/TheAirWeBreathe-NS-Air-Quality2000-2007.pdf [Accessed March 8, 2017]

626 Approval, Province of Nova Scotia, Approval holder: Northern Pulp Nova Scotia Corporation, March 9, 2015-January 30, 2020. Nova Scotia Environment. p 21. https://novascotia.ca/nse/issues/docs/2011-076657-A0 1NorthernPulpApprovalAmendmentsignedversionMar915.pdf [Accessed March 8, 2017]

627 In an email response received June 25, 2017, to a list of questions to the Department of Environment, the reply to a question to confirm these figures stated, "The tonnes of production used in the equations are the actual production for the year and not the maximum production limits of the Approval."

628 Hoffman, E., Bernier, M., Blotnicky, B., Golden, P.G., Janes, J., Kader, A, Kovacs-da Vosta, R., Pettipas, S., Vermeulen, S., and Walker, T.R. Assessment of public perception and environmental compliance at a pulp and paper facility: A Canadian case study. *Environmental Monitoring and Assessment*, 2015, Dec. 187: 766 (https://link.springer.com/article/10.1007/s10661-015-4985-5)

629 Air Quality Regulations, made under Sections 25 and 112 of the Environment Act, amended November 12, 2014. https://www.novascotia.ca/just/regulations/regs/envairqt.htm [Accessed March 8, 2017]

630 Approval, Province of Nova Scotia, Approval holder: Northern Pulp Nova Scotia Corporation, March 9, 2015-January 30, 2020. Nova Scotia Environment. Table 5, p 53

631 Hoffman, E., Bernier, M., Blotnicky, B., Golden, P.G., Janes, J., Kader, A, Kovacs-da Vosta, R., Pettipas, S., Vermeulen, S., and Walker, T.R. Assessment of public perception and environmental compliance at a pulp and paper facility: A Canadian case study. *Environmental Monitoring and Assessment*, 2015, Dec. 187: 766 (https://link.springer.com/article/10.1007/s10661-015-4985-5)

Chapter 16 (pages 215-225, notes 632 to 663)

632 Bousquet, Tim. The politics of bullshit. *The Coast*. October 3, 2013. http://www.thecoast.ca/halifax/the-politics-of-bullshit/ Content?oid=40915471003 [Accessed March 11, 2017]

633 Cadogan, George. What Scott does not pay for water and disposal, N.S. taxpayers must pay. *The Pictou Advocate*

634 http://inflationcalculator.ca/ [Accessed March 10, 2017]

635 Harder, Steve. Boat Harbour: Environment department looks for new operator. September 9, 1989. *The Chronicle Herald*

636 Nova Scotia and Northern Pulp agree on water use rules. February 8, 2016. CBC News. http://www.cbc.ca/news/canada/nova-scotia/northern-pulp-water-usage-appeal-decision-1.3438549 [Accessed March 9, 2017]

637 Confirmed during a telephone call on March 8, 2017 by Marc Theriault, Nova Scotia Environment Inspector Specialist, Pictou

638 Nova Scotia and Northern Pulp agree on water use rules. February 8, 2016. CBC News. http://www.cbc.ca/news/canada/nova-scotia/northern-pulp-water-usage-appeal-decision-1.3438549 [Accessed March 9, 2017]

639 Indemnity Agreement between Province of Nova Scotia and Scott Maritimes, December 31, 1995

640 Foshay, Rae. Program for Scott pollution control. September 18, 1970. *The Chronicle-Herald*

641 Taylor, Wilkie. Record production at Scott mill during 1980. January 19, 1980. *The Mail-Star*

642 Taylor, Wilkie. Scott cancels plans for $51 million modernization. May 25, 1983. *The Chronicle-Herald*

643 Ward, Brain and Harder, Steve. Province pours $17 million into Scott mill. October 16, 1993. *The Chronicle-Herald*

644 Neenah land purchase. Nova Scotia Department of Natural Resources. 2010. http://novascotia.ca/natr/land/neenah-2010/ [Accessed January 11, 2017]

645 The Canadian Press. Nova Scotia government helps fund upgrades at Northern Pulp mill. April 5, 2013. *Canadian Business*. http://www.canadianbusiness.com/business-news/nova-scotia-government-helps-fund-upgrades-at-northern-pulp-mill/ [Accessed February 8, 2017]

646 Beswick, Aaron. N.S. loans over $20 million to pulp mill. April 5, 2013. *The Chronicle Herald*. http://thechronicleherald.ca/novascotia/1121876-n.s.-loans-over-20m-to-pulp-mill [Accessed February 17, 2017]

647 Energy: Natural gas coming to Pictou County (press release). Nova Scotia Government, Department of Energy, n.d. https://www.novascotia.ca/nse/ea/pictou-county-natural-gas-pipeline/AppA_press_rls.pdf [Accessed February 6, 2017]

648 Government of Nova Scotia Environmental Assessment: Pictou County natural gas pipeline. n.d. https://www.novascotia.ca/nse/ea/pictou-county-natural-gas-pipeline.asp [Accessed February 6, 2017]

649 Beswick, Aaron. N.S. loans over $20 million to pulp mill. April 5, 2013. *The Chronicle Herald*. http://thechronicleherald.ca/novascotia/1121876-n.s.-loans-over-20m-to-pulp-mill [Accessed February 17, 2017]

650 Ibid

651 Historical substance reports, Northern Pulp Nova Scotia Corporation, National Pollutant Release Inventory, Environment and Climate Change Canada. http://ec.gc.ca/inrp-npri/donnees-data/index.cfm?do=facility_history&lang=En&opt_npri_id=0000000815&opt_report_year=2015 [Accessed March 8, 2017]

652 Letter From Bobbi Morrison, Clean The Mill, to Director Public Services, Pictou County Health Authority and Medical Officer, Colchester East Hants, Cumberland and Pictou County Health Authorities. July 13, 2014

653 A request to Nova Scotia Business Inc. (formerly JobsFund) for details on the repayment schedules and terms of these loans was made on February 16, 2017. The response, on March 20, 2017, was that "The company is in compliance with the terms and conditions of its loans. NSBI is not able to provide the details of the loan terms outside of the Freedom of Information Protection of Privacy Act." A Freedom of Information request for this information was submitted on March 20, 2017, and after two extensions, partial information was released on June 8, 2017. The $15 million loan issued in 2009 over a 10-year term had been amended on January 1, 2013, to commence on that date. "Severed" in the results were the interest rates for the loans. A request for a review to the Information and Access Privacy Commissioner was submitted, requesting this omitted information, on June 13, 2017. The Freedom of Information Office says this review can take between 90 days and two years.

654 Beswick, Aaron. N.S. loans over $20 million to pulp mill. April 5, 2013. *The Chronicle Herald*. http://thechronicleherald.ca/novascotia/1121876-n.s.-loans-over-20m-to-pulp-mill [Accessed February 17, 2017]

655 Taylor, Roger. Firms steamed over Northern Pulp Aid. April 12, 2013. *The Chronicle Herald*. http://thechronicleherald.ca/business/1123134-taylor-n.s.-firms-still-steamed-over-northern-pulp-aid [Accessed February 9, 2017]

656 Ibid

657 Gorman, Michael. Group calls for audit of funds for pulp mill. March 19, 2013. *The Chronicle Herald*

658 NP ordered to fix pollution problem again. March 18, 2013. CBC News. http://www.cbc.ca/news/canada/nova-scotia/northern-pulp-ordered-to-fix-pollution-problem-again-1.1340641 [Accessed February 9, 2017]

659 National Pollutant Release Inventory, Northern Pulp Corporation, Environment and Climate Change Canada. http://ec.gc.ca/inrp-npri/donnees-data/index.cfm?do=facility_history&lang=En&opt_npri_id=0000000815&opt_report_year=2015 [Accessed March 9, 2017]

660 Wilson, Rita. NDP using jobs as an excuse for inaction. April 17, 2013. *The Advocate*

661 MacInnis, Adam. Balancing concerns. August 28, 2013. *The News* (New Glasgow) http://www.ngnews.ca/News/Local/2013-08-27/article-3365859/MLAs-meet-with-Northern-Pulp-directors/1 [Accessed February 9, 2017]

662 Ibid

663 A letter requesting an interview with Premier Stephen McNeil for this book was emailed on January 26, 2017, and an automatic confirmation of its receipt came back, but the request itself went unanswered.

Chapter 17 (pages 226-238, notes 664 to 704)

664 Cited by Sandberg, L. Anders and Clancy, Peter. 2000. *Against the grain: foresters and politics in Nova Scotia*. Vancouver, BC: UBC Press, p 62

665 Video available at: https://www.youtube.com/watch?v=cvQmzfjxqfc [Accessed September 25, 2016]

666 https://www.facebook.com/groups/545965902107532/

667 http://cleanthemill.com/

668 Clean The Mill, Our Concerns, Health. http://cleanthemill.com/ [Accessed June 30, 2016]

669 Hewitt, Mark et al. Altered reproduction in fish exposed to pulp and paper mill effluents: role of individual compounds and mill operating conditions. *Environmental Toxicology and Chemistry*, 2008. Vol 27(3): 682-697. Available at: http://bit.ly/2mKB6HY [Accessed March 9, 2017]

670 Clean The Mill, Our Concerns, Economy. http://cleanthemill.com/ [Accessed June 30, 2016]

671 Keats, Paul (Inspection, Compliance and Enforcement Division, Nova Scotia Department of Environment, District Manager, Antigonish, Acting Regional Director Northern Region), March 23, 2017. Emailed response to questions.

672 Howe, Miles. Where it goes, somebody knows ... Pictou County Watershed Coalition gets conflicting stories as to final resting place of Boat Harbour dredge. February 12, 2012. *Halifax Media Co-op*. http://halifax.mediacoop.ca/story/where-it-goes-somebody-knows/9886 [Accessed March 9, 2017]

673 Pöyry (Vancouver) Inc. Northern Pulp Nova Scotia Corporation, Air Emission Management Plan. September 25, 2009

674 Northern Pulp ordered to fix air pollution problem. April 21, 2012. CBC News. http://www.cbc.ca/news/canada/nova-scotia/northern-pulp-ordered-to-fix-air-pollution-problem-1.1169785 [Accessed March 1, 2017]

675 Howe, Miles. Exclusive: All reports and directives from Nova Scotia Environment on Northern Pulp's emissions. 1989-2014. July 23, 2014. *Halifax Media Co-op*. http://halifax.mediacoop.ca/story/exclusive-all-reports-and-directives-nova-scotia-e/31256 [Accessed March 10, 2017]

676 Andreatta, David. In Nova Scotia town, local residents fight pulp mill's pollution. September 13, 2013. *The Globe and Mail*. http://www.theglobeandmail.com/news/national/in-nova-scotia-town-residents-fight-local-mills-pollution/article14324606/ [Accessed February 11, 2017]

677 Gorman, Michael and Zaccagna, Remo. No bailout for NP McNeil vows. January 30, 2014. *The Chronicle Herald*. http://thechronicleherald.ca/novascotia/1183166-no-bailout-for-northern-pulp-mcneil-vows [Accessed February 13, 2017]

678 Ibid

679 Brannen, John. Hope for Boat Harbour. February 6, 2014. *The News* (New Glasgow)

680 Zaccagna, Remo. Northern Pulp deal rapped. February 24, 2014. *The Chronicle Herald*

681 Gorman, Michael. N.S. rapped for hiring former Bowater manager in renewables role. April 28, 2014. *The Chronicle Herald*

682 Ibid

683 Howe, Miles. Exclusive: All reports and directives from Nova Scotia Environment on Northern Pulp's emissions. 1989-2014. July 23, 2014. *Halifax Media Co-op.* http://halifax.mediacoop.ca/story/exclusive-all-reports-and-directives-nova-scotia-e/31256 [Accessed March 10, 2017]

684 Ibid

685 Project to improve mill's environmental performance ready. June 4, 2014. *The Advocate*

686 Effluent leak at pulp mill shuts down plant temporarily. June 11, 2014. *The Advocate*

687 Beswick, Aaron. N.S. likely liable for cleanup. June 14, 2014. *The Chronicle Herald.*

688 Goodwin, Steve. Pulp mill faces golden rule. August 6, 2014. *The Advocate.*

689 Farrell, Gerry. It's time to say enough is enough: clean the mill or close it. August 6, 2014. *The Advocate*

690 Businesses join forces to promote clean air in Pictou area. July 8, 2014. *The Chronicle Herald.* http://thechronicleherald.ca/novascotia/1221440-businesses-join-forces-to-promote-clean-air-in-pictou-area [Accessed February 13, 2017]

691 MacLean, Stirling. Letter to Randy Delorey, Nova Scotia Environment Minister. July 14, 2014

692 Provincial ministers join discussion as concerns over mill emissions continue. July 16, 2014. *The News* (New Glasgow)

693 Northern Pulp won't be shut down despite emissions, stench. July 30, 2014. CBC News. http://www.cbc.ca/news/canada/nova-scotia/northern-pulp-won-t-be-shut-down-despite-emissions-stench-1.2722855 [Accessed February 17, 2017]

694 Ibid

695 Beswick, Aaron. Northern Pulp concedes emissions on the rise. July 30, 2014. *The Chronicle Herald.* http://thechronicleherald.ca/novascotia/1226454-northern-pulp-concedes-emissions-on-rise [Accessed February 13, 2017]

696 Ibid

697 Paul Sobey lashes out at Northern Pulp Mill over smell. July 29, 2014. CBC News. http://www.cbc.ca/news/canada/nova-scotia/paul-sobey-lashes-out-at-northern-pulp-mill-over-smell-1.2722044 [Accessed February 13, 2017]

698 *Defenders of the dawn: green rights in the Maritimes* (a film by Silver Donald Cameron and Chris Beckett, Anhinga Films). CBC Absolutely Maritimes. September 5, 2015. Available at: http://www.cbc.ca/player/play/2674956490 [Accessed February 19, 2017]

699 Brannen, John. Pictou businesses unable to clear the air after meeting with mill. July 31, 2014. *The News* (New Glasgow)

700 Northern Pulp: Peter MacKay says collaborative efforts are crucial. July 31, 2014. CBC News. http://www.cbc.ca/news/canada/nova-scotia/northern-pulp-peter-mackay-says-collaborative-efforts-are-crucial-1.2723671 [Accessed February 13, 2017]

701 Anderson, Steven. Northern Pulp projects receive boost. News Within The Pulp And Paper Industry. January 24, 2011. http://beta.pulppapernews.com/20161229/2565/northern-pulp-projects-receive-boost [Accessed February 20, 2017]

702 Ibid

703 Northern Pulp: Peter MacKay says collaborative efforts are crucial. July 31, 2014. CBC News. http://www.cbc.ca/news/canada/nova-scotia/northern-pulp-peter-mackay-says-collaborative-efforts-are-crucial-1.2723671 [Accessed February 13, 2017]

704 Northern Pulp mill: what's in the smelly haze? July 31, 2014. CBC News. http://www.cbc.ca/news/canada/nova-scotia/northern-pulp-mill-what-s-in-the-smelly-haze-1.2724460 [Accessed February 13, 2017]

Chapter 18 (pages 239-248, notes 705 to 731)

705 Interview with Terry Mosh Dunbrack, resident of Pictou and member of the Clean Up The Pictou County Pulp Mill Facebook Group, October 16, 2016

706 Interview with Don MacKenzie on CBC Halifax *Information Morning*. July 13, 2014 http://www.cbc.ca/player/play/2480091236 [Accessed February 20, 2017]

707 Unifor national representative Tom McNamara was contacted for an interview by telephone and email on January 26, 2017; he provided the telephone number for Don MacKenzie, president of Local 440 that represents workers at the mill, and an email for Unifor's communications person in Halifax, Shelley Amyotte. Two phone calls to Mr. MacKenzie (January 26 and 30, 2017) were not returned, nor were two emails (January 26 and February 20, 2017) to the communications person.

708 Beswick, Aaron. N.S. loans over $20 million to pulp mill. April 5, 2013. *The Chronicle Herald.* http://thechronicleherald.ca/novascotia/1121876-n.s.-loans-over-20m-to-pulp-mill [Accessed February 17, 2017]

709 Loans support cleaner air, rural jobs (Nova Scotia government news release). April 5, 2013. http://novascotia.ca/news/release/?id=20130405008 [Accessed February 16, 2017]

710 Province making final disbursement to Northern Pulp under now-closed Jobs Fund (Nova Scotia government news release). October 2, 2015. http://novascotia.ca/news/release/?id=20151002005 [Accessed February 17, 2017]

711 Union expresses concern over pollution from mill. March 20, 1970. *The Evening News*

712 Northern Pulp mill situation is 'very dire' says Peter MacKay. August 5, 2014. CBC News. http://www.cbc.ca/news/canada/nova-scotia/northern-pulp-mill-situation-is-very-dire-says-peter-mackay-1.2728289 [Accessed February 20, 2017]

713 Goodwin, Steve. No response given to Clean Air pleas. August 6, 2014. *The Advocate*

714 Cameron, Aaron. Residents continue with pulp mill protest. August 20, 2014. *The Advocate*

715 Taylor, Roger. N.S. must fix environmental rules: province can't be held hostage by Northern Pulp with health of residents at stake. August 23, 2014. *The Chronicle Herald*

716 Connections revealed between high-ranking bureaucrat and Northern Pulp: Former Northern Pulp lawyer now high-ranking Nova Scotia bureaucrat. August 26, 2014. CBC News. http://www.cbc.ca/news/canada/nova-scotia/connections-revealed-between-high-ranking-bureaucrat-and-northern-pulp-1.2747606 [Accessed March 24, 2017]

717 Ibid

718 Nova Scotia Registry of Lobbyists, Northern Pulp. https://novascotia.ca/sns/lobbyist/search.asp and https://novascotia.ca/sns/lobbyist/consultant/confirmation.asp [Accessed March 29, 2017]

719 MacGregor, Andy. "We cannot afford to lose Northern Pulp." August 23, 2014. *The Chronicle Herald*

720 Clean The Mill group offering free concert. September 3, 2014. *The Advocate*

721 Those who appeared at the concert included Matt Anderson, Thom Swift, Joel Plaskett, J.P. Cormier, Bruce Guthro, Mary Jane Lamond, Wendy MacIssac, Catherine McLellan, Garnet Rogers, Jim Dorie, Fleur Mainville, Dolores Dagenais, Machete, Grabrielle Papillon, Jon Raven, Trevor Stanley, Kent Vodden, and Wabanaki Confederacy. See: Cameron, Aaron. Thousands turn out for Clean The Air concert. September 17, 2014. *The Advocate*

722 In a telephone conversation on July 5, 2016, Jack Kyte declined to be interviewed for this book.

723 http://www.davegunning.com/mediatools/ [Accessed June 27, 2017]

724 Desborough, Rod. Early letters a foreshadow of today. September 3, 2014. *The Advocate*

725 Goodwin, Steve. Concert has real meaning. September 3, 2014. *The Advocate*, p 6

726 Langille, Ella. Gov't has the power to correct wrongdoings at the pulp mill. September 3, 2014. *The Advocate*

727 Felderhof, Dr. Catharina. Community must address injustices exhibited by mill. September 3, 2014. *The Advocate*

728 Fraser, Colin. Lack of political interest in Clean Air photo exhibit disappointing to reader. October 1, 2014. *The Advocate*

729 Cameron, Aaron. Clean The Air photo exhibit opens at deCoste. October 1, 2014. *The Advocate*

730 Two requests sent by email (June 23 and August 12, 2016) to Premier McNeil for details of this meeting went unanswered. A letter to the office of the premier requesting an interview for this book, emailed on January 26, 2017, received only an automated reply acknowledging receipt.

731 Premier to Paper Excellence: Comply or be shut down. September 18, 2014. *Cape Breton Post*. http://www.capebretonpost.com/news/local/2014/9/18/premier-to-paper-excellence-comply-or-b-3873497.html [Accessed March 23, 2017]

Chapter 19 (pages 249-264, notes 732 to 790)

732 Submission to Northern Pulp Nova Scotia Corporation Public Consultation. November 7, 2014. http://bit.ly/2obyXpn [Accessed March 17, 2017]

733 Kwasnik, Dr. Anne, quoted in Clean Pictou Air Group of Businesses advertisement. October 29, 2014. *The Advocate*

734 Bingley, Kent. Northern Pulp: Clean The Air Group pollutes the news media. November 5, 2014. *The Advocate*

735 Brannen, John. Report shows heavy metals in mill effluent. November 7, 2014. *The News* (New Glasgow)

736 Paul Sobey speaks out against Northern Pulp emissions. October 17, 2014. CTV Atlantic. http://atlantic.ctvnews.ca/paul-sobey-speaks-out-against-northern-pulp-mill-emissions-1.2057840 [Accessed February 13, 2014]

737 Krawczyk, Dr. John. Interviewed along with Dr. Gerry Farrell by Bob Murphy on CBC Halifax Nova Scotia *Information Morning*. September 7, 2014.

738 Northern Pulp emissions data gets mixed review. November 28, 2014. *The Chronicle Herald*. http://thechronicleherald.ca/novascotia/1254152-northern-pulp-emissions-data-gets-mixed-reviews [Accessed February 17, 2017]

739 Ibid

740 Ibid

741 Ibid

742 Brannen, John. Department releases draft approval for Northern Pulp. December 2, 2014. *The News* (New Glasgow)

743 Brannen, John. Gunning: Government forgot to add teeth to approval. December 4, 2014. *The News* (New Glasgow)

744 Ibid

745 Nova Scotia Department of Environment. Approval: Province of Nova Scotia, Environment Act, S.N.S. 1994-95, c.1, Northern Pulp Nova Scotia Corporation. Approval No. 2011-076657-R03. January 29, 2015

746 Nova Scotia Department of Environment. 2015 Industrial Approval for Northern Pulp Nova Scotia Corporation – Summary. n.d. http://www.novascotia.ca/nse/issues/docs/2015-ns-environment-northern-pulp-approval-summary.pdf [Accessed February 23, 2017]

747 Paul Sobey speaking in *Defenders of the dawn: green rights in the Maritimes* (a film by Silver Donald Cameron and Chris Beckett, Anhinga Films). CBC Absolutely Maritimes. September 5, 2015. Available at: http://www.cbc.ca/player/play/2674956490 [Accessed February 19, 2017]

748 Goodwin, Steve. Responses mixed to mill's approval. February 4, 2015. *The Advocate*

749 Ibid

750 Goodwin, Steve. Opinion: Stakes rising over pulp mill. February 4, 2015. *The Advocate*

751 Ibid

752 Hoffman, E., Bernier, M., Blotnicky, B., Golden, P.G., Janes, J., Kader, A, Kovacs-da Vosta, R., Pettipas, S., Vermeulen, S., and Walker, T.R. Assessment of public perception and environmental compliance at a pulp and paper facility: A Canadian case study. *Environmental Monitoring and Assessment*, 2015, Dec. 187: 766 (https://link.springer.com/article/10.1007/s10661-015-4985-5) (https://www.ncbi.nlm.nih.gov/pubmed/26590146)

753 Musick, Sueann. February 26, 2015. Northern Pulp will appeal limits. *The News* (New Glasgow), p 2

754 Ibid

755 Northern Pulp union and management challenge McNeil gov't. February 24, 2015. CBC News. http://www.cbc.ca/news/canada/nova-scotia/northern-pulp-management-and-union-challenge-mcneil-gov-t-1.2970516 [Accessed February 24, 2017]

756 An unsigned copy of this letter is available at: http://halifax.mediacoop.ca/sites/mediacoop.ca/files2/mc/fpans_petition_letter_draft.pdf [Accessed February 23, 2017]

757 Devet, Robert. Stick to facts, activist tells NP supporters. April 13, 2015. *Halifax Media Co-op*. http://halifax.mediacoop.ca/story/stick-facts-activist-tells-northern-pulp-supporter/33380 [Accessed February 23, 2017]

758 Clean The Mill. Comments on Northern Pulp IA appeal "fact" sheet. March 28, 2015. http://halifax.mediacoop.ca/sites/mediacoop.ca/files2/mc/comments_on_forest_products_association_np_ia_fact_sheet_2015_final.pdf [Accessed February 23, 2017]

759 Stantec. Source emissions testing – recovery and power boiler. Winter 2015. http://www.novascotia.ca/nse/issues/docs/stantec-source-emissions-testing-winter-2015.pdf [Accessed February 24, 2017]

760 Houston, Tim. Delorey should be transparent with regard to mill's IA. April 1, 2015. *The Advocate*

761 Delorey, Minister Randy. Letter to Brian J. Hebert, Counsel for Pictou Landing First Nation. June 8, 2015. http://www.novascotia.ca/nse/issues/docs/northern-pulp-pictou-landing-first-nation-decision-june-8-2015.pdf [Accessed February 24, 2017]

762 Pulp mill poised to restart in June. June 10, 2015. *The Advocate*

763 Delorey, Minister Randy. Letter to Terri Fraser, Northern Pulp Nova Scotia Corporation from Environment Nova Scotia. July 9, 2015.

764 Northern Pulp appeal leads to changes in industrial approval. July 9, 2015. CBC News. http://www.cbc.ca/news/canada/nova-scotia/northern-pulp-appeal-leads-to-changes-in-industrial-approval-1.3144550 [Accessed February 24, 2017]

765 Henderson, Jennifer. Northern Pulp mill takes Nova Scotia to court over operating permit. August 21, 2015. CBC News. http://www.cbc.ca/news/canada/nova-scotia/northern-pulp-mill-takes-nova-scotia-to-court-over-operating-permit-1.3199310 [Accessed February 24, 2017]

766 Nova Scotia Environment. Redacted PowerPoint. 2015. FOIPOP Application Number 2016-076 submitted by Andrew Younger.

767 Northern Pulp. Northern Pulp economic impact results released. September 17, 2015. http://northernpulp.ca/media/press-releases/gardner-pinfold-consultants-release-study/ [Accessed February 24, 2017]

768 Goodwin, Steve. Northern Pulp: communication key. October 14, 2015. *The Advocate*

769 Withers, Paul. Northern Pulp emissions prompt directive from Nova Scotia. October 21, 2015. CBC News. http://www.cbc.ca/news/canada/nova-scotia/northern-pulp-emissions-results-1.3290322 [Accessed February 24, 2017]

770 Northern Pulp completes precipitator project. October 28, 2017. *The Advocate*

771 Pöyry (Vancouver) Inc. Northern Pulp Nova Scotia Corporation, Air Emission Management Plan. September 25, 2009

772 Northern Pulp, website. 2013. Environmental: Power boiler scrubber. http://northernpulp.ca/environmental [Accessed June 20, 2013]

773 David Kerr interviewed by Stephanie Domet on CBC Halifax *Mainstreet*. August 6, 2014. http://www.cbc.ca/player/play/2483547416 [Accessed February 24, 2017]

774 Henderson, Jennifer. Northern Pulp disagrees with CBCL's findings. January 26, 2016. CBC News. http://www.cbc.ca/news/canada/nova-scotia/ northern-pulp-can-meet-conditions-cbcl-report-1.3419669 [Accessed February 24, 2017]

775 Hoffman, E., Bernier, M., Blotnicky, B., Golden, P.G., Janes, J., Kader, A, Kovacs-da Vosta, R., Pettipas, S., Vermeulen, S., and Walker, T.R. Assessment of public perception and environmental compliance at a pulp and paper facility: A Canadian case study. *Environmental Monitoring and Assessment*, 2015, Dec. 187: 766 (https://link.springer.com/article/10.1007/s10661-015-4985-5) (https://www.ncbi.nlm.nih.gov/pubmed/26590146)

776 Miller, Margaret, Letter to Terri Fraser, Technical Manager, Northern Pulp Nova Scotia Corporation from Nova Scotia Environment Minister. February 8, 2016.

777 Nova Scotia and Northern Pulp agree on water use rules. February 8, 2016. CBC News. http://www.cbc.ca/news/canada/nova-scotia/northern-pulp-water-usage-appeal-decision-1.3438549 [Accessed February 24, 2017]

778 Withers, Paul. Nova Scotia accused of major concessions in Northern Pulp deal. February 11, 2016. CBC News. http://www.cbc.ca/news/canada/ nova-scotia/northern-pulp-deal-report-wastewater-paper-1.3443094 [Accessed February 24, 2017]

779 Ibid

780 Emailed response from the Department of Environment. June 23, 2017

781 Kelly, Ron. Premier should stand up to the mill and stand for the people of the county. March 2, 2016. *The Advocate*, p 18

782 Letter from Margaret Miller, MLA, Minister of Environment. March 16, 2016

783 Northern Pulp Nova Scotia Corporation. Notice in *The Advocate*, April 13, 2016, p 22

784 Dunbrack, Terry Mosh. August 29, 2016. https://www.facebook.com/ groups/545965902107532/ [Accessed February 25, 2017]

785 Northern Pulp, Environment, Community Liaison Committee. http:// northernpulp.ca/environment/community-liaison-committee/ [Accessed May 29, 2017]

786 Letter from Margaret Miller, MLA, Minister of Environment. July 21, 2016

787 Gunning provided Minister Miller with a link to the news story about the exceedances, but at the time of this writing, that link is no longer active: http://www.bigdog1009.ca/news/story.aspx?ID=2198912

788 Gunning, Dave. Letter to Environment Minister Margaret Miller. July 28, 2016. Posted at: https://www.facebook.com/groups/545965902107532/permalink/1058145424222908/

789 It emerged in September 2017, after Northern Pulp again failed an emissions test, that NS Environment had withdrawn that summary ticket in 2016, saying there had been "technical difficulties" with the June and August testing. Withers, Paul. $697 air pollution fine levied – then withdrawn – against Northern Pulp last year. September 20, 2017. CBC News. http://www.cbc.ca/news/canada/nova-scotia/northern-pulp-pollution-fine-withdrawn-1.4297297 [Accessed September 20, 2017]; Campbell, Francis. Northern Pulp handed nominal fine for exceeding emission approval. September 7, 2017. Local Xpress. https://www.localxpress.ca/local-business/northern-pulp-handed-nominal-fine-for-exceeding-emission-approval-407496 [Accessed March 1, 2017]

790 The Nova Scotia Legislature, Nova Scotia House of Assembly – Law Amendments Committee Submissions, Assembly 62, Session 2, Boat Harbour Act- Bill 89. April 27, 2015 http://nslegislature.ca/index.php/committees/submissions/C96/89/ [Accessed May 29, 2017]

Chapter 20 (pages 265-277, notes 791 to 848)

791 Interviewed by Haley Bernard and Christian Francis in the film *A'se'k*, 2013. https://www.youtube.com/watch?v=6AdxlcF3Lzl [Accessed March 23, 2017]

792 Pictou Landing Native Women's Group (c/o Sheila Francis, Past President), Castleden, H., Lewis, D., Jamieson, R., Gibson, M., Rainham, D., Russell, R., Martin, D., and Hart, C. (2016). "Our Ancestors Are in Our Land, Water, and Air": A Two-Eyed Seeing Approach to Researching Environmental Health Concerns with Pictou Landing First Nation – Final Report, p 2

793 Hoffman, E., Bernier, M., Blotnicky, B., Golden, P.G., Janes, J., Kader, A, Kovacs-da Vosta, R., Pettipas, S., Vermeulen, S., and Walker, T.R. Assessment of public perception and environmental compliance at a pulp and paper facility: A Canadian case study. Environmental Monitoring Assessment, 2015, Dec. 187: 766 (https://link.springer.com/article/10.1007/s10661-015-4985-5) (https://www.ncbi.nlm.nih.gov/pubmed/26590146)

794 Scott, Murray K. Letter to Chief Anne Francis-Muise, Pictou Landing Band Council from Office of the Minister of Transportation and Infrastructure Renewal. December 4, 2008.

795 A Boat Harbour update from Chief and Council, Chief and Council Message. *A'Se'K News*, February 2009. Issue No. 3

796 Scott, Murray K. Letter to Chief Anne Francis-Muise, Pictou Landing Band Council from Office of the Minister of Transportation and Infrastructure Renewal. December 4, 2008.

797 Accommodation Agreement between Northern Pulp Nova Scotia Corporation and Pictou Landing Indian Band. December 31, 2008.

798 University of King's College Investigative Workshop. Closed-door negotiations underway to end Boat Harbour controversy. April 23, 2009.

799 Interview with Brian Hebert, legal counsel for the Pictou Landing First Nation. March 2, 2017

800 The University of King's College Investigative Workshop. Closed-door negotiations underway to end Boat Harbour controversy. April 23, 2009

801 Ware, Beverley. Boat Harbour cleanup in doubt. March 3, 2010. *The Chronicle Herald*

802 Musick, Sueann. Community rallies to rid itself of effluent plant. May 4, 2010. *The News* (New Glasgow)

803 Pictou Landing Band Council. Pictou Landing Band Council files lawsuit against Nova Scotia: Press Release. July 8, 2010. Available at: http://halifax.mediacoop.ca/fr/newsrelease/4323 [Accessed February 27, 2017]

804 Supreme Court of Nova Scotia, Notice of Action. September 9, 2010. http://canadianaboriginallaw.com/wordpress1/wp-content/uploads/2012/06/Boat-Harbour-Lawsuit-Statement-of-Claim1.pdf [Accessed February 27, 2017]

805 Howe, Miles. Pictou Landing votes "NO": Band votes resoundingly against taking provincial hush money. January 26, 2012. *Halifax Media Co-op*. http://halifax.mediacoop.ca/story/pictou-landing-votes-no/9727 [Accessed February 26, 2017]

806 Beswick, Aaron. Band council seeks way to fund suit. June 22, 2012. *The Chronicle Herald*

807 Beswick, Aaron. Plant effluent into Boat Harbour sparks threat. April 17, 2014. *The Chronicle Herald*. http://thechronicleherald.ca/novascotia/1201592-plant-effluent-into-boat-harbour-sparks-threat [Accessed February 26, 2017]

808 Ibid

809 Ibid

810 Interview with Jonathan Beadle, June 27, 2016

811 Provincial Court of Nova Scotia. R. v. Northern Pulp Corporation, Sentencing Decision. May 11, 2016. p 4. http://www.courts.ns.ca/Decisions_Of_Courts/documents/2016nspc29.pdf [Accessed February 28, 2017]

812 Ibid

813 Pictou Landing Band Office. R. v. Nova Pulp Nova Scotia Corporation: Victim impact statement. February 17, 2016. http://canadianaboriginallaw.com/wordpress1/wp-content/uploads/2016/02/PLFN-Victim-Impact-Statement-2016-02-221.pdf [Accessed February 28, 2017]

814 Pictou Landing First Nation. Pictou Landing erects blockade against Northern Pulp mill. June 13, 2014. NB Media Co-op. http://nbmediacoop.org/2014/06/13/pictou-landing-erects-blockade-against-northern-pulp-mill/ [Accessed February 28, 2017]

815 Provincial Court of Nova Scotia. R. v. Northern Pulp Corporation, Sentencing Decision. May 11, 2016. http://www.courts.ns.ca/Decisions_Of_Courts/documents/2016nspc29.pdf [Accessed February 28, 2017]

816 Ibid p 6

817 Beswick, Aaron. First Nation stands firm on effluent issue. June 11, 2014. *The Chronicle Herald*. http://thechronicleherald.ca/novascotia/1214026-first-nation-stands-firm-on-effluent-issue [Accessed February 26, 2017]

818 Ibid

819 Ibid

820 Brannen, John. Updated: Pictou Landing agrees to accept government offer, dismantle blockade. June 16, 2014. *The News* [New Glasgow] http://www.ngnews.ca/news/local/2014/6/16/updated-pictou-landing-votes-to-accept-3765124.html [Accessed February 28, 2017]

821 Provincial Court of Nova Scotia. R. v. Northern Pulp Corporation, Sentencing Decision. May 11, 2016. http://www.courts.ns.ca/Decisions_Of_Courts/documents/2016nspc29.pdf, pp 6,7 [Accessed February 28, 2017]

822 Lees, Matt, Kavanagh, Sana, and Perrier, Erika. Northern Pulp effluent spill: MCG test results report. Prepared for Pictou Landing First Nation by the Mi'kmaw Conservation Group, the Confederacy of Mainland Mi'kmaq. October 31, 2014.

823 Brannen, John. Environmental report released on effluent leak. August 1, 2014. *The News* (New Glasgow)

824 Ibid

825 Ibid

826 Ibid

827 Provincial Court of Nova Scotia. R. v. Northern Pulp Corporation, Sentencing Decision. May 11, 2016. http://www.courts.ns.ca/Decisions_Of_Courts/documents/2016nspc29.pdf [Accessed February 28, 2017]

828 Pictou Landing Band Office. R. v. Nova Pulp Nova Scotia Corporation: Victim impact statement. February 17, 2016. http://canadianaboriginallaw.com/wordpress1/wp-content/uploads/2016/02/PLFN-Victim-Impact-Statement-2016-02-221.pdf [Accessed February 28, 2017]

829 Ibid p 8

830 Ibid p 15

831 Ibid pp 12-13

832 Pictou Landing Native Women's Group (c/o Sheila Francis, Past President), Castleden, H., Lewis, D., Jamieson, R., Gibson, M., Rainham, D., Russell, R., Martin, D., and Hart, C. (2016). "Our Ancestors Are in Our Land, Water, and Air": A Two-Eyed Seeing Approach to Researching Environmental Health Concerns with Pictou Landing First Nation – Final Report

833 Ibid

834 Ibid p 35

835 Nova Scotia Government Bill 89, Boat Harbour Act. http://nslegislature.ca/legc/bills/62nd_2nd/3rd_read/b089.htm [Accessed February 28, 2017]

836 Nova Scotia House of Assembly- Law Amendments Committee Submissions Assembly 62, Session 2. Boat Harbour Act- Bill 89. April 27, 2015. Dave Gunning's submission available at: http://nslegislature.ca/pdfs/committees/62_2_LACSubmissions/Bill89.pdf [Accessed May 30, 2017]

837 Kyte, Jack. Won't be easy to fix wastewater from Northern Pulp, former employee. April 20, 2015. CBC Halifax *Information Morning*. http://www.cbc.ca/player/play/2664862121 [Accessed March 1, 2017]

838 Fendick, Reg. Scott pulp mill cleanup to cost $74 million. November 28, 1991. *The Daily News*, p 3

839 Kyte, Jack. Won't be easy to fix wastewater from Northern Pulp, former employee. April 20, 2015. CBC Halifax *Information Morning*. http://www.cbc.ca/player/play/2664862121 [Accessed March 1, 2017]

840 Gorman, Michael. Cost of new Boat Harbour site, who will pay, still up in air. February 22, 2016. *Local Xpress*. https://www.localxpress.ca/local-news/cost-of-new-boat-harbour-site-who-will-pay-still-up-in-air-298219 [Accessed March 1, 2017]

841 Musick, Sueann. Consultant selected for Northern Pulp treatment facility replacement study. December 15, 2016. *The News* (New Glasgow) http://www.ngnews.ca/news/local/2016/12/15/consultant-selected-for-northern-pulp-treatment-facility-replace.html [Accessed March 1, 2017]

842 KSH submission the NS Legislature, Law Amendments Committee, April 23, 2015. Available at: http://nslegislature.ca/pdfs/committees/62_2_LACSubmissions/Bill89.pdf [Accessed May 30, 2017]

843 MacInnis, Adam. Testing to begin this year on Boat Harbour cleanup. June 9, 2017. *The News* (New Glasgow). http://www.ngnews.ca/news/local/2017/6/9/testing-to-begin-this-year-on-boat-harbour-cleanup.html [Accessed June 13, 2017]

844 Withers, Paul. Officials with $133 million Boat Harbour cleanup get first look at contaminated sediment. CBC News. http://www.cbc.ca/news/canada/nova-scotia/boat-harbour-clean-up-estimated-133-million-1.2423846 [Accessed June 26, 2017]

845 Withers, Paul. Northern Pulp submits plans to replace notorious Boat Harbour facility. September 1, 2017. CBC News. http://www.cbc.ca/news/canada/nova-scotia/northern-pulp-proposal-boat-harbour-waste-water-facility-1.4270995 [Accessed September 1, 2017]

846 Speaking in the film *A'se'k (The Other Room)*, edited by Barrie Bernard, Haley Bernard, and Christian Francis. 2013

847 Harvie, Debbi. Ceremony aims to cleanse polluted waters. November 16, 2016. *The Advocate*

848 Campbell, Francis. Pictou Landing Band optimistic that things "actually happening" with Boat Harbour cleanup. December 28, 2016. *Local Xpress.* https://www.localxpress.ca/local-news/pictou-landing-band-optimistic-that-things-actually-happening-with-boat-harbour-cleanup-498246 [Accessed March 27, 2017]

Epilogue (pages 278-282, notes 849 to 856)

849 Wohlleben, Peter. 2016. *The hidden life of trees: What they feel, how they communicate.* Vancouver, BC: Greystone, p 242

850 Prest, Wade. Nova Scotia forestry: Seize the moment. July 19, 2012. *The Chronicle Herald.* http://thechronicleherald.ca/opinion/118614-nova-scotia-forestry-seize-the-moment [Accessed June 28, 2017]

851 Ecology Action Centre, Eastern Shore Forestry Watch, Nova Scotia Woodlot Owners and Operators Association. https://ecologyaction.ca/event/otter-ponds-demonstration-forest-opdf-biota-survey [Accessed June 28, 2017]

852 Community Forests International, Dale Prest. http://forestsinternational.org/our-team [Accessed June 28, 2017]

853 Interview with Dale Prest, June 28, 2017

854 Pross, Paul. Coordinator's report: March 2016-June 2017. Healthy Forest Coalition

855 Pannozzo, Linda. Biomass, freedom of information and the silence of the DNR company men, part 4: The case of the disappearing forest age class data. April 16, 2016. *Halifax Examiner.* https://www.halifaxexaminer.ca/province-house/biomass-freedom-of-information-and-the-silence-of-the-dnr-company-men-3/ [Accessed March 17, 2017]. The five articles in the series can be accessed on the *Halifax Examiner* website.

856 Pannozzo, Linda. Testing the limits: Part 2. The Examiner goes on the road in search of an endangered lichen (a photo essay). March 30, 2017. *Halifax Examiner.* https://www.halifaxexaminer.ca/province-house/testing-the-limits-2/#comments [Accessed March 30, 2017]